W9-AKV-367

THE
INTERNET
HANDBOOK
FOR
Writers,
Researchers,
AND
Journalists

Mary McGuire
Linda Stilborne
Melinda McAdams
Laurel Hyatt

THE GUILFORD PRESS
New York London

To all my journalism students, whose hunger to learn new skills has inspired me. —
M. McGuire

For Alex Spencer, who helps me make sense of the world. —
L. Stilborne

For N'Gai, Noah, Scoot, and Tracy. —
M. McAdams

Published in the United States by **The Guilford Press**
A Division of Guilford Publications Inc.
72 Spring Street, New York, NY 10012

First published in Canada by Trifolium Books Inc.
Copyright © 1997 Trifolium Books Inc.

All rights reserved.

Permission is not granted for institution-wide, or system-wide, reproduction of materials presented herein. No part of this publication maybe reproduced, stored in a retrival system, or transmitted, in any form or by any means, electronic, mechanical, photocopying, microfilming, recording, or otherwise, without written permission from the Publisher. Care has been taken to trace ownership of copyright material contained in this book. The publishers will gladly receive any information that will enable them to rectify any reference or credit line in subsequent editions.

This book is printed on acid-free paper

Last digit is print number: 9 8 7 6 5 4 3 2 1

Library of Congress Cataloging-in-Publication Data available from the Publisher

Internet handbook for writers, researchers, and journalists

ISBN 1-57230-331-X (hard)
ISBN 1-57230-332-8 (paperback)

Editing/production coordination: *Francine Geraci*
Cover and text design/layout: *Jack Steiner Graphic Design*

If you would like to know about other Guilford titles, please visit our Web site at **http://www.guilford.com**

Acknowledgments

The authors and publisher would like to thank the Unisys Corporation for granting permission to include in our book its excellent Glossary, *Information Superhighway Driver's Manual: Key Terms and Concepts That Will Put You in the Passing Lane.* Special thanks to James B. Senior and Michael Heck of Unisys Corporation for providing us with all the material we needed on such a timely basis, and to Jim Chiponis for his delightful cartoons.

Mary McGuire would like to thank her family for putting up with her spending endless hours online, and her colleagues for putting up with her enthusiasm about the Internet long before it was easy to use. She also owes special thanks to her colleague, Prof. Jay Weston, whose advice and support helped launch a new course in online journalism at Carleton University so that students could learn many of the skills covered in this book.

Stay on top of what's on the net...on the net

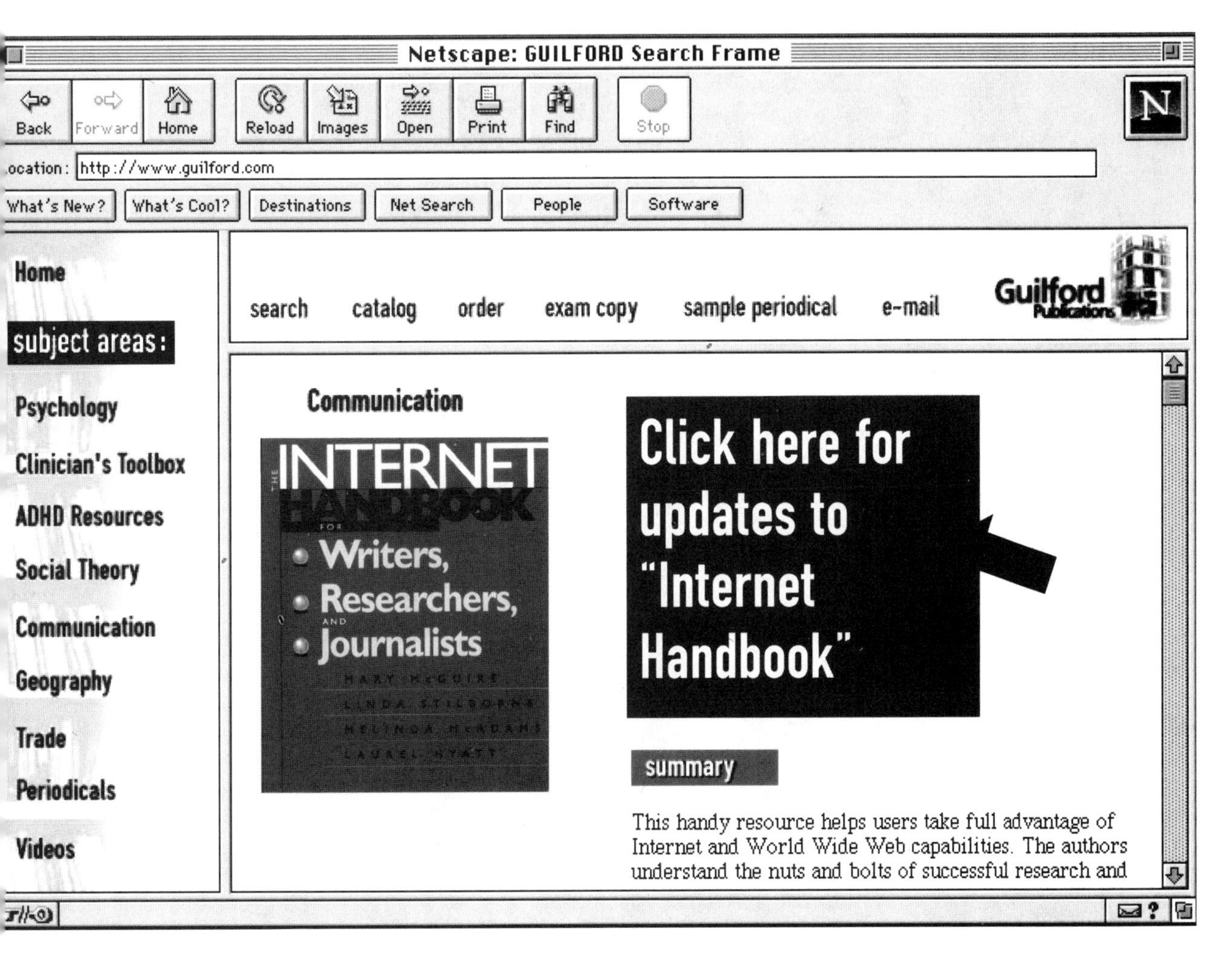

'isit the "Internet Handbook" online update page to stay current on additions and changes to the resources in this edition

http://www.guilford.com/writernet

Contents

Introduction

The Internet is a tool that media and other information professionals need to use with skill. *The Internet Handbook for Writers, Researchers, and Journalists* is for people who want to develop that skill.

To put it simply, information professionals find things out, check them out, and tell others about them in clear and compelling ways. The Internet has changed the way we do all those things and, as it becomes more sophisticated, will doubtless continue to pave the way for change.

It is easy to be excited by the Net's potential, and tempting to say it will help us do our jobs better. That's still debatable — just as it's debatable whether writers produce better writing with computers than they did with typewriters, or whether reporters produce better journalism now that they can send reports live via satellite from around the world. Whether our product is better or not, word processors, satellites, and the Internet are here to stay, and it only makes sense to learn to use them well.

Skillfully used, the Internet gives writers and other researchers wider access to more information and expert sources much more quickly than any other means. Instead of going to the library to find the latest government policy on health care, you can stay at your desk and bring it up on your own computer screen with just a few keystrokes. Instead of scouring local newspapers for stories on a topic you are researching, you can search hundreds of newspapers from around the world in just seconds by visiting the right Web sites. Instead of spending all day on the phone trying to find the leading experts on right-wing militia groups in the United States, you can post a query to the proper mailing list and gets lots of useful leads from people with first-hand knowledge of the issue. Instead of playing telephone tag with someone who has information you need, you can communicate more efficiently with them via electronic mail.

It is important for us, as information professionals, to understand just what the Internet has to offer if we are going to provide products that are useful to our audience. If everyone has easy access to the vast information resources of the Internet, writers, researchers, editors, and journalists will have to provide something more — some added value. More than ever, we need to put all that information into context, to provide analysis and perspective, and to present it in an interesting and compelling way. Certainly, if we provide little more than is already accessible on the Internet, we won't survive for long.

We have designed this book to help you — as writers, researchers, editors, and journalists — understand the Internet and use it efficiently and effectively to find the information, services, and experts you need quickly. Although we have written it especially for people who are new to the Internet, it should also prove helpful to anyone who is currently using the Net and wants to avoid wasting time figuring out how to use it well. Also, our book is written in plain language — since writers, researchers, and journalists don't usually have the time or inclination to become technogeeks.

Chapters 1 through 3 give you all the information you need to log on, start exploring the Internet, and try some of the most important applications, such as a Web browser. Chapter 4 helps you develop and refine your search strategies and techniques. The chapters that follow give an overview of the most helpful Internet resources for writers, researchers, and journalists: Chapter 5 covers Web sites for libraries, databases, media, and government; Chapter 6 tells how to use e-mail, newsgroups, and mailing lists to find ideas, tips, information, resources, and experts. Chapter 7 offers practical suggestions for avoiding the two biggest hazards of the Internet — information overload and difficulty in separating the treasures from the trash. Chapter 8 will help those who want to publish information on the World Wide Web to get started.

Throughout the book you'll also find these other useful features:

FYI. Helpful hints and practical suggestions for learning about the Net and making the most of your time online.

Tech Talk. Technical points that are not essential, yet are useful to know about. If a particular point seems obscure at first, you can highlight it and return to it once you've gained more experience. It's not necessary to understand everything all at once. In fact, we hope this guide will continue to be useful to you over the long term.

INFOnuggets. Facts and figures that illustrate current trends and offer insights into this fascinating medium.

Focus On... These special features look at Internet applications and technologies, showing you how to get the most from them quickly and easily.

Appendices. Here you'll find quick references for using Lynx, the text-based Web browser; citing online sources; dealing with copyright and censorship issues, and more.

Resources on the Web. Our unique index of Web sites puts hundreds of professional and general interest Internet resources at your fingertips.

Associated Press Policy for Using Electronic Services. An example of how one organization deals with online information as it pertains to news gathering.

Glossary. For quick reference, check the handy glossary of Internet terms in the back of the book.

The Internet Handbook for Writers, Researchers, and Journalists is chock-full of useful advice for anyone who wants to know how to locate the best resources of the world's largest library without leaving home. We hope this book, together with these resources, help you become an even better writer, researcher, editor, journalist, or student than you already are.

Chapter 1 Coming to Terms with Cyberspace

“[My problem with] the Internet is that it’s about facts and figures and information. But without the flesh and blood and the breathing that goes on, who am I talking to? What do they look like? Is it a multitude? Are there 25 people there? … That part — the human touch, that’s what’s missing.”

— From “An Interview with Studs Terkel,” *Mother Jones*, September/October 1995, p. 22.
http://bsd.mojones.com/mother_jones/SO95/eastman.html

OK — so the Internet isn’t everyone’s favorite hangout. Some people love it; others hate it. Most of us are still reserving judgment. We just want to know more about it.

Most of us already know that the Internet is a great new medium for information and communication. But even experienced cybernauts are often torn between appreciation for the many positive things about the Internet and frustration over the negatives.

Here are some of the things we *like* to do on the Net:

- visit virtual museums
- buy books
- hear about jobs
- do research
- network with other professionals
- get news from around the world tailored to our interests
- take courses through distance education
- consult with educators, academics, health professionals, and other experts
- find health information
- rediscover old friends and make new ones
- find out about restaurants, vacation destinations, and other travel information
- check schedules for buses, trains, and airplanes
- get the latest government information
- let the government know what we think.

And here are some of the things that we *dislike* about the Internet:

- reading text on a screen
- graphics that take forever to load
- Web addresses that are constantly changing
- finding 300 messages in our e-mail box
- finding that 200 of those messages are much longer than they need to be (some folks have not yet grasped the difference between e-mail and letters!)
- dealing with people in "not-real time"
- having to distinguish between "real time" and some other kind of time
- flaming and other forms of electronic nastiness
- the sense that because things change so quickly on the Internet, we have to struggle to keep up just so we won't be left behind.

If you are currently using the Internet, you can probably add to both these lists.

Those who have spent time on the Internet often feel overwhelmed by its vastness. Even though it has been around for a number of years (1994 marked its twenty-fifth anniversary), the Internet is still evolving. It is multifaceted and complex, and in many ways it remains a vast, uncharted frontier. It's great fun to explore, but there are also bound to be challenges and even a few unpleasant surprises along with the thrills.

Despite that, there are solid reasons for getting onto the Net. If you are a professional researcher, a writer, a journalist, an editor, or a student, you can't afford not to use the Internet. In the end, two things will help to overcome some of the difficulties that people sometimes encounter with the Internet — one is the technology itself, which is constantly improving; the other is learning to use the Internet efficiently.

> "More and more journals are reviewed and published electronically, giving faster turnaround and quicker feedback. I can reach a researcher directly, and perhaps get an answer within an hour ... Networks are terrific.
>
> "On the other hand, I've watched researchers waste morning after morning, reading irrelevant net news, plowing through e-mail and fine tuning their screen savers."
>
> — Clifford Stoll, *Silicon Snake Oil: Second Thoughts on the Information Highway.* New York: Doubleday, 1995, p. 91.

The Internet Handbook for Writers, Researchers, and Journalists will show you how to use the Internet efficiently as a research tool. It's not necessary to understand everything about the Internet, but it is important to be able to select and make use of the kinds of features and resources that will be of most value to you.

The first step is to get an overview of what's available on the Net. The second is to start learning about the tools that will get you where you want to go.

Chapter highlights

- Beyond the hype: What's really available on the Net?
- Internet tools: Keys to unlock the world of information
- Challenges and opportunities in electronic communications
- Looking ahead: What does the future hold?

Technogeek

Beyond the hype: What's really available on the Net?

The Internet is an extensive system of interlinked yet independent computer networks. In less than two decades, the Internet has evolved from a highly specialized communications network used mostly for military and academic purposes into a massive electronic bazaar. Today, the Internet includes:

- academic and government computers
- computers from research institutions
- computerized library catalogs
- corporations
- community-based computers (sometimes called *freenets*)
- diverse small, local computers (called *bulletin boards*) where technogeeks are known to hang out.

Anyone who has an account on one of these computers can send electronic mail throughout the network and access resources from thousands of other computers on the network.

Because of the free-wheeling culture of the Internet and its overall lack of structure and external controls, it is tempting to dismiss it as a novelty. Those who take time to learn about it soon discover, however, that the Internet is a microcosm of our society.

The following "snapshots" of daily activities on the Internet reveal a cyberworld that is as dynamic, varied, and controversial as the world reflected in print or broadcast news. They also suggest the richness of the Internet as a source of information for students and researchers, as well as its potential as a tool for writers and journalists with its wealth of contacts, story ideas, and background information.

Business on the Net

Your local bagel shop may not be on the Internet, but thousands of other businesses are. Yahoo, a popular Internet search engine, lists more than 120,000 companies on the Internet. These include legal firms, advertising agencies, car dealerships, financial institutions, publishers, and bookstores. (And, yes, there are even a few bagel shops: Bagel Oasis in New York will ship bagels to your home or office.)

Amazon.com (pronounced "Amazon-dot-com"), one of a number of virtual bookstores on the Net, is an example of a particularly

INFO*nugget*

Fulton McDonald, a retail consultant from the International Business Development Corporation, predicts that "the Internet is going to drive half of today's retailers out of business by 2010." However, another research executive, Seymour Merrin, maintains that "the buying population on the Net is essentially social misfits. People who are comfortable in public will go to a store."

— Noted in *Yahoo Internet Life*, January, 1997, pp. 39, 41.

successful online business. It's located — sort of — in Seattle, Washington, but its services are available almost anywhere around the globe. Amazon claims to offer more than five times as many titles as its nearest (non-cyber) competitor, so it is not surprising that one patron recently managed to locate two books that he been seeking for five years, while another successfully tracked down a book from the 1970s (which arrived with its original price tag still in place!).

On the Internet, researchers and journalists can also tap into the latest economic, business, or stock market news. They can talk to small business owners or sample discussion groups on controversial topics, such as the advantages and disadvantages of a flat tax or the future of work. There are many resources providing information on setting up a small business or on telecommuting — two important business trends.

Health information on the Net

The Internet is a terrific source for the latest medical news, and for sharing medical opinions and research. There are an estimated 500 health-related discussion groups on the Internet, and likely even more health-related resources on the World Wide Web. Premier health agencies such as the Mayo Clinic, the U.S. Centers for Disease Control, and Health Canada provide research information online. Journalists can find out about exciting new areas of research, such as DNA vaccines, or they can consult medical specialists to verify information about bone marrow transplants. Researchers are able to access study results and health information databases.

Alternative health information can also be found in abundance on the Net. In fact, practitioners involved in alternative approaches to health care have benefited greatly from being able to use the Internet as a resource for sharing information and lobbying for their discipline. The Internet makes available information about acupuncture, chiropractors, herbs, vitamins, iridology, gemstone therapy, and even a traditional favorite — leeches. Increasingly, scientists and researchers use the Internet to share information and ideas. A project from the National Library of Medicine has produced a spectacular resource consisting of 21,000 pictures of the human body. The Visible Human Project (http://www.nlm.nih.gov/research/visible/visible_human.html) provides a complete, anatomically detailed, three-dimensional representation of the human body. The project is, among other things, a prototype for the development and dissemination of a medical image library. The Internet is truly a gateway to understanding the latest developments in science and medicine.

Education on the Net

While there are hundreds of useful resources for teachers and nearly 6,000 elementary and secondary schools posting information on the Internet, the power of this technology is particularly evident in two areas of alternative education: distance education and home schooling. The Virtual Online University (http://www.athena.edu/) is an example of a distance education institution available on the Internet (Figure 1-1). The electronic campus is open twenty-four hours a day, seven days a week, and offers such courses as Macroeconomics, Freshman Composition, History, and Latin. The Internet University (http://www.caso.com/iuhome.html) lists over 700 college courses available over the Internet, including studies in arts, business, mathematics, psychology, and education. Students from around the world can enroll in these courses. Some students will use them to supplement courses from local institutions, while professionals pursuing life-long learning opportunities value the flexibility of distance learning. There are even a number of primary and secondary schools now offering high school courses over the Internet.

Similarly, the Internet has become a major resource for home schoolers. On the Internet, home schoolers can connect to courses, online tutors, and learning services. Once isolated in their own communities, such students can now participate in live online discussion groups, projects, and activities with other kids being schooled at

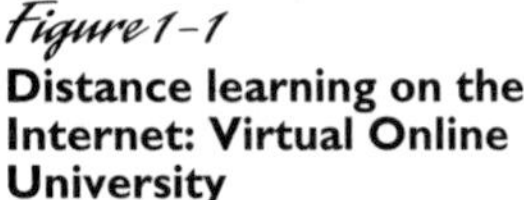
Figure 1-1
Distance learning on the Internet: Virtual Online University

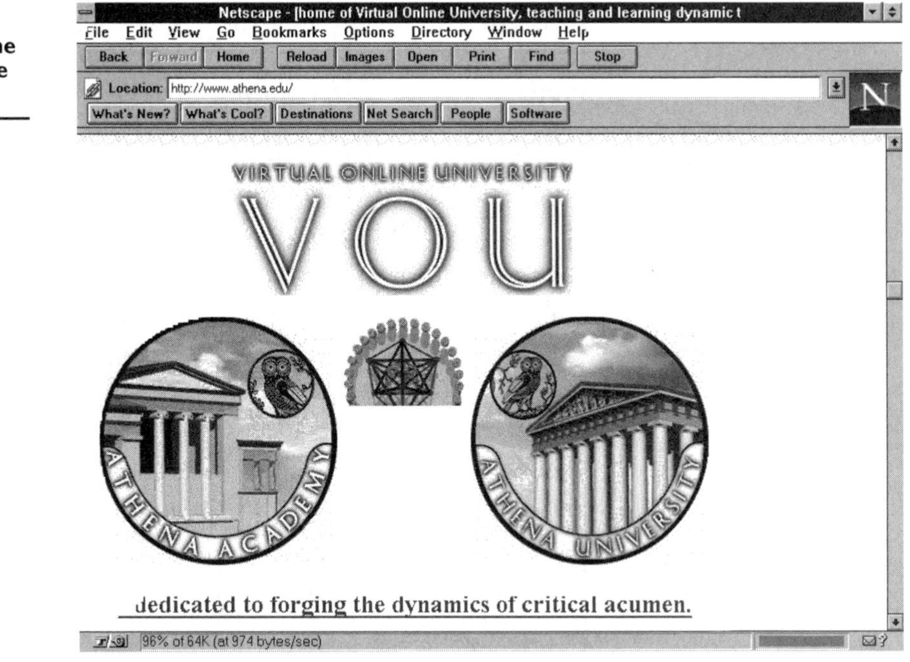

home. In the United States the number of students being taught at home has increased from roughly 18,000 in the late 1970s to an estimated 800,000 today (some claim this figure is closer to one million). If you are a journalist or a social science researcher, you will be intrigued by the broad social changes signaled by this kind of growth. Undoubtedly, the Internet will fuel even greater growth in alternative and distance learning in the years ahead.

Media on the Net

No area of endeavor has been more profoundly affected by the Internet than the media. Traditional print and broadcast sources are now "reinventing" themselves online. Change is further fueled as existing print and broadcast agencies merge and media conglomerates compete with telephone companies for dominance on the information highway.

Radio has been on the Internet since 1993. The first-ever Internet video broadcast of a rock concert featured the Rolling Stones in November, 1994.

There are several hundred newspapers on the Net, as well as news services such as AP and Reuters. News is available on the Internet from over eighty countries in the world. The Ecola Newsstand (http://www.ecola.com) lists over 2,300 print publications that now maintain an active presence on the Web. This total does not include the hundreds of publications that exist only online.

The online versions of many publications (also called *cybergeists*; Figures 1-2 and 1-2A) usually give you a sampling of their latest issue and sometimes offer complete back issues. These publications also provide online links that relate to current features, invite dialogue, offer online interviews with authors or guest "speakers," and in some cases facilitate discussion groups related to topics of interest to readers. Increasingly, publications on the Internet are developing multimedia formats that integrate text, sound, graphics, and animation.

It is speculated that, over the next several years, press releases and newswire services will become available, with the Internet as the preferred (if not exclusive) point of access.

INFO*nugget*

Summary results from a 1995 survey of 197 responses from journalists:

- 38% of newsrooms are connected to the Internet
- 81% of respondents using the Net or online services do so at least once a week
- 67% of respondents said Internet usage makes them more productive
- 39% said research is their primary reason for hooking up to the Internet

— Ernst & Young and Canada NewsWire, *The Media and the Internet: 1995*.
http://www.newswire.ca/interest/ernst.html

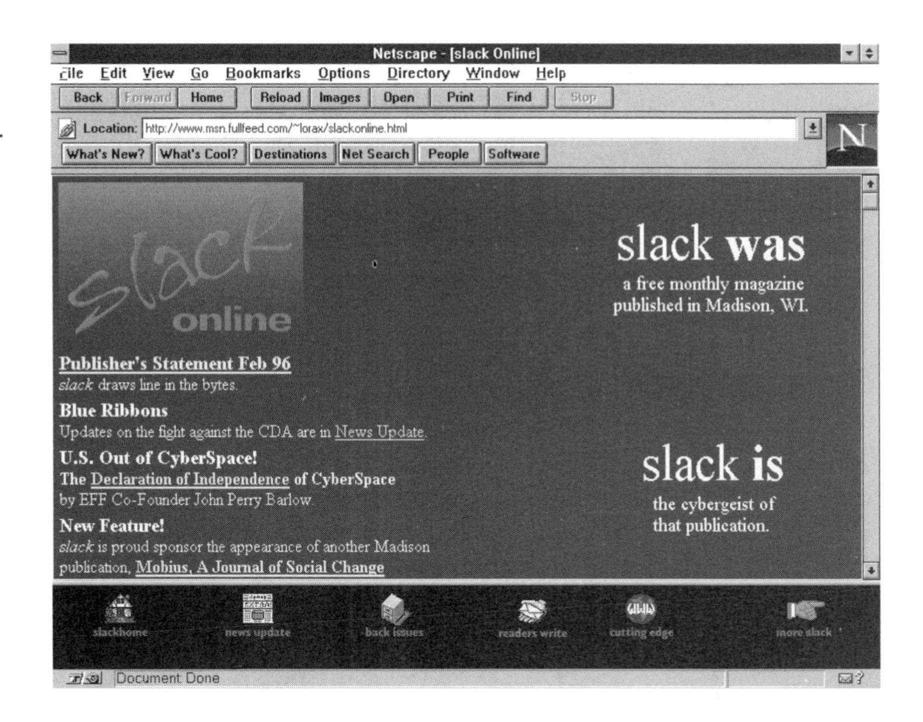

Figure 1-2
Newsmedia on the Internet: slack online

Figure 1-2A
Café Utne, cybergeist of *The Utne Reader*

Internet tools: Keys to unlock the world of information

Journalists and researchers need to know more about the Internet than simply how to find information and contacts. They also need to know about the social and economic trends and changes represented in the day's events. Students, too, are expected to develop an up-to-date awareness of many different fields as they pursue a diploma or a degree. Freelance writers and editors will find many new opportunities by learning about telecommunications technologies and incorporating new media into their work lives.

Media professionals also have a substantial contribution to make in helping to shape the online world. Journalists in particular will appreciate becoming actively involved in the creation of a new medium that has the potential to reach millions of people around the globe, and everyone will want to have at least a general understanding of the technology that makes this possible.

As with any learning venture, success depends on mastering the basics. Currently, the two biggest applications of Internet technology are the World Wide Web and electronic mail.

INFO*nugget*

"... the true extent of the stampede from newsprint to hypertext has become clear. Since September [1995], 864 newspapers have gone online ... A total of 768 commercial newspapers are online today in the United States. Nine months ago, there were only 154."

— Eric K. Meyer, "All the Newspapers That Fit: New Numbers Show the Extent of the Trend — Or Is It a Fad?" NewsLink. http://www.newslink.org/

World Wide Web

The World Wide Web is a vast collection of text, graphics, sound, and occasionally, video files. With special software called a *Web browser* you can view the material on the Web by pointing the cursor and clicking your mouse button. Among the millions of Web pages you will find news stories, online museum exhibits, art gallery displays, government information resources, distance learning courses, weather maps, online catalogs, and interactive computer games, to name just a few possibilities.

You can also use a Web browser as a communications tool — for example, to send electronic mail or to participate in online discussions. Technologies such as *Web conferencing*, in which messages are posted to the Web for ongoing discussions, and *push technology*, which allows customized data delivery, have greatly enhanced the relatively static presentation of text and graphics.

Electronic mail

Electronic mail rivals the Web as the most common Internet application; some consider it the most powerful application on the Net.

Electronic mail allows you to send and receive individual messages over the Internet, as well as participate in group discussions. Many people with limited Internet access rely on electronic mail to obtain online publications, software, and even information from Web pages.

Electronic mail lets you communicate with anyone who has an

Internet address. For journalists, electronic mail can be a method for making contacts with experts, conducting interviews, and networking with colleagues. Many researchers use electronic mail contacts to conduct surveys or focus groups and to locate information sources.

Through electronic mail, researchers, writers, and students can also join worldwide discussion groups. There are close to 40,000 different discussion groups on the Internet. Participants use them to keep abreast of professional news, to gain background on particular topics, and to pursue personal interests. Journalists might join JOURNET, a discussion group for journalism educators, or CARR-L, which discusses the use of computers in journalism. YAFICT-L offers writing tips, market possibilities, workshops, and personal support for writers of young adult fiction. An Internet mailing address gives you access to discussion groups in business, politics, arts, health, humanities, science, nature, and recreation. Today, Internet newsgroups and listservers are valuable communications tools. (We discuss newsgroups and listservers in detail in Chapter 6.)

Other Internet applications

Although the Web and electronic mail are currently the two most important technologies on the Internet, there are other Internet tools as well. Most of these are accessible using just your Web browser, although some require more specialized software. (Web browsers and related helper applications are described in Chapters 2 and 3.)

Online chat and conferencing. It is possible to participate in real-time communications on the Internet by using a "chat" program such as Global Chat or Internet TeleCafe. These give you access to Internet Relay Chat (IRC) networks or "chat rooms," where users engage in social conversation or take part in scheduled events, such as online discussions with politicians or bestselling authors.

Another form of Internet communication is group conferencing based on stored text messages. Web conferencing software is used for "town hall" meetings and online class discussions. A number of

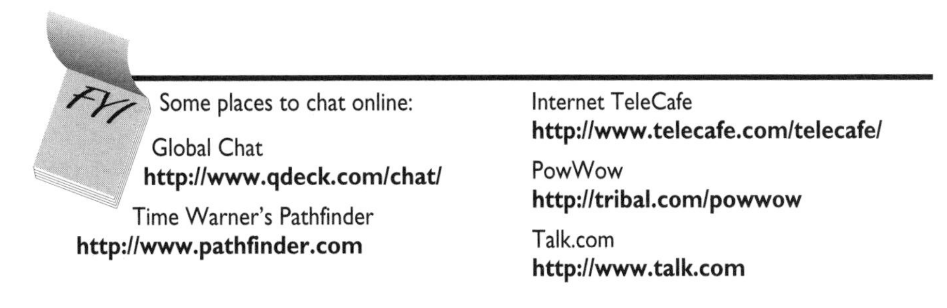

online magazine sites sponsor Web conferences; a few conference sites, such as ICS Netropolis (http://chat.acmeweb.com/), let you set up your own conference room on the Web.

Audio and interactive video. With the proper computer setup (including speakers, a sound card, and Web phone software, which you can buy at your local computer store), you can also use the Internet in place of the telephone. While this technology is not yet common, it is estimated that more than one million people currently use it.

You can also have instant access to radio and other audio broadcasts with technologies such as *RealAudio*. (We discuss RealAudio in Chapter 3.) Desktop videoconferencing and video over the Internet are still limited on slower-speed networks (such as those dependent on ordinary telephone lines), but new techniques for compressing and transmitting data may make these high-end applications widely available in just a few years.

FYI Some newer browsers, such as Microsoft's Internet Explorer 3.0 and Netscape Communicator, allow you to use text or audio and an online "whiteboard" to interact with people over the Internet.

The proliferation of cable television services, set-top boxes (for Internet access via your television), and satellite communications technologies may facilitate the development of an all-purpose tool that will one day bring interactive audio, video, and broadcast services to average technology users.

Gopher, FTP, and telnet. These are older technologies that you may have heard about. All are still available on the Internet. A Gopher site on the Internet is like a Web site without the pictures. FTP is used to transfer files from one computer to another, and telnet is used to search library catalogs or interact with those computers that are on the Internet, but are not readily accessible through a Web page. We discuss these three technologies further in Chapter 3 (Gopher and FTP) and Chapter 5 (telnet).

Challenges and opportunities in electronic communications

As the technology continues to develop, the Internet promises radical changes in the way we communicate, at work and at play. The Internet holds exciting possibilities for news gathering and other mass media. It also poses a number of challenges.

Although the Internet offers a wealth of information, much of it is of questionable value. Most of us like our information served up in carefully selected and easily digestible bites. We don't necessarily want to know when *Sailor Moon* broadcasts in Tokyo, or which San Diego grocery stores deliver. While it's thrilling to be able to send messages to people all over the world via the Internet, it is less of a thrill to have hundreds of people we don't know sending messages to us.

10 new ways to get the news

Many newspapers and news broadcast sources offer online versions of the news. Quite a few of these are free, while others charge a modest fee.

NewsHound (http://www.sjmercury.com/hound.htm)
The *San Jose Mercury News* has developed NewsHound, which searches newspapers and wire services for topics of interest to you. With a subscription, you can specify up to five different topic profiles. Topics can range from computers to garage sales. NewsHound scans its news sources every hour on the hour, and sends the most relevant articles to your electronic mailbox.

Reuters News Headlines (http://www.yahoo.com)
You can access news headlines and summaries from Reuters News Service at Yahoo. This service offers the day's top stories as well as business news, technology, sports, entertainment, politics, health, and weather around the world. At Yahoo you can also click on Xtra! for quick access to the day's headlines or register for My Yahoo, which will provide personalized news based on your interests. For serious news addicts, My Yahoo also offers a news service that scrolls horizontally across the bottom of your Windows 95 screen, even while you're working in a non-Internet application.

ClariNet e.News (http://www.clari.net)
This is an electronic newspaper that delivers professional news and information to your computer in the Usenet news format. To receive ClariNet news, your Internet access provider must subscribe to the ClariNet service. Many universities and some freenets offer ClariNet news. ClariNet draws from UPI, Reuters, BizWire, and Newsbytes. You can sample ClariNet e.News from the newsgroup *biz.clarinet.sample*.

NewsPage Direct (http://www.netcom.com)
NewsPage Direct will deliver a customized news page to your e-mail box. Once you have created your personal news profile based on the subjects that you are interested in, informative daily briefings will be delivered every weekday by 7 A.M. Use your Web browser to jump to full-text versions of the stories.

PointCast Internet Broadcast (http://pioneer.pointcast.com)
PointCast is a free Internet broadcast service. Headlines scroll across your computer screen 24 hours a day. This service is free (watch for ads!) and offers headline news, stock information, industry updates, weather, and sports. You can even get a customized version featuring the kinds of stories that are of most interest to you.

TimesFax (http://nytimesfax.com)
TimesFax is a brief news update from the *New York Times*, delivered in Portable Document Format (PDF). With TimesFax, you access the news through a Web site or have it delivered via electronic mail. Then, you must download the file and call it up in a special PDF viewer (such as Adobe Acrobat or Envoy) to read or print the document on your local printer. The advantage to PDF is that the original column format, along with photos or diagrams, is preserved. PDF viewers are "freeware," software that may be downloaded from the Internet at no charge.

CNN (http://www.cnn.com)
CNN provides access to headline news and complete transcripts of their news broadcasts.

AP (http://www.trib.com/NEWS/APwire.html)
You can access the Associated Press directly on the Internet. The service lets you browse or search the latest news.

CBC Radio News (http://www.radio.cbc.ca/)
The Canadian Broadcast Corporation delivers hourly news reports in text and downloadable audio format.

NewsLink (http://www.newslink.org/)
The *Wall Street Journal*, the *Los Angeles Times*, and the *Calgary Herald* are all now online. Many weekly newspapers, community papers, university papers, and even high school papers have found their way into cyberspace. You can find out about many of these at NewsLink.

A big challenge for writers and journalists is how to attract and sustain an audience. Someone has estimated that the average amount of time spent on a Web page is about 15 seconds — not much time in which to build readership. Journalists are used to developing material that springs from the interests of their readers. How do you write a story that will capture the attention of even a fraction of the millions of people who use the Internet? And how will anyone find an article you've written in a technology-mediated universe that must be navigated by computerized search engines, and where your piece may well be served up along with hundreds of others on the same topic?

> "Most houses have a catch-all closet, or attic, or junk drawer — a disorganized space strewn with dozens of odds and ends. We tolerate this messiness because it is our messiness. But imagine that people from all over the world could toss items into your junk drawer at will — and imagine that every item came wrapped in virtually identical fashion, so that you couldn't tell a knickknack from a jewel from a lewd postcard without first opening the package. Welcome to the Internet."
>
> — Herb Brody, *Technology Review*, Vol. 99, No. 1 (January 1996), p. 11.

FYI Editors are used to sifting through content to determine a story's "angle" — what's relevant and what's not. Now there's a company on the Internet that provides this service. **BroadVision Technologies (http://www.theangle.com/)** devises a "personality profile" for you based on your interests, then preselects Web pages that are tailored to your profile.

But the Internet also represents new markets for many writers. Journalists in small communities and those working for smaller publications can draw on a much broader range of sources than were previously readily available. Electronic communications provide unique opportunities for interviews, and story ideas abound.

For researchers, the Internet poses some new challenges as well, such as mastering the many different ways to search the Web and keeping abreast of what's available. While this takes time and effort, most researchers will benefit from the mushrooming of resources that are accessible online.

The most important factor in mastering the electronic universe is learning to use the Internet well. It's a cinch to call up your Web browser and start surfing, but it takes time and a deeper understanding of what the Internet is all about to use it effectively.

Looking ahead: What does the future hold?

We have talked about some of the good things on the Internet, and acknowledged a few of the negatives. But what does the future hold? It's easy enough to predict that the technology will continue to develop so that people will be able to do more and more things on the Internet — watch movies, play 3D chess, book a business trip, order take-out food. We believe, however, that the two most important applications for the Internet will continue to be information exchange and global communications. Both areas offer phenomenal opportunities for Internet-savvy reporters and information professionals.

We anticipate that there will be increased demand for non-technicians to participate in developing services on the Internet. To some extent, content on the information highway has been neglected in favor of technical development. But the focus is beginning to shift from laying the tarmac to sprucing up the destinations. This shift represents a prime opportunity for journalists, writers, and information specialists to become content creators and experts on the Net.

Interestingly, much of the future demand for writers and content experts will come not from the traditional publishing community (though publishers too are finding a place on the Web), but from other kinds of companies with products to sell. Whereas traditional print publications control content but need commercial advertisers to cover printing costs, advertising online needs useful, informative articles to attract readership. Commercial sponsors are therefore becoming more involved in developing online publications and information sources. For example, Toyota sponsors six different electronic magazines; L.L. Bean provides access to a database of national parks; and Molsons, the Canadian beer company, provides listings for upcoming concerts across Canada.

The Internet remains in many ways unpredictable. Who would have guessed, just a few years ago, that electronic mail would edge out the post office ("snail mail") as the primary vehicle for business communications? Figuring out just where the opportunities will be is one of the things that makes the Internet interesting and fun.

Ultimately, there are probably only two things we can say for certain about the Internet: it's bound to keep on growing, and it will offer the best opportunities to those who become most skilled at using and developing material for this new medium.

> "Computers are incredibly fast, accurate and stupid; humans are incredibly slow, inaccurate and brilliant; together they are powerful beyond imagination."
>
> — Albert Einstein

Further reading

Botkin, Jim, and Davis, Stan. *The Monster Under the Bed: How Business Is Mastering the Opportunity of Knowledge for Profit*. New York: Touchstone Books, 1995.

Brockman, John. *Digerati: Encounters with the Cyber Elite*. San Francisco: Hardwired, 1996.

Information Highway Advisory Council. *Connection, Community, Content: The Challenge of the Information Highway. Final Report*. Ottawa: Supply & Services Canada, 1995. http://info.ic.gc.ca/info-highway/ih.html

McQueen, Rod, and Tapscott, Don. *The Digital Economy: Promise and Peril in the Age of Networked Intelligence*. New York: McGraw-Hill, 1995.

Stoll, Clifford. *Silicon Snake Oil: Second Thoughts on the Information Highway*. New York: Doubleday, 1995.

Chapter 2

First You Have to Connect

"...Many people, including some experienced Net riders, don't have a good grasp of what the Internet really is. [For them] it's sort of a virtual embodiment of Gertrude Stein's description of Oakland, California: there's no 'there' there. Strip away the peels of the Internet onion, and all you have are layers of technology — a bunch of rules for moving data around."

— STEVEN LEVY, *NEWSWEEK*, FEBRUARY 25, 1995, P. 22.

Not very long ago, if you wanted to get online you had to know something about all those layers of technology tucked into the Internet onion (and you could expect to shed a few tears once you started peeling). Luckily, connecting to the Internet is now much easier. Where once you had to find your way through a confusing maze of options, today it is possible to buy software from a local computer vendor or bookstore that will have you connected in less than an hour. There are, however, a few things to think about before you buy. What equipment do you need? What factors should you consider in choosing a service provider? Which software is best, and how can you obtain it?

This chapter is primarily for newcomers to the Net: it will help you make the necessary decisions to get you up and running. If you're already connected to the Internet, you may want to move directly to Chapter 3. You can always consult this chapter at a later date if you decide to change Internet providers, or if you wish to upgrade your Internet software.

Chapter highlights

- **Hardware requirements for getting online**
- **Getting an Internet account**
- **Dialing in to your account**
- **Internet software: Client/server computing, Web browsers, electronic mail, and more**

Hardware requirements for getting online

Computer

You can have simple access to electronic mail even with an old computer and a slow modem. But for surfing the World Wide Web, you'll need, at a *minimum:*

- a 386 PC or Macintosh 680040 central processing unit (CPU)
- a 100-megabyte (MB) hard drive with 8 MB RAM
- a 14,400-baud modem.

While this equipment will do the job, it is preferable to have a more powerful computer with the fastest modem and the largest hard drive you can afford. If you are buying a new computer, consider an IBM-compatible multimedia Pentium, or a Macintosh PowerPC. Such attributes as the amount of available RAM (Random Access Memory) and the size and speed of the hard drive inevitably have an effect on your computer's performance on Internet tasks. As a general rule, you will want eight or sixteen megabytes of RAM.

If you are a researcher, you will also require a substantial hard drive, particularly if you are planning to run Windows 95 or Windows NT. A one-gigabyte (or more) hard drive is increasingly standard fare. To access video and multimedia applications, you will require a video adapter card with one megabyte or more of video memory and an SVGA monitor. If these options are currently beyond your budget, you can still comfortably use the Internet for research without these expensive options.

If it's not possible to purchase a new computer, consider upgrading your current system. You can add memory to your CPU and a second hard drive for less money than it would cost to buy a new computer. Your local dealer can inform you of the range of options for upgrading.

Modem

The rule of thumb for buying a computer for Internet access is: Buy the best you can afford. Purchasing a modem, however, presents another series of questions. The options include internal modems, external modems, fax/modems, and cable modems.

The purpose of a modem is to change computer data signals into analog signals so that they can be sent over the telephone lines. Here are several features that you will want to be aware of in shopping for a modem:

Speed. The speed of a modem is known as the *baud rate*. The baud rate tells you how many computer bits can be transmitted per second (bps). Although a 14,400 bps modem is acceptable, it is preferable to have a faster modem, such as 28,800 or 33,600 bps.

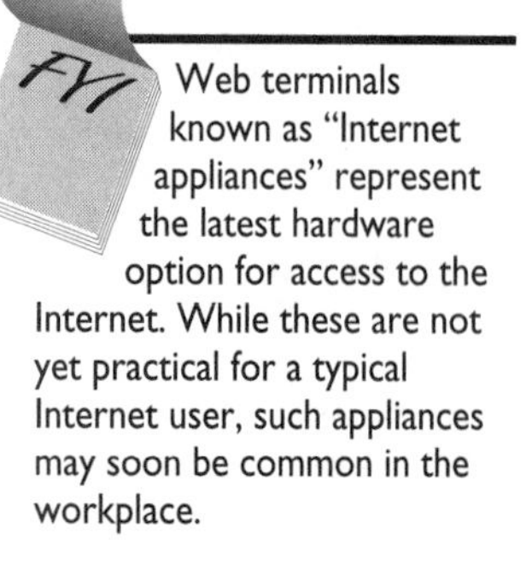

Web terminals known as "Internet appliances" represent the latest hardware option for access to the Internet. While these are not yet practical for a typical Internet user, such appliances may soon be common in the workplace.

Modems are no longer expensive: most are in the US$100 to $300 range. The faster the modem, the more expensive it will be. In assessing the overall cost, consider that having a faster modem can help reduce your online costs. Speed will become increasingly important as more and more video and multimedia resources appear on the Internet. Cable modems and modems for use with high-speed ISDN lines are not yet in general use, but both these technologies promise very fast access in the not-too distant future.

Two further decisions that need to be made before you purchase are whether to purchase an external or internal modem, and whether to purchase a fax/modem.

Remember that your data transfer speed will be affected by the speed of the modem at the other end. A 28,800-baud modem is considered standard these days, and most Internet service providers should be able to offer access at this speed. A university computer, however, may only offer dial-in access at 9,600 baud. Any modem can accommodate speeds slower than its maximum, so that a 33,600-baud modem will be able to step down to slower speeds.

Internal vs. external. Deciding between an internal and an external modem is largely a matter of personal preference. Some people find external modems easier to install, and it can be reassuring to see the flashing lights signal that something is happening when you use an external modem. Another plus is that an external modem is portable, so that you can use it on different computers. On the other hand, internal modems are slightly less expensive and do not require a separate cable or power adapter. They also do not take up space on your desktop.

Fax/modem. A fax/modem is a good option for what is usually a small additional investment. These days, most modems do include fax capability. While a fax/modem may not replace a physical fax for heavy users of fax transmission, it is entirely adequate for most people's fax needs. With a fax/modem, faxes are delivered to your computer. Fax software (which comes with the modem) allows you to print the fax using your computer printer. With a laptop or a powerbook, a fax/modem will let you use any fax machine as a printing device. This can be a great advantage when you are working away from your usual base of operations.

Remember that phone lines can be "tone" or "pulse." Most people today have tone dial service, but if you live in a rural area you may have pulse. When installing your modem, be prepared to specify your dialing service — as well as any special codes you need to use (such as dialing 9 for an outside line). For example, if you must dial 9, you would type in your modem's dialing protocol using a comma to indicate a brief pause in the sequence. Thus, typing "9,1-800..." instructs your modem to pause briefly after dialing the 9. For a longer pause, insert two commas.

Installation. Your modem comes with a detailed manual describing how to install and use the product. Frequently, a diskette is provided that walks you through the installation on your system. Newer operating systems, such as OS/2 Warp and Windows 95, provide communications services (like Internet access) as an integral part of the operating system, and this makes things even easier. Windows 95 streamlines modem setup by including auto-configure utilities for installing many different kinds of modems.

Modems come with many standard settings already in place. Most of the time, the factory settings will work just fine, but if you run into difficulty, check to see if your modem manufacturer offers a 1-800 help desk service. You can also ask your dealer for help. Some computer dealers will even install the modem for you, though they may charge a small fee for this extra service.

INFO*nugget*

Boardwatch Magazine reports that, as of August, 1996, there were 2,900 Internet service providers in the United States, and 3,100 when Canadian providers are included in the total. Watch for these numbers to decrease as competition heats up!

What you'll need for cruising the Internet

	SLOW	ACCEPTABLE	GREAT PERFORMANCE
Computer			
PC	386	486	Pentium
Macintosh	680040	PowerPC 603	PowerPC 604
Operating system			
PC	Windows 3.1	Windows 95	Windows 95
Macintosh	7.5.1	7.5.3	Open Transport
Hard drive	100 MB	810 MB	1–2 GB
RAM	8 MB	16 MB	32 MB
Modem speed	14,400 bps	28,800 bps	33,600 bps or ISDN

If you are a student or a faculty member at a university, you may get free Internet access from your institution's computing services, but it may not include graphical capability. This type of non-graphical account is sometimes called a *shell account*. With a shell account, you will not be able to use Windows or Mac software to interact with the network unless the university is also running a special Internet adapter program. You can find out about an adapter program called **SLiRP at: http://www.webcom.com/~||arrow/tiarefg.html**

Getting an Internet account

An Internet service provider (or ISP) is a company or agency that sells or makes available accounts that allow you to dial in to the Internet. Some ISPs also offer a link to the Internet through some form of permanent connection, such as a dedicated phone line. As an individual user, you will be most interested in a type of access called PPP or SLIP. These acronyms simply refer to two different ways to get Windows-based or other graphical access to the Net. Your ISP will offer at least one type of access, and possibly both. SLIP is the older of these two technologies and is now almost obsolete. For most individual users, it doesn't matter which protocol is used, since they both do essentially the same thing: They allow your computer to talk to your ISP's computer as though you were both on the same hard-wired network — when actually you are using a modem connection via telephone lines.

The two features to look for in an Internet service provider are reliability and value for money. This can mean a bargain-basement, no-frills local provider. Or it can mean paying more money, but receiving more service options — such as support for your personal Web page, a reliable help desk service, or an opportunity to connect through a high-speed ISDN line. Provider options range from small local providers (some of whom have fewer than 1,000 customers) to national services, such as AT&T's WorldNet service, Netcom, or Sympatico in Canada. You can also purchase Internet access through traditional commercial online services, such as CompuServe or America Online. These offer Internet access plus many extra services that are not available from other providers, such as online encyclopedias or special financial information services.

Although there are a number of resources on the Internet that provide information on ISPs (such as **The List** at **http://thelist.com**), you will have difficulty obtaining these unless you already have some way to access the Internet. A better way is to look for lists of service providers in computer magazines. *Boardwatch Magazine* publishes an annual directory of ISPs. You can also check business magazines, Internet books, phone or business directories, and newspapers. Frequently, you can get leads on ISPs from your local computer store, or you can ask friends who already have a service provider for their recommendations. Your friends may also be able to warn you about providers to avoid.

One of the simplest ways to connect is to buy one of the "off the shelf" Internet packages from your local computer dealer. These packages usually contain all the software you need, and they will automatically connect you to an Internet provider. Just make sure that the provider is one you would choose to use, or that you can change easily to another provider, should you find one that offers better value.

Cost. Costs for Internet access vary widely and commonly range from US$15 to $35 for thirty hours or more. Some providers offer unlimited access for approximately US$20 per month. While some local bulletin board services offer inexpensive access to the Internet, they may provide only electronic mail. Others may include access to the Web, but they may restrict total hours available to subscribers.

Commercial online services are usually the most expensive, but their additional data resources may justify the additional cost to a

Quick reference guide to North American Internet providers

Access in the United States:		
America Online	800-827-6364	http://www.aol.com/
CompuServe	800-848-8199	http://world.compuserve.com/
Microsoft Network	800-386-6399	http://www.msn.com/
Prodigy	800-PRODIGY	http://www.prodigy.com/
AT&T WorldNet	800-967-5368	http://www.att.com/
Netcom	800-777-9638	http://www.netcom.com
SpryNet	800-777-9638	http://www.sprynet.com
GNN	800-819-6112	http://www.gnn.com
PSINet	703-904-4100	http://www.psi.net/
OnRamp	1-888-GET-1495	http://www.theonramp.net/
Access in Canada:		
Sympatico	1-800-773-2121	http://www1.sympatico.ca
iStar	1-888-Go-iSTAR	http://www.istar.ca/
Hookup Communication	1-800-363-0400	http://www.hookup.net/
CNet (rural communities)		http://cnet.unb.ca/cnet/

For detailed information about commercial providers, try **Jay Barker's Online Connection** at: **http://www.barkers.org/online/**

student or researcher. CompuServe, for example, offers access to a full-text magazine database and Grolier's Multimedia Encyclopedia.

At the moment, the ISP marketplace is very competitive, with larger, international services squeezing out smaller, local providers. This intense competition should ultimately benefit consumers. Unlimited access at an affordable price will soon be available across the continent.

To determine which ISP is most suitable for your needs, consider how many hours you are likely to spend online. You may have to guess, but be generous. Many people are amazed to discover how frequently the intention to spend ten minutes online looking for one piece of information turns into two hours of "surfing." Next, compare the costs of the options available, including those services that involve long distance charges. Remember that a fast modem can reduce long distance costs, and will sometimes be less expensive, overall, than a slow local service.

Freenets

Freenets are community-based, computerized bulletin boards designed to provide local residents with a forum in which to share information. Freenets exist in many urban communities in North America. The greatest advantage of freenets is that they are free!

It's easy to join a freenet. Usually, you just dial in using your

10 tips for finding a good service provider

1. **Seek a provider who advertises "no busy signals."** You can test the claim by obtaining the access number and dialing in from your telephone. Pick times of the day when you anticipate using the service.
2. **Your provider should offer at least 28,800-baud access.** A few also offer very high-speed access over ISDN lines, though the cost for this is high relative to the needs of most individuals.
3. **Look for a provider with an automated registration process.** This reduces the likelihood of problems in getting connected.
4. **Your provider should offer a phone-in help desk.** What are their hours? Is there any additional charge for help? Is the desk staffed by a machine or a person?
5. **If you travel a lot, consider getting an account with a major national provider.** This will allow you to dial in to the account from a local number in most cities.
6. **Find out what documentation and software are provided with your account.**
7. **Ask around.** Your friends or your local computer dealer might have some good suggestions. Seek opinions from more than one source.
8. **Watch for free trial offers that allow you to sample a service.** Some services offer money-back guarantees. Quite a few commercial online services provide diskettes for easy access and ten or fifteen hours of free Internet time.
9. **Unless you are on a tight budget, make sure your provider offers comprehensive Internet service.** This should include graphical access to the World Wide Web.
10. **Spend adequate time researching which provider is best for you.** It's tempting to go with the least expensive option, but if you make a mistake and later want to switch providers, it's a hassle to have to change your e-mail address.

modem, log in as a guest, and follow the online instructions to register. After a few days, you'll be given your own login and password.

However, a freenet account will not meet the needs of the average researcher or journalist. The limitations of a freenet account include:

- a time limit online (often only one hour per day)
- limit on services, such as FTP
- limited mailbox size
- difficulties in establishing a connection due to a shortage of lines
- usually, only non-graphical access.

Despite these limitations, journalists and writers may want to sign up for a freenet account *in addition* to an account with a commercial access provider. Freenets are an excellent source of local information that may not otherwise be available on the Web. Through a freenet you can track local issues, hear about school board meetings, check the activities of business associations and benevolent groups, obtain municipal information, and generally keep up with what's happening in your community.

Dialing in to your Internet account

The next step in connecting to the Internet is to dial in to your account. If your ISP has provided you with preconfigured dial-in software, dialing in for the first time can be reasonably easy, but sometimes you need to add setup information to your software. In the Windows environment, this dialer software is known as Winsock (for *Win*dows *Sock*et). If you have a Macintosh you'll be using MacTCP together with InterSLIP, MacSLIP, or MacPPP.

TCP/IP (Transport Control Protocol/Internet Protocol) is a term you will likely bump into. This is the set of computer rules that govern the way data get moved around from place to place on the Internet. Simply put, TCP/IP is how computers on the Internet talk to each other. You don't have to know much about TCP/IP, because your Internet dial-in software does, but it's a good term to know because it helps you understand how the Internet works.

The TCP part packages up the bits of information, while the IP adds the address. One of the pieces of information you may need to insert into your software program is the IP address for your Internet provider. This set of four numbers (e.g., 130.142.79.225) tells other computers on the Internet exactly where in the network universe to find the computer you wish to connect to.

One Internet author has offered a vivid analogy for how TCP/IP works:

> "Say you wanted to take apart an old covered bridge in New England and move it lock, stock and barrel to California (people do these things). You would dismantle the sections, label them very carefully, and ship them out on

Windows 95 has built-in (32-bit) Winsock. You can access a helpful file that explains TCP/IP access with Windows 95 at: **http://www.windows95.com/connect/tcp.html**

three or four, maybe even five different trucks. Some take the northern route and some the southern route, and one just has to go through Texas. The trucks get to California at various times with one arriving a little later than the others, but your careful labels indicate which section goes up first, second, and third."

— Tracy LaQuey, *The Internet Companion*. New York: Addison-Wesley, 1993, p. 25.

If your Winsock or other dialer software is not already preconfigured by your provider (as in Figure 2-1), you will need to obtain documentation that specifies the appropriate IP numbers and settings for establishing your connection. Your access provider should give you specific directions on how to configure your software if the settings are not already in place.

To configure your dialer software, you will require the following information:

- Your user name
- Your password
- Your ISP's local telephone number for Internet access
- Your host name (this will usually match your user name)
- Your ISP's domain name
- Their IP subnet mask
- Their gateway IP address
- Their Domain Name System (DNS) address.

FYI

If your access software is already configured for connecting to a particular ISP, make sure this provider is in fact the best choice for you. For example, a recent version of Mosaic in a Box comes preconfigured with ready access to CompuServe. If your choice of vendors is not CompuServe, but you still want to use the Mosaic product, you will need to reconfigure the settings. Your preferred access provider should be willing to help you do this.

Internet software

The software that is used to access and navigate the Internet is based on *client/server* technology. Client/server is another important

Network Configuration 7:47 AM

IP address 192.0.4.1
Netmask 255.255.255.0 Default Gateway 205.207.219.65
Name server 204.208.229.20 Time server
Domain Suffix dialnet.com
Packet vector 00 MTU 256 TCP RWIN 848 TCP MSS 216
Demand Load Timeout (secs) 5 TCP RTO MAX 60

☒ Internal SLIP ☐ Internal PPP
SLIP Port 2
Baud Rate 19200
☐ Hardware Handshake
☐ Van Jacobson CSLIP compression

Online Status Detection
◉ None
○ DCD (RLSD) check
○ DSR check

Ok Cancel

Figure 2-1

Trumpet Winsock network configuration box

concept because it helps you to understand the relationship between your computer and the Internet. It's common for people, when they first start using the Internet and have "surfed," say, from New York to Brussels and then to a computer in Japan, to imagine that they have opened up connections around the world that remain open until the surfers backtrack or log off. In fact, this is not the case, because of the client/server relationship.

Client/server computing

Simply put, in a client/server environment, two pieces of software work together as a team.

The *client* is responsible for:

- the user interface (what the software looks like to you on your desktop)
- initiating the communications process
- displaying information sent from the server.

The *server*:

- retains information (such as Web pages and related files)
- analyzes requests coming from the client
- responds to requests by sending information back to the client.

In a nutshell, the client is the program that you use locally, and the remote server does what the client says.

An advantage to client/server computing is that it allows information to be passed back and forth over the Internet without the connections between computers having to remain open. The connection to a remote computer, which could be located anywhere in the world, stays open only long enough to respond to your immediate request for a menu or file. You, in turn, read the item only after it has been sent to your (local) computer. Your phone connection to your access provider, though, will remain open until you actually log off.

FYI: ZD Net is the Web site for Ziff-Davis publishing, which publishes such popular computer magazines as *MacWeek* and *PCWeek*. This site offers current magazine features that will keep you up to date about new Internet sites and products. **ZD Net** is located at: **http://home.zdnet.com**

Another advantage to client/server computing is that you can select whatever client software is most useful for you. You are not necessarily stuck with the software selection provided by your Internet service provider if you find something better or more up to date. Following are some of the current software options for Internet access.

Web browsers

The client software you use to access the World Wide Web is called a *browser*. Increasingly, Web browsers are designed to be an all-purpose Internet tool, so that the most recent browsers have a mail feature that lets you send messages directly from your browser. Where previously individual software programs handled such tasks as accessing Gophers, reading newsgroups, or transferring files, most

Figure 2-2
Microsoft Explorer is the browser of choice for many people

Microsoft Internet Explorer Home Page - Microsoft Internet Explorer

File Edit View Go Favorites Help

Address: file:C:\IEXPLORE\start.htm

Microsoft Internet Explorer

Welcome to Microsoft Internet Explorer

Microsoft Internet Explorer provides a fun and easy way to access and display Web pages, whether they are stored locally on your computer, your local network, or on the Internet. This page is stored locally on your computer.

Once you are connected to the Internet, you can use Internet Explorer to view a huge variety of information. You can also incorporate this information into your documents or save it to a file on your computer.

Start exploring now!

- To browse the Web pages on a server installed on your local network, type the name of that server in the Address box at the top of this window. For example, if the server is named \\CorpNet, type: **Corpnet**
- To view World Wide Web pages on a server that is on the Internet, type the address of the server in the Address box.
- If you are connected to the Internet and need a place to begin browsing, click the following link, www.msn.com, to find information about Microsoft products and some links to other useful sites.

For more information about Microsoft Internet Explorer, see Getting Started, or the Help Contents.

Today, you can even access the Internet through your television! For this you need a "set-top box," which replaces your computer, and a WebTV browser. This is not the best way for a researcher to access the Net, but if you're curious, you can find out more about **WebTV** at:
http://webtv.net

of these jobs can now be done easily with a Web browser. Your ISP will provide you with a Web browser or will recommend a particular one to use.

Once you are comfortable using the Web, feel free to explore the range of browser possibilities. New and improved Web browsers are always on the horizon.

Electronic mail software

Another primary tool you will want to be familiar with (in addition to your Web browser) is electronic mail software. The ease with which you can compose and send messages over the Internet will depend on the electronic mail software you select. Some Web browsers can send and receive mail, but many people still prefer to use a separate mail package, which may offer a few additional features.

In a Windows or Macintosh environment you will have a choice of user-friendly mail packages (such as Eudora Mail, Claris Emailer, or Pegasus). Commercial services such as America Online, Prodigy, and the Microsoft Network integrate mail programs into their customized software programs. Most come preconfigured with your return address. AOL even lets you use different fonts within an electronic message, which can be viewed by others using the AOL mail program. If you are working in a non-graphical computer environment, a popular electronic mail program is Pine.

The latest versions of most Web browsers attempt to keep in step with current Internet applications, but not all will support the newest features on the Web. Keep up with the newest browsers (and new versions of your old favorites) at **David J. Graffa's Browser Watch** page:
http://browserwatch.iworld.com

Web browsers

Netscape Navigator (http://home.netscape.com/)
Netscape has dominated the browser market for several years and remains one of the most popular and powerful browsers. The Netscape Web browser incorporates a newsgroup reader and an electronic mail manager. One of the latest versions of Netscape, Netscape Communicator, will even let you chat with people directly if both of you are online at the same time. (Because Netscape Navigator is currently the browser used by most people, it will be discussed in detail in Chapter 3.)

Netscape Gold (ftp://ftp2.netscape.com/pub/)
This version of Netscape includes an HTML editor. HTML (Hypertext Markup Language) is the coding used to format pages on the World Wide Web. (We discuss HTML in Chapter 8.) Netscape Gold would be a good choice for someone intending to do a lot of Web page development.

Microsoft Internet Explorer (http://www.microsoft.com/ie/)
Microsoft Internet Explorer (MIE) is Netscape's primary rival in the browser marketplace. Originally developed as a complement to Windows 95, the browser is now available for Windows 3.1 and even the Macintosh computer platform. MIE is currently available for free. An important plus for this browser is that it makes help files available on your system's hard disk, rather than on a remote server. This is an important plus if you are paying for access time while trying to master the use of your browser.

The MIE browser has a feature called ActiveX, which allows you to display other Windows applications over the Internet. This promises to be an important feature, but there are currently not a lot of Web sites that incorporate this application. Other browsers will likely follow suit once this becomes a more significant demand. The popularity of MIE is rapidly increasing, as a number of online providers have adopted it as their browser of choice.

Opera (http://traviata.nta.no/opera.htm)
This is a very good browser from Norway. It loads pages very quickly and, for this reason, may be of interest to those using an older computer (such as a 386). Opera provides the option of automatically saving a site you are exploring from one session to the next. It will also allow you to open up to four different "surfing" windows at any one time.

Cyberdog (http://cyberdog.apple.com/)
Cyberdog is a browser for Macintosh computers. With it you can read and write electronic mail, participate in Usenet discussion groups, and use FTP and telnet, in addition to cruising the Web. Cyberdog also lets you enjoy movies, playback sounds, and QuickTime movies without the need for additional applications. Its notebook file stores Web addresses (called URLs), e-mail addresses, and notes.

Lynx (http://www.nyu.edu/pages/wsn/subir/lynx.html)
Lynx is a text-only browser and is commonly available on university- or library-based computers. While it is not a browser that you would likely choose for your personal computer, you may need to use Lynx as your

Web browser if you are accessing the Web through a shell account (rather than a PPP or SLIP connection). Access to Lynx is quick, and it has a number of useful features (such as the ability to mail a file directly), but the fact that Lynx does not handle graphics will make it less attractive for most users. (For a more detailed discussion of Lynx, see Appendix A at the back of this book.)

Browsers are available for many different computer platforms. If you are still running a DOS-based computer, you can try **NetTamer**, which can be found at: **http://www.delphi.com/people/davidcolston/** or **Minuet**, which can be found at: **ftp://minuet.micro.umn.edu/pub/minuet/**

There are many sources on the Internet for information about electronic mail software:

Eudora
http://www.eudora.com/

Claris Emailer
http://www.claris.com

Pegasus Mail by David Harris
http://www.cuslm.ca/pegasus/

Elm — Electronic Mail for UNIX
http://www.myxa.com/elm.html

Pine Information Center
http://www.washington.edu:1180/pine/

Most e-mail programs allow you to:

- send electronic mail
- send one or more carbon copies to different addresses
- reply to electronic mail sent to you
- forward electronic mail
- save messages to a file
- send enclosures or attachments
- automatically include a customized signature
- delete electronic messages.

More advanced mail software may include such features as a built-in spell-checker, filters that file incoming messages into different folders, or access to Web sites by simply clicking on the address. Some packages even let you send and receive faxes.

Chapter 6 provides more detailed information on sending and receiving electronic mail.

Other Internet software

Your Internet software may or may not include newsreader, telnet, and FTP software. In the chapters that follow, we will explain how to obtain these through your Web browser, but you can also sample these applications using the various software packages offered by your Internet service provider.

Here are some of our favorite sources for finding Internet software online:

Tucows (Windows and Macintosh)
http://www.tucows.com/

Stroud's Consummate Winsock Apps List
http://www.stroud.com/cwsa.html

Windows95.com 32-bit Shareware Collection
http://www.windows95.com/apps/

University of Texas Macintosh Archives
http://wwwhost.ots.utexas.edu/mac/main.html

Suite software

Another option for obtaining Internet software is to purchase some type of suite software package. Suite software integrates a number of different Internet tools for easy transition between Internet applications — such as Web browsing, electronic mail, and online chat. Major commercial online providers (e.g., CompuServe or America Online) generally offer some type of suite software designed to streamline access to their particular service. For example, with the integrated package from America Online, you can enter a real-time online chat group with a simple click, rather than having to call up a separate chat program.

You can also buy suite software off the shelf. Various "in-a-box" products are designed to work as an integrated suite of programs. Examples include *Internet in a Box* from O'Reilly and Associates, *Netscape in a Box*, and *Graphix Zone ExpressNet Suite*. With the increasing availability of sophisticated browsers that integrate applications, purchasing a separate suite package for Internet access may become less attractive. However, the promise of easy set-up remains appealing for many non-technically inclined people. One "all-in-one" package will automatically set up and configure over twenty-five Internet applications, such as Internet phone software, document readers, audio and video players, learning tutorials, and site directories.

You can find out about suite packages by browsing through computer magazines or checking for boxed Internet software at a computer store.

Further reading

"E-Mail Moves Beyond the LAN." *PC Magazine*, Vol. 14, No. 8 (April 25, 1995).

"Getting up to Speed." [Advice on cable modems.] *Newsweek*, Vol. 128, No. 10 (March 4, 1996), p. 46.

"Internet Access: Cable Modems."
http://www.zdnet.com/wsources/960617/featsub4.html

"Online Services in an Internet World." *PC Magazine*, Vol. 15, No. 11 (April 25, 1995).

Prendergast, Richard A. *Learn to Use Your Modem in a Day*. (Popular Applications Series.) Plano, Texas: Wordware, 1995.

University of Chicago Campus Computer Stores. "Introduction to Modems."
http://www-ccs.uchicago.edu/technotes/Modems.html

Chapter 3

Tip-Toeing Onto the Web

"[The Web] is simply amazingly complicated despite the seductive simplicity of its easy-to-use hypertext human interface. One wag compared WWW navigation to trying to get from one part of a city to another by moving through a series of tunnels connecting the basements of the city's buildings."

— THOMAS COPLEY, MAKE THE LINKS WORKSHOP, TUTORIAL NO. 4, NOVEMBER 3, 1996.

The Web is seductive. Once you've connected for the first time, the temptation is to start "surfing" the universe. This is not difficult to do; most Web browsers are designed to help you find your way around. Netscape, for example, gives simple, point-and-click access to the Web, using buttons labeled "What's New," "Directory," and so on. Highlighted links to other Web pages and browser toolbars make it a snap to continue gliding around, sampling everything from the Ottawa Senators Hockey team to Hillary's Hair (a site that features hairstyles worn by Hillary Clinton). The only hazard here is the fallout that might result from neglecting your family, your job, your sleep, and other aspects of the "real" world competing for your attention.

As tempting as it is to continue randomly sampling the wealth of goodies on the Net, sooner or later you will want to move beyond this and learn how to use the Web efficiently as a research tool. You will want to find the best sites for your area of interest, know how to return to important resources, go directly to a resource that a colleague has recommended, and make use of links that download files rather than display Web pages.

This chapter covers the mechanics of Web browsers and the World Wide Web (WWW).

Chapter highlights

- **WWW: An overview**
- **Browsers: Netscape vs. Explorer**
- **Navigating the Web: Netscape, URLs, bookmarks, browser helper applications**
- **Other Internet applications: RealAudio, computer conferencing, Gophers, FTP**

WWW: An overview

The World Wide Web provides easy access over the Internet to a variety of media. Web pages can display text, pictures, sound, video, and animated graphics.

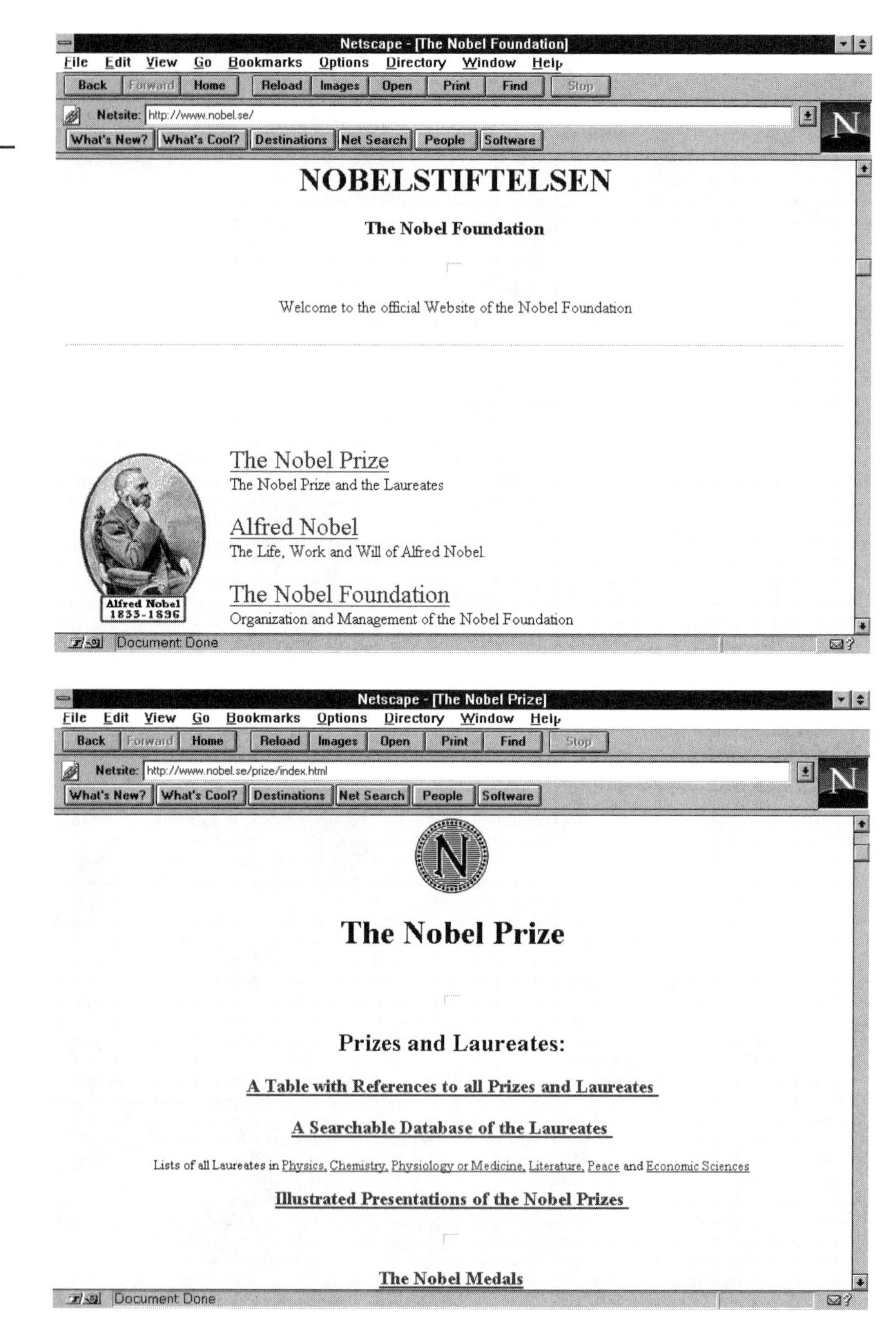

Figure 3-1
Clicking on highlighted hyperlinks brings up a new page (below).

One common feature of Web pages is *hypertext links* (or *hyperlinks*). These are spots on which you can click to move from one page to the next. Clicking on a link brings up a screen (or more) of information related to that link.

INFO*nugget*

Q. Who invented the Web, anyway?

A. Tim Berners-Lee. In 1989 Berners-Lee was working at CERN, a high-energy physics lab in Switzerland, when he got the idea for a system that would link scientific documents via the Internet, making them available to researchers worldwide. By the end of 1990, the Web consisted of one server at the CERN lab in Switzerland and one file, the CERN phone book. Today, the number of files is approaching 30 million and there are more than 200,000 servers. Today, Berners-Lee heads the World Wide Web Consortium in Cambridge, Massachusetts.

— From "A Short, Clickable History of Hypertext," *Yahoo Internet Life*, November 1996, p. 65.

Hypertext links lead you to more information whenever you choose to follow them. A simple example of a hypertext link would be a highlighted word within a document onscreen. You can click on that word to find its definition. Or, you might be viewing a document about health and nutrition, and discover a link to another document that provides in-depth information about vitamins.

Hypermedia is another term you will encounter on the Web. Hypermedia is similar to hypertext in that both denote the ability to access further information from a document. But hypermedia makes it possible to access other kinds of media besides text, such as pictures or sound files.

Increasingly, Web pages are interactive in design. Web-based forms invite visitors to provide information by filling in blank fields displayed on the screen. The computer customizes its responses based on how you have filled in the fields. You can ask the computer to send you an electronic mail reminder for an important date, or to create a personalized edition of today's news tailored to your needs or interests.

Multimedia formats (combining graphics, sound, and animation) are delivered over the Web via special helper software called *plug-ins*. These are programs specifically designed to work with particular kinds of files, such as movie files or audio files. Web pages can also "talk to" software on your desktop, and your desktop software can be used to download information from a Web page.

Browsers: Netscape vs. Explorer

Although we will talk primarily about Netscape in this chapter, remember that it is just one of many browsers available (see Chapter 2). Netscape was an early favorite that has retained its popularity, but Microsoft's Internet Explorer is currently giving Netscape a run for its money.

Both Netscape and Explorer offer many of the same features, and versions are available for both Macintosh and Windows operating systems. Both provide a toolbar for easy navigation and accept plug-ins for access to many different types of files. With either browser you will be able to track sites you've visited in the current session, save and print documents, and save references to sites you want to visit again. If you have configured your browser with information on how to locate news and mail on your Internet service provider's computer, you can also read and post to newsgroups, and receive and send electronic mail.

Because Netscape and Explorer offer very similar features, the choice between them is mostly a matter of personal preference. It's easiest to stick with the browser that is supplied or recommended by your Internet service provider (ISP), but don't be afraid to down-

The term *home page* refers to the first page that introduces you to a particular site. It can also refer to the first page that your browser loads when it starts up. Many people have personal home pages to tell people about themselves.

load and try out another browser. Chapter 2 describes where to obtain both of these popular browsers, as well as others.

Many of Netscape's features are similar to those of other Web browsers. If you are not using Netscape, locate each of the features discussed below on your own browser, and then use the Help menu to find out about additional features and options. In Lynx (the non-graphical browser that is commonly used in universities) typing **h** will bring up a list of help topics. (More detailed information about Lynx is included later in Appendix A.)

Navigating the Web

If you have successfully connected to the Internet through an ISP, chances are you've already sampled the Web. If not, just double-click on your Netscape (or other) browser icon and have a look around.

When you first start your Web browser, it will connect to a Web server and display an initial (or "home") page. Depending on the browser you are using and your ISP, the home page may be that of your service provider, or it could be the Netscape start-up page (or Microsoft Explorer's, if you're using that browser). (Later on we'll show you how to change the page that comes up first.) Generally, these home pages have been set up to make it easy for you to find useful information. For example, your ISP may provide links to local businesses and government services, as well as a gateway link to one of the popular Internet directories. Both Netscape and Explorer provide you with navigation buttons for easy access to searching tools and new or popular resources. Use whatever links are available from your browser to sample Net resources.

The links to new pages of information are highlighted — that is, they are generally brighter and often larger than other text. Sometimes they are underlined. Pictures also can be links. If you're not sure if something is a link, try clicking on it. You can also move your mouse slowly over the mouse pad and notice when the cursor on the screen changes to a hand icon (for grabbing!). When the hand appears, you can click to move to that site.

Once you've clicked on an active link, the cursor will change to an hour glass. BE PATIENT as your browser locates the computer on the other end and sends a request to it. If you are not yet used to working online, it's easy to become impatient with the length of time it takes for a page of information to come back and be displayed on your desktop. Clicking again won't help; it just confuses the computer. It takes especially long for pages to load if there are many pictures, or if you are connecting through a telephone line with a slower modem.

On Netscape the computer address for each link will appear at the lower left of your screen. This address, called a URL (for Uniform Resource Locator) changes as you move your cursor over different links on a page. Once you've clicked on a link, you can watch this spot to monitor the progress of your request being transmitted.

URLs

URLs are "addresses" that specify the computer and location on the Internet for different types of documents and resources. The first part of the URL (before the colon) indicates the access method or the type of resource you want to retrieve. The part of the URL that follows the double slash (//) specifies a machine name or site. Here are some examples:

http://www.clark.net/pub/robert/home.html This is a Web site. (The *http://* stands for *hypertext transfer protocol.*) Many URLs for Web pages include *www* after the *http://.*

gopher://unix5.nysed.gov This is a Gopher site.

file://wuarchive.wustl.edu/mirrors/msdos/graphics/gifkit.zip A URL that starts with *file://* is used to access a specific file on the Internet. A slightly different format is used to access a file on your own hard drive.

file:///c|/netscape/bookmark.htm This is an example of a URL that might be used to retrieve a file from your computer's C drive. Notice that, in this case, there are three slashes after the colon rather than two.

ftp://www.xerox.com/pub/ URLs starting with *ftp://* are used to access and transfer files. This URL would get you into the file listing for the "pub" directory at this site.

telnet://dra.com A *telnet* URL will access a login screen for a remote computer. In order to access a telnet site, you will need to have telnet software, and then set up your Web browser to call up the telnet software as a helper application (see Chapter 5).

news:alt.hyptertext If your browser has been configured to point to your newsserver (or a public newsserver), an address like this gives you access to newsgroups via your Web browser.

Browsers have other features in addition to hyperlinks that help you navigate. Both Netscape and Microsoft Explorer use a toolbar at the top of the screen. The arrow keys (bearing small icons pointing backwards and forwards) will move back and forth through pages that you have already accessed. In Netscape you can use the **Window | History** option from the pull-down menu to track which

Figure 3-2
The Netscape toolbar

Back | Forward | Home | Reload | Images | Open | Print | Find | Stop

Figure 3-3
The Netscape button bar

What's New? | What's Cool? | Destinations | Net Search | People | Software

sites you've already visited. Double-click on any you want to return to. The button that depicts a house will take you back to the opening (home) page.

Navigating with Netscape*

You can navigate at any point using hyperlinks, but Netscape also provides browsing options on its button bar. Using the button bar is a good way to get started "surfing."

What's New is a random compilation of some the newest sites on the Net, and **What's Cool** is a collection of sites that are... well, "cool." (Cool is what you want to be on the Net.) What's Cool includes a question-and-answer "Science Behind the News" site from the National Science Museum, a great site for getting free or inexpensive software and continuously updated camera shots of tropical fish. (Don't ask what the point is — either you like it or you don't, and lots of techies seem to like this one.) Many of these sites will not be of particular interest to journalists or researchers, but they offer a glimpse of some of the clever things that can be found on Web sites.

The **Destinations** button features some of the latest technologies on the Web, such as LiveVideo and Live3D. Sites apply to be listed here, and the Netscape company evaluates them partly on the basis of how well the sites make use of the latest Netscape features. Although you may not be interested in these sites from a technical point of view, the 500 sites included here are all of high quality, and many are worth knowing about.

Clicking on the **Net Search** button will bring up the Netscape Search Sampler. Netscape offers access to several very good search engines and rotates the featured search engine regularly. You can click on any of the search options listed across the top of the search frame to select another Internet search engine. Each covers the Internet in a slightly different way. (Chapter 4 describes several search engines in detail.)

A neat feature of the Netscape search screen is that you can click on the Site Sampler to set up a search engine to run in the back-

FYI

A good source for keeping up to date on Macintosh technology and the Internet is the long-standing electronic magazine *TidBits*. You can subscribe to receive weekly issues of *TidBits* via electronic mail, or you can access their Web site and search back issues at:
http://www.tidbits.com

If you are a Mac user, you will also want to check out one of the best Macintosh information sources on the Net — **The Ultimate Macintosh** at: **http://www.velodrome.com/umac.html**

* The examples in this chapter are for Netscape 3.0, which was the version of Netscape that most people had at the time of writing.

ground on your desktop. In Windows, you can use the **Alt Tab** function to bring up the search window quickly. This involves simply holding the Alt key down and tapping the Tab key to move between Windows applications.

To learn how different search engines work, try searching the same term using several of the various search engines listed here. Some offer more comprehensive services, while others are more selective. Some search engines provide a rating suggesting the relevance of a particular reference based on the terms that you keyed in for your search. Many search sites also offer directories to the Internet — a list of topics with pointers to selected sites. Using the Site Sampler, you might choose your favorite search engine on the basis of which directory you'd like to have sitting in the background.

If you scroll down the Netscape search page, you will find some additional searching resources. Some of these are search engines also, and some are special services such as WhoWhere (http://www.whowhere.com/), which will search for electronic mail addresses, business addresses, and shareware.

If you prefer, you can use the **People** button to access some tools for locating people. Some of these, such as the Four11 service, will also find phone numbers.

Clicking on the **Software** button on the Netscape button bar will bring up a Netscape setup screen where you can register your copy of Netscape and acquire a number of helper programs, which work with Netscape for accessing certain types of files. If you are looking for software programs to download for other purposes, check out *shareware.com* on the Netscape search screen.

Using the choices available on the Netscape button bar is a nice way to sample the Net. It also is an easy way to search for information.

To make the best use of Netscape's capabilities, you need to be aware of several other browser features. The Netscape menu provides features similar to those available in other Windows programs, including the choices **Save As** and **Print**. To save a copy of a file on your hard drive, click on **File | Save As**. You can choose to save a file as a Web page. You can also save a page as plain text.

When you save a Web page to your hard drive or a floppy disk, only text information is saved. Pictures must be saved separately using your right mouse button. To save text and graphics simultaneously, you will need to use an offline reader (see the FYI on page 55 of Chapter 4).

In Netscape, clicking on **View | Document Source** displays a document complete with HTML codes. HTML (Hypertext Markup Language) is the set of codes that your browser reads to determine how a Web page should be displayed. For example, HTML tells your browser to display some things in large lettering, other things as a list or in columns and rows.

To learn more about HTML, see Chapter 8. Although the codes will at first seem unreadable, eventually you may enjoy using your browser to see how they have been used to achieve different effects.

FYI

The toolbar for Microsoft Internet Explorer also offers a "Search the Internet" option. Here you can choose your favorite search engine and designate it as the one you'd like to use each time. With Explorer, click on the **Directory** option on the search page to access a topical gateway to the Net.

The file extensions *.htm* or *.html* are used when saving Web pages. These codes tell your browser how to display certain segments of a page. You can also save a page as plain text (*.txt*). If you save a file as plain text, the HTML tagging is eliminated.

Save files according to how you intend to work with them. If you plan to work on a file from within your browser, save it as HTML, but if you'll be working on it in your word processing program, save it as plain text.

FYI

If you want to download a file using Netscape, simply click on the file while holding the **Shift** key down and Netscape will ask you where you want to save the file.

The **File | Print** option will print a Web page from your printer. You can also highlight and copy a section of text from a Web page by highlighting the text and using the **Edit | Copy** menu option.

Navigating via URLs

Once you have clicked on a link to access a new Web page, the URL for that page will also appear in the window near the top of your browser (labeled "Netsite" in Netscape). Click on a link, and watch as the URL changes to match that of the document being retrieved. Most browsers will let you access a URL of your choice by clearing this field and typing in a new URL. (To do this, simply place your cursor in the field and click. The click highlights the existing URL. Clear the field by using the **Delete** key on your computer keyboard. With the cursor still in the field, you can now simply type in the URL for the Web page you want.)

Netscape will also allow you to access a new Web location using a URL by clicking **Open** on the toolbar, filling in the URL for the site you want to go to, and then clicking on **Open**. Most newer browsers let you drop the *http://* part of a Web address, but you must type in the address for your site very carefully. Computers on the Internet cannot locate a site if a character is missing, or if you don't use upper- and lowercase letters correctly, or if you've typed a hyphen (-) instead of a tilde (~). Every page on the World Wide Web has its own unique address. (This accounts for the excessive length of some Web addresses!)

Initially, you may not know many URLs. But once you start surfing the Internet, you will quickly develop a growing list of interesting sites and potential resources. These days, URLs are visible everywhere. Watch for them in newspapers, in magazines, and on television. Radio programs, too, often mention their Web address at the end of a show. You will see URLs displayed and exchanged at conferences, and students will be referred to useful URLs by their instructors.

If you are anxious to try accessing a site using a URL, check a local newspaper or magazine for URLs of sites that seem interesting. Columnists sometimes publish the URL for their Web page, and there may be URLs for businesses and products that are advertised.

You may also wish to try accessing some the following sites. These are well-established Internet resources that are important to know about. Some are comprehensive starting points for information about the Net, and a couple are pages of links to sources that have been selected by some very knowledgeable users.

Figure 3-4
Beginner's Luck

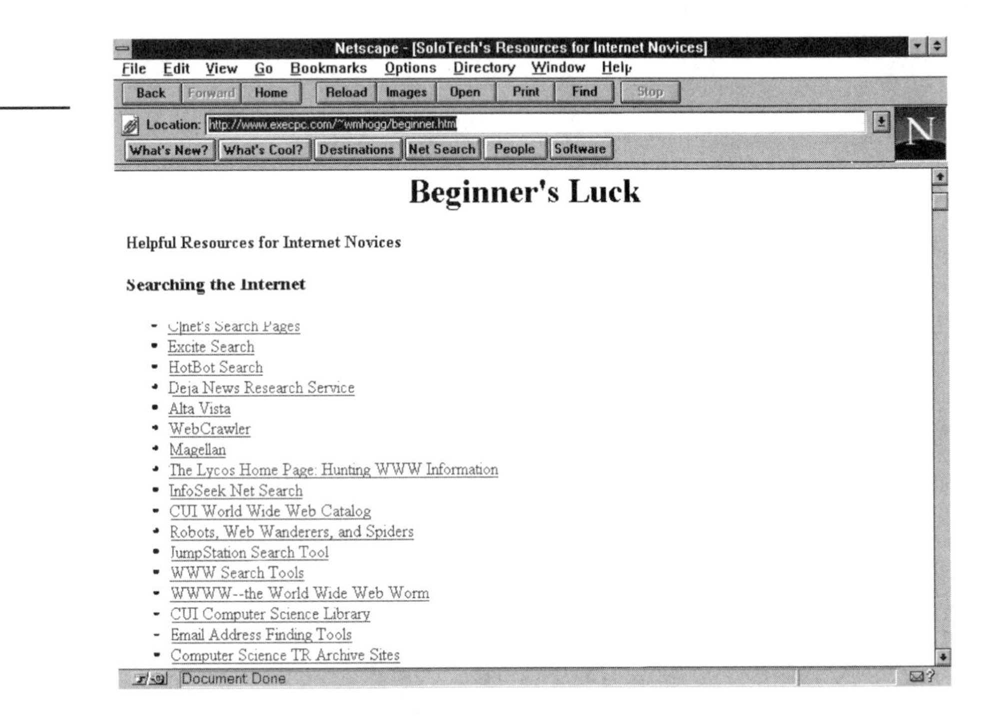

Yahoo
http://www.yahoo.com
For many people, Yahoo is a favorite starting point on the Web.

Beginner's Luck
http://www.execpc.com/~wmhogg/beginner.html
This is a great site for beginners; it includes online magazines and Net tutorials.

Awesome List
http://www.clark.net/pub/journalism/awesome.html
Outstanding list of useful sites developed by Internet trainer and columnist John Makulowich.

Yanoff's Internet Services List
http://www.spectracom.com/islist/
At one time, Yanoff's list was the one of the few ways to locate subject information on the Net.

Web Text
http://www.december.com/web/text/
This is one of a number of useful references by John December. (If you like this resource, you should also check out December's Internet Tools Summary at: **http://www.december.com/net/tools/index.html**).

FYI Be aware that Web sites are constantly changing. In particular, directory names and filenames may quickly go out of date. If a URL does not seem to work, check each character to be sure that you have entered it accurately. Then, try deleting the final filename and/or directories. Once you've accessed a specific location, you can often find the exact information you're searching for just by following the links. If you still are not successful, try finding the item using a search engine such as AltaVista or HotBot (see Chapter 4).

Scout Report
http://rs.internic.net/scout/
Weekly newsletter of new sites of interest on the Net. Also check out InterNIC's daily update, Net Happenings, and the Scout Toolkit.

Magellan
http://www.mckinley.com/
Database of reviewed sites. Good place to browse.

Point: Best of the Web
http://www.pointcom.com
Annotated list of the top five percent of sites on the Web.

NetGuide Magazine Online
http://techweb.cmp.com/ng/home/
Another useful source for keeping up to date.

NBNSoft Content Awards
http://www.tricky.com/liz/
Monthly reviews of the best on the Net.

Looksmart
http://www.looksmart.com
Internet subject directory from *Reader's Digest*.

B&R Samizdat Express
http://www.samizdat.com/
A site with lots of personality; lists full-text sources available on the Net, and other jewels.

Netscape bookmarks

Most browsers have a feature that allows you to save a list of sites that you want to return to. In Microsoft Internet Explorer, this list is called "Favorites"; some other browsers use the term "hotlist." Netscape calls this list "Bookmarks." Having a well-organized set of bookmarks is a great time saver — in effect, it gives you a personalized slice of the Internet.

To add a bookmark to your personal list, use the **Bookmark | Add** feature at the top of your screen. You can also click on the right mouse button. This will bring up a pull-down menu with a number of different options, including **Add Bookmark**. If your cursor is positioned randomly on the page, clicking on the Add Bookmark (mouse options) will save the current page, but if your cursor is positioned directly over a link, a bookmark to the link will be saved. The simplest way to be sure of what's being saved is to use the Bookmark option at the top of the screen.

Once you have set up a bookmark, you can access it by clicking on **Bookmark | Go to Bookmarks**. If you double-click on a Web

The *right* mouse button offers a number of handy features, including **Move Forward** or **Move Back** and **Add Bookmarks**. The options in the pull-down menu change, depending on where your cursor is positioned on a Web page. If the cursor is positioned on a link, the right button will let you open a link in a new window or access and download the Web page for the link. If the cursor is sitting on top of a picture, you can save the picture to your hard drive.

page reference in your list of saved bookmarks, Netscape will retrieve the page.

Setting up a bookmark is really easy. What's not so easy is to avoid amassing an unwieldy list of 5,000 bookmarks. In Chapter 7, we discuss how to manage information overload, including how to organize a bookmark list.

Setting browser preferences

The Netscape **Options** menu has a number of important functions.

On/off (toggle) options. One important toggle option is **Auto Load Images**. If you click on this item (listed in the Options menu), you can turn it off. Click again to turn it on. This is called a *toggle switch*. When you turn Auto Load Images off (i.e., leave its box unchecked), Netscape will load the Web page without displaying the graphics. This will greatly speed up the time it takes for pages to load, and since good page designers usually include an explanation of what's missing, you can still find your way around. Unfortunately, however, this is not always the case, so when you run into a screen where you can't figure out what's going on with only text showing, click on the **Images** button on the toolbar and the page will load again, this time with the pictures in place. If your focus is research and transmission speed is a priority, it can be an advantage to turn off the images.

The Options menu also lets you increase the size of your screen display by turning off the Toolbar, Location, and Directory buttons. To use this function, go to the Options menu and click on each of these menu choices. If you turn off the Toolbar, use your right mouse button to navigate.

Take a shortcut — keep your bookmark file running in a background window. Once you've selected the **Bookmarks | Go to Bookmarks** option, leave the file open, using Window's **Alt Tab** to move between Netscape's main window and Bookmarks.

General options. Netscape lets you customize the look of your Web pages. You can change the default colors for the links, text, and background, and you can change the font size. Most of the time you will want to leave the default settings in place, but if you have any trouble reading the screen, consider changing some of these options.

Some people like to change the page that loads first when they call up their browser. Changing your browser's home page isn't difficult: the **Options | General Preferences | Appearance** option calls up a **Browser Starts With** field where you may type in a URL for whatever site you like. Or, you can start with a blank page. If you use Netscape's **File | Save** option to save a copy of your favorite Web page, you can have your browser access this file from your hard drive whenever you start. This will speed up the initial loading, but you will need to save the page again periodically from the actual Web site to make sure that it's up to date.

Netscape's **Mail** and **News** options are important if you will be using Netscape as your preferred mail software or are planning to

INFO*nugget*

According to a survey done in April 1996 at the Georgia Institute of Technology's Graphic, Visualization, and Usability Center (GVU), the average age of Net users is 33. Women are using the Net more and more. In the six-month period between October 1995 and April '96, women's use of the Internet increased from 29.3% to 31.5% of all users.

You can find more Internet statistics at: **http://www.cc.gatech.edu/gvu**

— Andrew Kantor and Michael Neubarth, "Off the Charts: The Internet 1996." *Internet World*, December 1996.

access newsgroups using Netscape. The Mail and News preferences under Netscape Options tell your computer where to go on the Internet to get your mail, and where to get newsgroup discussions.

Security preferences will become increasingly important as more and more financial transactions are carried out on the Internet. To find out more about the Network and Security features, as well as other options, access Help from within each of the windows for setting Options.

Browser helper applications

If you have used some of the options on the Netscape button bar or tried a Web search, you are probably comfortable with the basics of accessing hyperlinks and exploring the Web. But sooner or later you will arrive at a site where valuable information is packaged in a file format that your browser doesn't know how to display. When this happens, you need special software called a *helper application*, *viewer*, or *plug-in* in order to make use of these files.

Sound files and video files are two file types that require a helper application. To find out about some other types of file that require viewers, click on **Options | General Preferences | Helpers**. The list displayed in the **Preferences** window includes several different file types. Each is identified with a file extension. *File extensions* are the letters that appear after the dot in a computer filename. You are probably already familiar with file extensions from using your word processor, which may use a file extension such as *.wp* or *.doc*.

Here are a few of the most important file types you will find on the Web. The ones that require special helper applications are marked with an asterisk:

.html, .htm	HTML files — the basic file type for Web pages.
.gif	GIF graphic; a picture file.
.jpg, .jpeg, .jpe	JPEG graphic. Another type of picture file.
.au, .snd, .wav	Sound files.*
.qt, .mov	QuickTime movie files.*
.mpeg, .mpg	Another type of movie file.*
.hqx	Macintosh encoded file.
.ra, .ram	RealAudio; broadcast-type sound files.*
.txt	Unformatted text (ASCII) files.
.pdf	Portable Document Format.*
.sit	StuffIt file. A Macintosh compressed file.*
.zip	Zipped file; another type of compressed file.*

Dealing with many file formats may seem daunting at first. But once you've learned to set up one helper program, it's easy to add new plug-ins for other types of files as your needs change. Software developers are always launching new browser applications and making them available via the Internet.

An *ASCII* file is a text-only file, i.e., a readable file that contains no special characters or formatting codes. The file extension for an ASCII file is *.txt*. *Binary* files can be either files that perform a task (such as a software application) or specially coded files, such as word-processed files or compressed files.

To link your browser to a helper application, follow these steps:

Step 1. From the **Options** menu, select **General Preferences | Helpers.**

Step 2. From the list displayed in the window, click on the file type for which you will be adding a helper application. Note that some applications already read **Browser** in the Action column. This means that the Netscape browser will display the file directly, so you won't need to set up a separate application.

Step 3. The name of the file type you've selected will appear in the smaller file extensions window. At this point you can click on **Browse** and locate the viewer or helper on your hard drive. Once you have selected a viewer to use, click on **OK.** The next time that you call up that particular type of application, Netscape will recognize the file type by its extension and automatically launch the application you specified.

This procedure will be slightly different on a Macintosh computer, but the basic process is similar. In essence, you are telling your browser where on your hard drive to find a particular helper application.

You will find specific helper applications in various places on the Internet. If a site makes use of a particular application, such as a

Figure 3-5
Adding helper applications in Netscape

Preferences 10:33 PM

Appearance | Fonts | Colors | Images | Apps | Helpers | Language

File type	Action	Extensions
application/x-zip-compressed	PKUNZIP	zip
application/x-stuffit	Ask User	sit
application/mac-binhex40	Browser	hqx
video/x-msvideo		avi
video/quicktime		qt,mov,moov
video/x-mpeg2	Ask User	mpv2,mp2v
video/mpeg	Ask User	mpeg,mpg,mpe,mpv,vbs,m
audio/x-pn-realaudio	Ask User	ra,ram
audio/x-mpeg	Ask User	mp2,mpa,abs,mpega

File / MIME Type: application   Create New Type...

Subtype: x-zip-compressed

File Extensions: zip

Action: View in Browser Save to Disk Unknown: Prompt User

Launch the Application:

C:\PKUNZIP.EXE   Browse...

OK Cancel Help

FYI *File compression* is a process for shrinking the size of files to make them easier to transfer and store. There are a several ways to compress a file. In the Windows world, compressed files often have a *.zip* file extension. To uncompress a .zip file, you need to obtain a piece of software called PKUnzip, WinZip or similar. You will find **PKUnzip** at: **http://www.pkware.com**
Winzip is available from: **http://www.winzip.com/**
In the Macintosh world, compressed (.sit) files can be unpackaged using StuffIt Expander or StuffIt Lite. **StuffIt** can be found at: **http://www.aladdinsys.com**

FYI To get a complete list of all file compression/archiving methods and programs to decompress them, use FTP (described at the end of this chapter) to access the following site, and retrieve the file called *compression*:
ftp.cso.uiuc.edu directory: pub/doc/pcnet/ compression
This document also tells you where to go to get the proper software for decompressing. You can also locate a number of programs for decoding and decompressing files at **Tucows: http//www.tucows.com**
The files are listed under *Compression Utilities*.

sound file or a multimedia file, the site itself will often provide a link to the necessary plug-in. You will also find many applications at **Stroud's Consummate Winsock Apps** site (**http://www.icorp.net/stroud/**), where various helper applications are listed as graphics viewers, multimedia viewers, or plug-in modules.

Browser plug-ins are also available at **Tucows** (The Ultimate Collection of Windows Software — **http://www.tucows.com/**) and at **NetscapeWorld** (Netscape's online publication site — **http://www.netscapeworld.com/netscapeworld/common/nw.plugintable.html**). Netscape also gives you the option of downloading various plug-ins along with the latest version of the browser, though if your computer is not set up to handle applications such as Internet phone, Live 3D or video, you probably won't want to bother getting these. In Netscape, Click on **Help | Frequently Asked Questions** to find out more about helper applications. If you are using Microsoft Internet Explorer, you can learn about helper applications in the **Help** menu under **Configuring File Types**.

PDF files

If you are a journalist or a researcher, you will undoubtedly encounter PDF files. PDF stands for Portable Document Format. This file format is designed to preserve the original look of a print document (headlines, columns, graphics, etc.). Many agencies find it convenient to make information available as PDF files, rather than convert the files to the Web page file format known as HTML.

PDF can prevent illegal copying of material, and it ensures that a document will look the same regardless of which browser — or which computer platform — you are using. The *New York Times* delivers the **TimesFax** service (**http://www.nytimesfax.com**) over the Net using two different types of PDF file formats: Envoy and Adobe Acrobat.

PDF files require the use of a helper application known as a PDF viewer. These viewers are usually free. There are several viewer types available. Most sites that provide information in PDF format also provide a link to whatever viewer you will need. Usually, you need only click on the viewer link to download it to your own computer. Then, just install the viewer as a helper application, following the instructions outlined in the previous section. You can find out more about PDF files at these sites:

Adobe Acrobat
http://www.adobe.com

Envoy
http://www.tumbleweed.com

Common Ground
http://www.commonground.com/

Take time to explore the viewer's features, such as increasing the size of a display for easier reading. Editing features will vary. For example, although most PDF viewers will allow you to view and print a document, you may not be able to cut and paste from it.

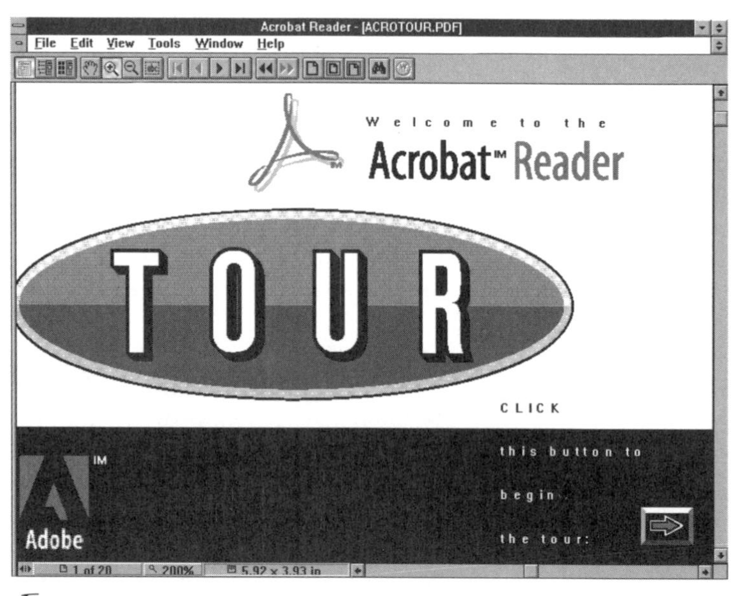

Figure 3-6
Introduction to Adobe's Acrobat Reader

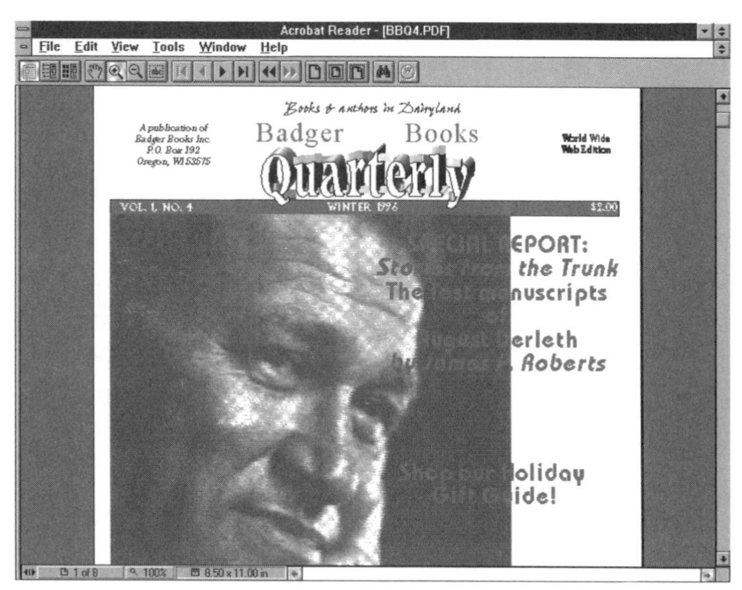

Figure 3-6A
PDF viewers enable you to see a document in its original format

FYI There are lots of sites offering Web tutorials and other guides to help you learn about the Internet. Below are a few locations with links to some of the best newcomer guides. Also, check out the "Internet and Computers" references in Part I of Appendix B.

Newbie Help Links
http://www.netlinks.net/netlinks/newbie.html

Charm Net Learning
http://www.charm.net/learning.html

Internet Resources on the Web
http://www.brandonu.ca/~ennsnr/Resources/

Internet Learner's Page
http://www.clark.net/pub/lschank/web/learn.html

Internet Learning Resources
http://www.rgu.ac.uk/~sim/research/netlearn/callist.htm

BPL Internet Index
http://www.ci.berkeley.ca.us/bpl/bkmk/internet.html

Other Internet applications

Web pages are rapidly growing beyond the simple display of text and still pictures. Today, audio, video, and computer conferencing applications are accessible over the World Wide Web. At the other end of the spectrum are two older Internet technologies: Gophers and FTP. Although these are used less often than Web pages, you will find them useful resources to know about. Here is a brief summary of some of the other technologies that are accessible using a Web browser.

RealAudio

RealAudio (as the name suggests) provides sound broadcasts over the Internet. With RealAudio you can sample the latest CD or catch a CBC radio interview. The *Christian Science Monitor* and ABC news offer RealAudio broadcasts, and the Continuing Legal Education Society of British Columbia, Canada makes available legal education courses in RealAudio format. Although listening to a rock concert as it is being broadcast requires a very fast connection to the Internet, with even a 14.4-baud modem you will be able to download files and play them at your convenience.

To listen to RealAudio, you must download and install a RealAudio player. This helper application is available free from:

http://www.realaudio.com/

Sites featuring RealAudio commonly provide a link to the player. In addition to the player, you will require, at a minimum:

- 486/33-MHz PC with 4 MB RAM (or Macintosh equivalent)
- sound card
- speakers
- 14.4-baud or faster modem connection (faster for music and higher-quality sound).

Broadcast radio on the Internet is not perfect, but like everything on the Net, it's improving. Researchers and journalists will soon be able to access an increasing number of news and educational broad-

Streaming audio is a term for sound files that play as they are downloading. RealAudio is an example of streaming audio. You will find other kinds of audio files on the Web, in addition to streaming audio. If you encounter a .wav or .au file, you can play the file as long as you have installed the appropriate type of helper application.

casts from around the world. Try these sites to sample some of the RealAudio broadcasts that are currently available:

AudioNet
http://www.audionet.com/

National Public Radio
http://www.npr.org

CBC Radio
http://www.radio.cbc.ca/

Monitor Radio–RealAudio http://www.csmonitor.com/monitor_radio/real_audio.html

INFOSEARCH Broadcasting Links
http://www.searcher.com/links.html

To find out more about how to use RealAudio and what's available, visit the Real Audio home page:

http://www.realaudio.com/index.html

Computer conferencing

As we have seen, communications can happen on the Internet in several different ways, the most common being electronic mail. There are also discussion forums — called newsgroups and listservers — that use mail servers to exchange messages. (We discuss these groups in Chapter 6.) Another way to participate in electronic discussion groups is to join a Web-based computer discussion.

In a Web conferencing environment, messages are grouped by topics and subtopics. You can review comments made by other contributors and submit your own comments — either to the group as a whole, or to an individual. The distinguishing features of Web conferencing are that commentary is usually structured (unlike the free-for-all style of newsgroups), and messages are posted directly onto the Web.

Conferencing is more formal than newsgroup forums. Conferences may be moderated; they may occur within a set time frame, and may be intended to facilitate discussion among a specific group, such as students enrolled in a distance learning course. To sample a Web-based conferencing system, try **NetForum** at:

http://www.biostat.wisc.edu/nf_home/

NetForum is just one of many conferencing software programs. You can locate lots of other conferences by searching the Forum Finder at **Forum One:**

http://www.ForumOne.com

Find out about a variety of Web conferencing programs at:

http://freenet.msp.mn.us/people/drwool/webconf.html

Figure 3-7
Conferencing on the Net: Forum One

FYI Chat software allows you to open up a channel on the Internet and converse in real time with someone else on the Internet. Some sites, such as Time-Warner's Pathfinder service, provide a group chat environment where you can interact with a guest speaker. Various software can be used for conversing with others on the Net. One well-designed program for individual or group chatting is **PowWow** at: **http://www.tribal.com/powwow**

With PowWow, you can participate in a text-based conversation involving two or more participants, exchange files, and tour the Web together. This type of chat is also available with Netscape's recent product, Netscape Communicator.

Gophers

This once very useful Internet tool was developed in 1991 at the University of Minnesota. The name is derived from the gopher mascot for the University's Golden Gophers athletic team. Happily (and not coincidentally), the name also describes exactly what Gophers do — they "go fer," or retrieve, information from the vast resources on the Internet. For many types of information, Gopher's method of presenting information — that is, in hierarchical lists — was admirably efficient.

Now, however, most agencies in North America that originally set up Gophers no longer strive to keep Gopher information up to date, and instead make their information available on the Web. Sometimes you may find a Web page that points to a Gopher. When this happens, your browser will handle the connection automatically. Gopher menu choices will be displayed as hyperlinks, and you can navigate by clicking on the link to the item you want to access. A URL for a Gopher site starts with *gopher://*. If you are given a URL reference for a Gopher site, you can access it using the same technique you use to access a Web site.

FTP

FTP is another older technology, but unlike Gopher, FTP sites remain very useful. Many, many files that are available in electronic format are never posted to Web pages directly. Instead, they are

Figure 3-8
File directory at obi, an FTP site

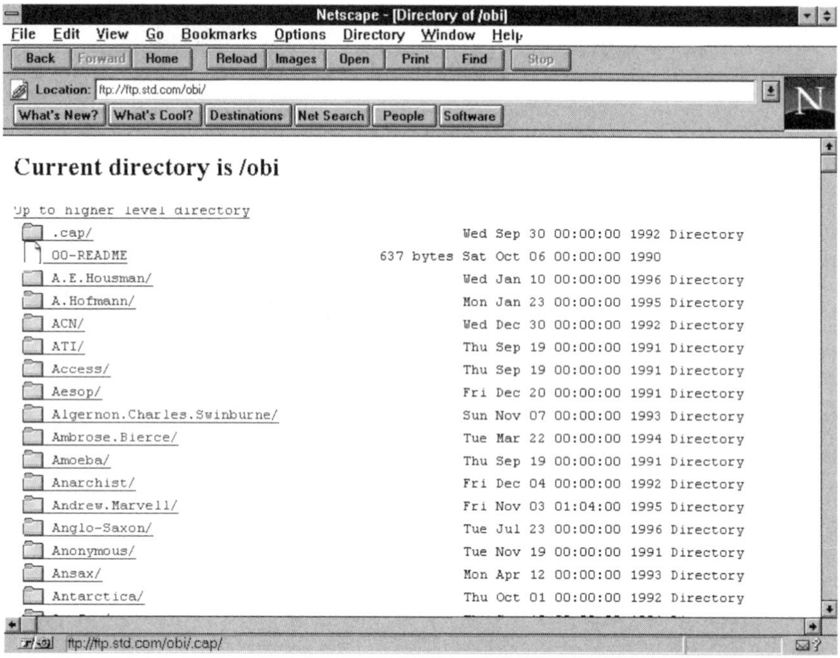

Netscape - [Directory of /obi]

File Edit View Go Bookmarks Options Directory Window Help

Back Forward Home Reload Images Open Print Find Stop

Location: ftp://ftp.std.com/obi/

What's New? What's Cool? Destinations Net Search People Software

Current directory is /obi

Up to higher level directory

.cap/		Wed Sep 30 00:00:00 1992 Directory
00-README	637 bytes	Sat Oct 06 00:00:00 1990
A.E.Housman/		Wed Jan 10 00:00:00 1996 Directory
A.Hofmann/		Mon Jan 23 00:00:00 1995 Directory
ACN/		Wed Dec 30 00:00:00 1992 Directory
ATI/		Thu Sep 19 00:00:00 1991 Directory
Access/		Thu Sep 19 00:00:00 1991 Directory
Aesop/		Fri Dec 20 00:00:00 1991 Directory
Algernon.Charles.Swinburne/		Sun Nov 07 00:00:00 1993 Directory
Ambrose.Bierce/		Tue Mar 22 00:00:00 1994 Directory
Amoeba/		Thu Sep 19 00:00:00 1991 Directory
Anarchist/		Fri Dec 04 00:00:00 1992 Directory
Andrew.Marvell/		Fri Nov 03 01:04:00 1995 Directory
Anglo-Saxon/		Tue Jul 23 00:00:00 1996 Directory
Anonymous/		Tue Nov 19 00:00:00 1991 Directory
Ansax/		Mon Apr 12 00:00:00 1993 Directory
Antarctica/		Thu Oct 01 00:00:00 1992 Directory

ftp://ftp.std.com/obi/.cap/

FYI You can locate a number of Gopher sources by subject category from the **Gopher Jewels** site at: **http://galaxy.einet.net/GJ/**

deposited in a computer directory somewhere, and listed by filename. A URL for an FTP site begins with *ftp://*. For example, the URL for the **Online Book Initiative** is:

ftp://ftp.std.com/obi

If you access this site, you will find the complete text of many full-length books. (Appendix B at the back of this book lists other sources for online books.)

Some Web pages include links to FTP sites. Selecting one of these links brings up a list of files and directories at that site. In this way, you may already have navigated some FTP sites.

For many people, it may not be necessary to go beyond the simple FTP navigation that is available through Web pages. If you do choose to access an FTP site directly, here are the steps to follow:

Step 1. Clear the location field and type in the URL, which in this case begins with *ftp://*. When you press **enter**, Netscape will retrieve an actual directory of files from the remote site. If the reference is to a folder, you will see an icon that looks like a folder. The filename will include the size of the file and indicate whether it is compressed.

Step 2. Scroll through the list to find the directory or file you would like to access. Then simply click on the filename to retrieve it. If the file is a text file, it will be displayed on the screen just as a normal file would that is part of a Web page. Other types of files,

Figure 3-9
Should the Unknown File Type dialog box appear, click on one of the options

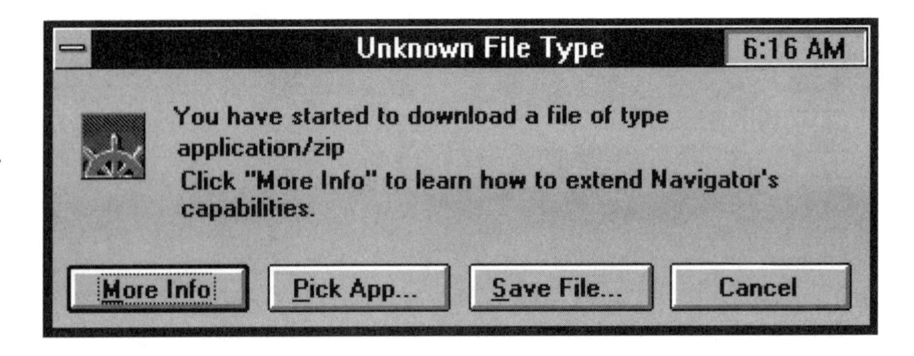

such as large-image files or PostScript (special printer) files, will display only if you have preconfigured your browser with an appropriate viewer (discussed above). In many cases, clicking on the file results in an Unknown File Type box being displayed.

Step 3. The Unknown File Type dialog box gives you three options: Save to Disk, Cancel Transfer, or Configure a Viewer. In most instances you will want to **Save to Disk.**

One of the challenges in accessing an FTP site is that the contents of files are sometimes hard to recognize based on the filenames or directory names. While it's easy enough to guess what might be contained in a file called *unabomber*, it's not so easy to discern contents from names like *shwtxt20.txt* or *nice205.zip*.

The feature box "6 Tips for Using FTP" offers some guidelines for accessing and obtaining files from an FTP site.

A last word

The Web is always changing. Newer technologies include Web phone, which lets you place phone calls over the Net (providing you know someone to call, who must have similar equipment). The drawback of this — and, indeed, of most new technologies — is that it takes a critical mass of people using the technology to make it a practical tool. Video is another new promising Net technology: one day we will be able to play video clips from the Net as easily as we now view still images. It is currently possible to view real-time video over the Net, but connections are still slow, quality is poor, and applications are few.

This introductory chapter on the Web has dealt with the fundamentals of Web navigation: browsers, URLs, and helper applications. You can build on this information as you become acquainted with other features of the Internet. Don't be overwhelmed by your technowhiz colleague's knowledge of the very latest Internet gizmo. The most important thing is to have a good understanding of how the Internet can be useful to you.

If you do not have graphical (Windows or Mac) access to the Internet, retrieving a file from a remote system may result in the file's being deposited somewhere on your ISP's computer. When this is the case, you will need to download the file to get it onto your own computer. Instructions for uploading and downloading a files will be explained in your communications software manual. But because things can go wrong when you are downloading for the first time, it may be a good idea to contact your service provider (or a knowledgeable friend or colleague) for help with this. With a graphical browser, files should download automatically to your local computer.

6 tips for using FTP

1. Always look for an Index or ReadMe file at a remote FTP site. An index will sometimes contain information about the contents of files at the site.
2. Many locations include their shareware and information files in a directory called *pub*. The pub directory is a good first place to look on an unfamiliar system.
3. If someone gives you the name of a file and its location, type in the URL with great care. Many computers on the Internet are *case sensitive* — i.e., they read capital letters differently from small letters. Filenames commonly use both.
4. You can search for software, graphics and other types of files using the **All-in-One Search Page** at: **http://www.albany.net/allinone**
5. If you are downloading software, download to a floppy disk whenever possible and *always* scan for computer viruses before running the program. To detect a virus, you will need to have computer virus software on your computer. A good place to learn more about computer viruses is at the **Symantec AntiVirus Research Center**, located at: **http://www.symantec.com/avcenter**

You can purchase anti-virus software from a local computer store. Remember to keep up with the latest upgrades for your virus software to ensure that your computer is protected against new viruses.
6. You will not be able to view all types of files automatically. For example, a word processed file must be downloaded and viewed from within a word processor. Familiarize yourself with various file extensions (such as those listed earlier in this chapter), particularly the extensions that indicate a compressed format. You can find out about different types of file formats at: **http://www.matisse.net/files/formats.html**

In the chapters to come, we'll discuss more ways to find what you're looking for on the Internet, and identify specific Web sites that are especially valuable for researchers and writers.

Further reading

Carroll, Jim, and Broadhead, Rick. *Canadian Internet Handbook*. Toronto: Prentice Hall, 1997.

The Internet Index Home Page
http://www.openmarket.com/intindex/

Internet Starter Kit for Macintosh
http://www.mcp.com/hayden/iskm/mac.html

Kantor, Andrew, and Neubarth, Michael. "Off the Charts: The Internet 1996." *Internet World*, December 1996, pp. 46–51.

Odd de Presno Online World Resources Handbook
http://login.eunet.no/~presno/index.html

World Wide Web FAQ Frequently Asked Questions
http://www.boutell.com/faq/

Chapter 4 Search Strategies and Techniques

“The Internet is not like the computer on Star Trek. You can't just say: 'Computer, who are the ten biggest crooks that donated money to the sleazebag politician in my city?' and wait a few seconds for the answer. The Internet will not make stupid reporters smart. But it will make smart reporters smarter. The Internet is a vast, largely unorganized, ever-changing library (in fact, many of the world's best libraries are actually on the Internet). And — like any library — you have to do the hard work to find the nugget of information you want. The books don't walk off the shelves into your hands.”

— JULIAN SHER, *MEDIA MAGAZINE*, WINTER 1995.

Trying to find information on the Internet is often described as trying to get a sip of water from a fire hydrant. With just a few keystrokes, it's easy to flood your computer screen with endless lists of possible references. Finding and isolating the useful material can seem daunting. Giving up and looking for that drink elsewhere can be very tempting.

There are, however, some simple techniques and sophisticated tools that you can use to make your searches productive and efficient. Once you develop some skill with them, the results will be rewarding. You will find what you need, and maybe even discover something you didn't know you wanted. You can satisfy your thirst, yet avoid the flood.

Not so long ago, you could search for information on the Net by "surfing" and making educated guesses about which links to follow from a few select Web pages to find the information you needed. But the phenomenal growth of the Internet makes that strategy about as successful as looking for a lost contact lens in the sand on the beach with your eyes closed. You may enjoy the heat of the sun and the sound of the waves, but you are not likely to find what you need.

This chapter will provide an overview of the tools and strategies you can use to make your searches both pleasant and successful.

Chapter highlights

- Searching the Web for information
- Starting pages: A place to browse
- Subject trees — a bird's-eye view: Yahoo, Galaxy, Magellan, and more
- Search engines — the most rewarding results: AltaVista
- More search engines: Excite, HotBot, Infoseek, Lycos, OpenText, WebCrawler
- Metasearch tools: Cyber 411, SavvySearch, MetaCrawler
- Comparing search tools

Searching the Web for information

> "While the ability to write is the most important qualification for a journalist, it's not enough any more — considering the number of good writers on the job market. Journalists who don't know about computer-assisted reporting, or how to surf the net, or who are reluctant to engage in the interactivity required in the online world will find it more and more difficult to find — or hold — a job."
>
> — Tom Regan, Webmaster, *Christian Science Monitor*, February 1996.

The Internet is a storehouse of information, pictures, sound, and even video, so vast it is difficult to comprehend.

You can log onto NASA's computers and look at the latest space pictures before they are published. You can read tomorrow's Jerusalem Post online hours before you can get a hard copy of it in North America. You can search a database at Johns Hopkins University for some of the latest research on prostate cancer. You can listen to radio shows from Dublin. You can even track the latest on an approaching hurricane before you hear about it on the evening news.

If you are a writer or a researcher, much of the information you need is probably out there — somewhere — online, and it is probably indexed or

Exploring cyberspace

catalogued somehow. But the Internet wasn't set up by librarians who organize things in a logical way and provide a central index to make them easy to find. Nor was it organized by journalists who need information quickly to meet tight deadlines. Still, it has become too valuable a resource for writers, researchers, and journalists to ignore.

There is no one right way to search the Internet for information. Instead, there are several different tools you can use and techniques you can develop to refine your searches. Try a few of the suggestions that follow. Find tools that work most of the time, but be prepared to use others if you are not satisfied with the results.

Starting pages: A place to browse

Starting pages are Web pages designed to provide you with a useful set of links to general reference information. All you have to do is scan the list of topics and select a link that interests you. No searching skills or strategies are required.

If you have access to the Internet at work, your place of employment may have a starting page with links to information you need on the job, such as the e-mail addresses of your colleagues. If you access the Internet through a commercial service or Internet service provider, you may get their page, or Netscape's home page, when you log on. These pages will provide you with useful links to explore. But for writers, researchers, or journalists, there may be more useful pages to start with.

The Virtual Library

If you are a professional researcher, then the library is probably one of the first places you go when you start a project. Instead of visiting traditional libraries, however, you can use the Internet to visit one of several virtual libraries. One is called just that — The Virtual Library. Here you will find an online version of a comprehensive subject catalogue covering topics from aboriginal studies to zoos. Select any topic for a long list of links to Internet resources on that subject. If you don't find anything useful here, you could try the link at the end of the first page to other virtual libraries. You will find **The Virtual Library** at:

http://www.w3.org/vl/

My Virtual Reference Desk

This is another useful site for researchers. It is the online equivalent of a library reference desk. The main page offers a set of choices including almanacs, encyclopedias, newspapers, reference guides, and lists of important Web sites. Choose any of them and you will be presented with a series of useful links to launch you on your

FYI There are lists of sites especially for professional researchers in various places on the Net. One is called **Marist 100** and is described as "the best 100 research sites." It is updated monthly and includes Academe This Week by the Chronicle of Higher Education at:
http://www.academic.marist.edu/mc100/mcalpha.htm

There is also a huge listing of more than 250 research sites on most topics, with a special emphasis on science and engineering at:
http://www.swin.edu.au/sgrs/research-sites.html

search. It is a handy way to find general information when you are in a hurry and don't have a lot of time to spend searching. You will find **My Virtual Reference Desk** at:

http://www.refdesk.com/main.html

Starting Point

A similarly useful starting page for researchers is called (aptly enough) Starting Point. It, too, includes many links to online sources for news, magazines, reference guides, and entertainment and business information. You will find **Starting Point** at:

http://www.stpt.com/

Julian Sher's Web Page

One of the most useful starting pages for journalists is produced by Julian Sher, an investigative journalist and television producer with the Canadian Broadcasting Corporation. His page provides links you can use to search the Net for information, phone numbers, e-mail addresses, experts, and much more. Many journalists in Canada make his page their first stop and use it to find much of what they are looking for on the Net. You can find **Julian Sher's Web Page** at:

http://www.vir.com/~sher/julian.htm

FACSNet

A similar resource designed more specifically for U.S. journalists and other researchers interested in public policy issues is FACSNet,

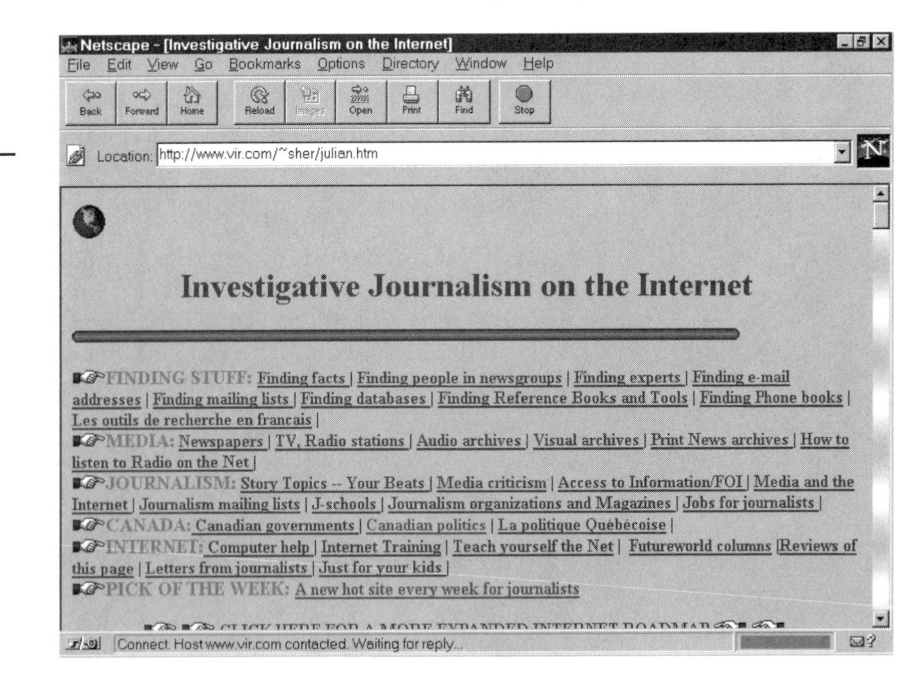

Figure 4-1
Julian Sher's starting page: Investigative journalism on the Internet

FYI

Offline readers are programs that let you download an entire Web site, including links and graphics, for viewing offline. You can use these to save on connection costs or to download a Web page for a presentation. *Freeloader, Web Buddy,* and *WebWhacker* are examples of this type of program. Some are available for a modest cost (US$10 to $50). Freeloader is available for free, but it regularly downloads pages of advertising as "required reading." Offline readers can be tricky to use and may eat up a lot of space on your hard drive, but they're worth checking out. You will find an article from *PC Magazine* about offline readers posted at:
http://www.pcmag.com/iu/browse/offline/_offline.htm
If you're venturesome, try downloading one of the following readers:

WebWhacker
http://www.ffg.com

Freeloader
http:///www.freeloader.net

Web Buddy
http://www.dataviz.com

produced by a group of journalists, scholars, and programmers at the *Detroit News*, the San Diego Supercomputer Center, and others. It provides background material on issues in the news, sources and contacts at all kinds of organizations, and think tanks and links to Internet resources to help track down information and contacts. You'll find **FACSNet** at:

http://www.facsnet.org/

FYI

Need census data or financial information? Check out a great collection of links to statistical resources at:
http://www.columbia.edu/cu/libraries/indiv/jour/subject/stats.html

One Stop Journalist Shop

Another starting page is put together by the Kennedy School of Government at Harvard University. Called the One Stop Journalist Shop, it is well organized, easy to navigate, and includes lots of good links to help journalists find background information, Internet resources, and even tips from other journalists on how to use the Internet. You'll find the **One Stop Journalist Shop** at:

http://ksgwww.harvard.edu/~ksgpress/journpg.htm

Subject trees — a bird's-eye view

Subject trees, like subject catalogs in a library, provide an organized hierarchy of categories with lists under each category of links to Web pages where you may find related information. They will help you find the haystack. Other tools will help you find the needle.

Yahoo

Once you've made the decision to search the Net for information, browsing a subject tree and following links related to your topic is usually the best way to begin. The best tree to start with is called **Yahoo** at:

http://www.yahoo.com

Figure 4-2
Yahoo's home page

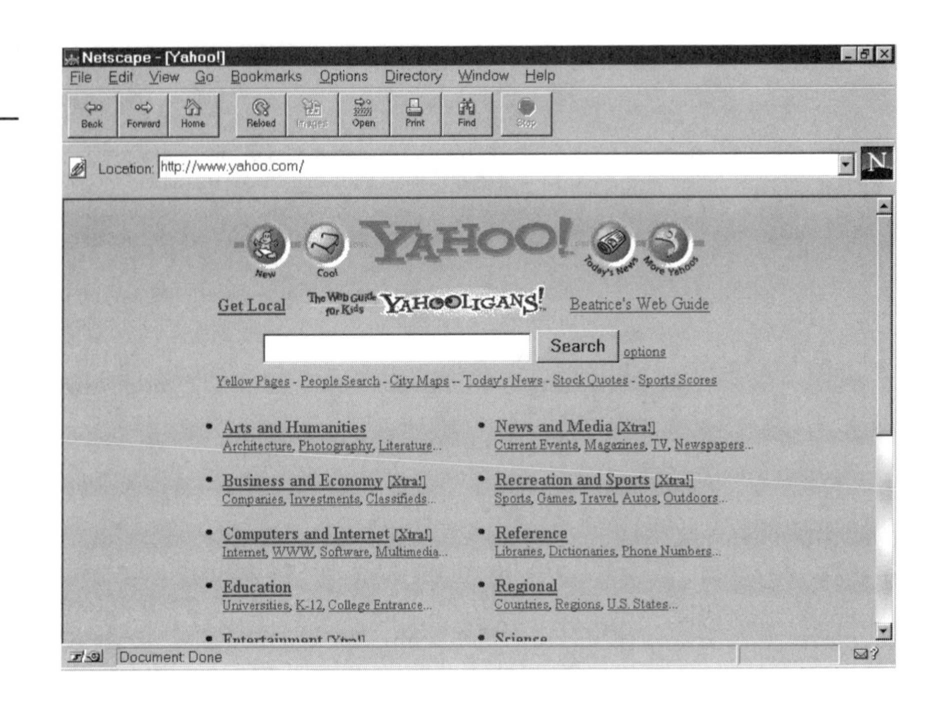

FYI

Yahoo has recently developed a subject tree for Canadian information which can be found at: **http://www.yahoo.ca/**

Yahoo is the most popular subject tree on the Internet, and not just because of its offbeat name. It is an extensive index of the best of the Web and can be searched by keyword. Although it is not a comprehensive search engine (discussed below), it deserves a prominent place on your bookmark list.

When you first go to Yahoo, you will find a general index of broad subjects such as Arts, Computers, Health, News, and Reference. Each heading is subdivided into forty to fifty subheadings that lead to further subheadings which you can follow until you get to the specific information you want. In all, tens of thousands of Internet sites are listed here with short descriptions of each of them. If you are looking for something useful to start your research you will probably find it here, or something close to it. It is an ideal place to quickly find general information and starter sites that can lead you to more specialized information.

Yahoo is also simple to use because at the top of each of page is a search box and links to show you how you got there. You can search all of Yahoo or just the specific category you are in.

Searching is straightforward and based on keywords. Just enter your search term in the search window and click **Search**. You can also limit your searches by clicking on the small **Options** link next to the main search window and making choices that will customize your search.

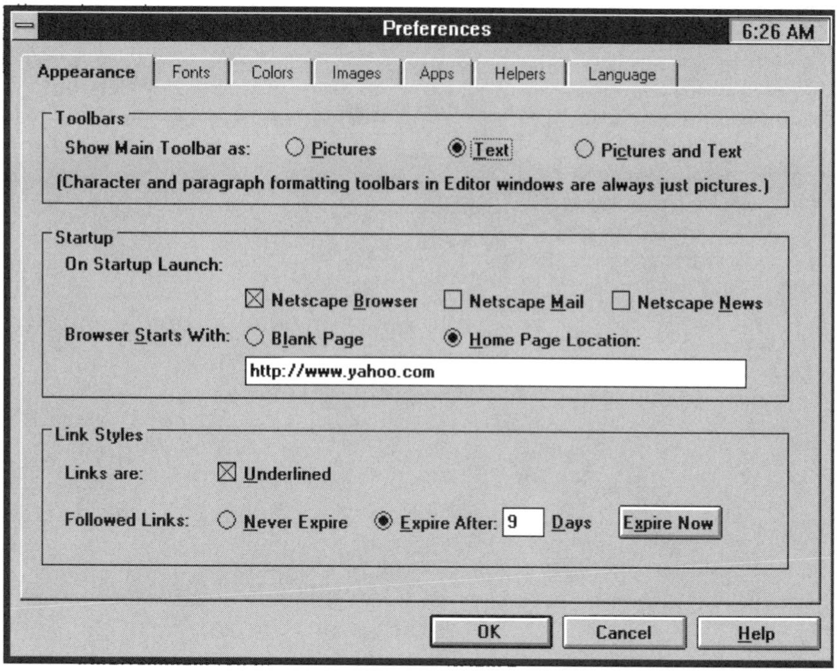

Figure 4-2A

Setting your Web browser to start up with a subject index such as Yahoo is easy and saves time

FYI

You can set up Yahoo as your default home page. Many people find it convenient to have their browsers start up with a subject index, such as Yahoo, displayed immediately. You can do this from Netscape by clicking on Options at the top of your screen. Choose General Preferences and in the box titled Browser, type: **http://www.yahoo.com/**

The results will give you both titles and descriptions of the pages that match your query. You will also get a link to the category from which those pages derive, enabling you to explore further information you may not have considered.

For example, if you type in the words *travel Hawaii* in the Search field and click the Search button, you will quickly be presented with a long list of links to travel information, maps, photographs, guides, and travel agents, and each link will be identified by the category or categories in which it was found.

If none of that works, the Options window includes links to several other search engines that you might try.

There are other subject trees as well, though none as popular as Yahoo.

Galaxy

Galaxy is another index of general topics that you can browse for reference information and relevant links. If you can't find what you want by topic, you can also search the entire index by keyword. Galaxy is located at:

http://galaxy.Einet.net/galaxy.html

Magellan

Magellan is another subject index that can be searched by keyword. What makes it different, however, is that it provides both ratings

FYI A great resource for factual information about countries around the world is the **CIA World Factbook**. No, it doesn't provide any classified information about spies, but it does offer political, social, and economic information about places you may not even have heard of. It is updated annually and is located at: **http://www.odci.gov/cia/publications/pubs.html**

and reviews for sites you find through its subject index. If you do a keyword search instead, it will also provide a brief description of the sites that come up. So, for example, from its main subject index you can choose Science, then choose Space Science. You will then be presented with a long list of great links to information about space science, each of which will be reviewed and rated to help you determine whether it is worth exploring. At the top of the list, for example, is an award-winning multimedia tour of the Sun. **Magellan** is located at:

http://www.mckinley.com/

Other subject trees

In addition to general-interest directories such as Yahoo, subject-specific directories cover everything from animals to zoos. The best way to find one of these specialized directories is to check the **Argus Clearinghouse for Subject-Oriented Internet Resource Guides at the University of Michigan** at:

http://www.clearinghouse.net/

If you're looking for U.S. government-sponsored Web sites, check out **Infomine** at:

http://lib-www.ucr.edu/govinfo.html

or the **Kennedy School of Government** at:

http://ksgwww.harvard.edu/~ksgpress/federal.htm

Some subject trees provide information related to a specific geographic area or country. For example, the **National Library of Australia** has a site that offers links to various other sites for information on Australia. You'll find it at:

http://www.nla.gov.au/

FYI Check out the National Library of Canada's subject tree, **Canadian Information By Subject**, located at: **http://www.nlc-bnc.ca/caninfo/ecaninfo.htm**

Subject trees are a great place to start; however, they are not comprehensive. They rely on human diligence to maintain them, and it is not humanly possible to keep up with the phenomenal growth of the Web. To conduct a more thorough search, you will have to use one or more of the Internet's search engines.

Search engines — the most rewarding results

Search engines are the most sophisticated tool you can use to search the Net for information. However, that doesn't mean they're difficult to use. In fact, they're very easy.

Search engines compile indexes of material on the Web. They search these indexes for the keywords or phrases you give them, and then provide a list of matches. It's a bit like hiring a private investigator to find all the women who graduated from Harvard law school in the last thirty years and went on to become judges.

The investigator would have to compile a list of all the female graduates and a list of all judges, and then try to find matches. Unlike the private investigator, however, the search engines provide you with results almost instantly. Just type the keyword in the search field and click on the **Search** button. In seconds you will get back a list of Web pages and other Internet resources that include your keyword or phrase. You will also get a few words about each page or link to help you assess its usefulness.

The search engines compile their indexes using software programs — sometimes called *robots, knowbots,* or *spiders* — that scour the Net. Quietly and persistently, they go from link to link, finding new documents and recording all or part of the contents of each new page to their indexes.

Each search engine, like each private investigator, works a little differently and gathers a different collection of raw data. So when you send a search engine out looking for a keyword, the results will vary depending on which search engine you use. You may have to learn to use several of them to find what you want. The search engines may also find links that look ideal, but turn out to be dead or unavailable when you go to use them. Pages go up and down on the Web more quickly than the search engines can update their databases. But all search engines have huge databases and will, most likely, return very long lists of matches or "hits." It is easy to be overwhelmed at the prospect of sifting through them all. For researchers and journalists, thousands of hits are almost as useless as no hits at all. So, you will need to develop a few strategies and learn a few tricks to get more manageable results.

A great place to find many of these search engines is through the Netscape browser. If you don't use Netscape, at least check out this page:

http://home.netscape.com/escapes/search/index.html

AltaVista

One of the most popular and comprehensive search engines on the Net these days is AltaVista. We will review its features in detail and then go on to describe other search engines. **AltaVista** can be found at:

http://www.altavista.digital.com

AltaVista has one of the largest indexes and returns consistently useful information at lightning speed. But that doesn't mean it is the only search engine you need, or the best to use in all situations. Different search engines using different indexing strategies will bring different results.

AltaVista began operating in December, 1995 and quickly became one of the most popular search engines because it is both comprehensive and fast. It claims to have indexed more than thirty million Web pages. It also indexes the entire text of newsgroup postings. The site receives several million search requests per day.

AltaVista allows you to conduct simple or advanced searches, and to have the results listed in summary or detailed form.

To make a simple query, just enter a keyword or phrase in the search window and click **Submit**. Seconds later, you will be presented with a list of hits that include all the keywords you entered, no matter the order in which you entered them. The list will provide hotlinked URLs which you can click on to go directly to the site. AltaVista, like other search engines, also ranks its results, usually according to how many times the search term appears in the document. So, you will generally find the best hits near the top of the page and less relevant ones farther down.

Be warned, however: simple searches using single words or series of words can result in thousands of hits. To get more manageable results, there are a several things you can do. You can direct AltaVista to search for phrases rather than individual words by putting the words in double quotes. For example, if you searched using the words *lung cancer* you would get thousands of references to lungs and thousands to cancer, but by using quotation marks around *"lung cancer"* you will get hits only on pages where both words are used together.

You can narrow your search even further by choosing to do an advanced, rather than a simple, search. Just select the **Advanced Search** button from the main screen. Advanced searches allow you to use what are called Boolean operators. That just means you can use the words *AND, OR, NOT,* and *NEAR* to refine your searches. For example, you could search for *"lung cancer" AND treatment AND NOT tobacco*. AltaVista also lets you use symbols instead of words: + (for AND), | (for OR), – (for AND NOT) and ~ (for NEAR).

You can use advanced techniques to search only for pages with the keyword in the title of the page. To try this, type in the Search field: *Title: "children's television"* and you will get only pages whose title includes those words and whose main focus, therefore, is probably children's television.

You can search for a Web page even if you don't have the URL. For example, let's say you figure that the American Medical Association (AMA) probably has a Web page, but you don't know the address. You can use AltaVista to find it by typing in the search window: *URL: AMA*. You will get a list of hits, and one of the first will be Web page for the American Medical Association.

With AltaVista you can choose to have your search results listed in a *compact form* that will give you the page title, the date the page was created, and the first few words on the page. Or, you can choose the *standard* or *detailed form*, which will give you the first several sentences of the page to help you assess its usefulness.

Figure 4-3
AltaVista's home page

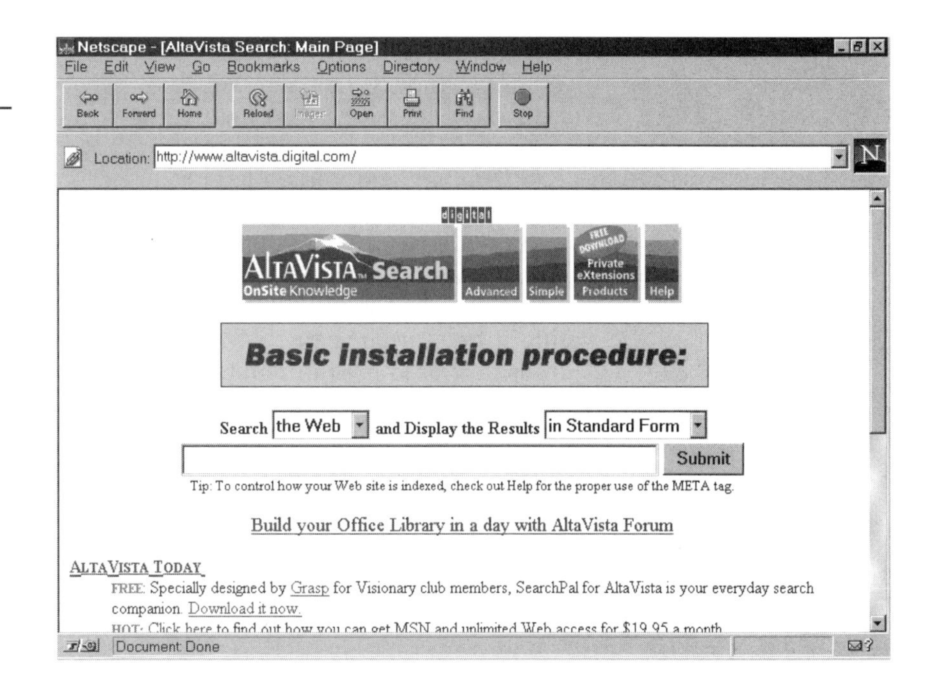

It's also possible to use a *wildcard* when searching AltaVista to ensure that a number of possible variations on a word are included in search results. The wildcard symbol is the asterisk (*), and means "anything can go here." For example, if you are looking for information about Mexico, you could type in the search window *Mexic** to ensure you get hits that include the words *Mexico, Mexican,* and *Mexicans*.

With advanced searches you may also specify keywords you wish AltaVista to use in order to rank your results. This is a very powerful feature that lets you control which items are ranked at the top of the hit list. Type the terms you wish AltaVista to weight more heavily in the **Results Ranking Criteria** field on the Advanced Search screen before submitting the search. Then, even though the search will find the same information, the first hits listed will fit your needs more closely. For example, if you search on the terms *women* and *engineering* you will get a lot of hits about women and a lot about engineering, but nothing that jumps out clearly as being about women engineers. However, if you do an advanced search and use the field marked Results Ranking Criteria to type in the word *women*, your search results will be much more relevant. Your first page of hits will probably include a page called "Women in Engineering."

You can even direct AltaVista to search by date. For example, you could use the advanced features to request a search on *"baby boomers" AND money AND NOT health* between the dates 1/Jan/96 and 20/Dec/96. You will get many interesting hits about how baby boomers were managing their financial affairs that year. Turn it around and search on *"baby boomers" AND health AND NOT money* and you will get a lot of hits about how they are dealing with balding and osteoporosis.

But AltaVista has its quirks, too. For one thing, it is case sensitive. So, if you search on *"John Lennon"* you may not find the transcript of an interview he did with Playboy magazine. But you would find it by searching on *"JOHN LENNON"* because the title of the transcript used his full name in upper-case letters.

You can also get hits that don't appear to be relevant to your search terms, or hits in which the search term is not at all obvious when you open the page or click on the hit. In those cases, you can use the command **Control F** to bring up a box that allows you to search for the term on that page.

More search engines

Excite

Excite is located at:

http://www.excite.com/

Excite is different from other search engines in that it searches not just by keyword, but by concept. In other words, it tries to find *what* you want, not just what you *say* you want. In librarians' terms, it uses "fuzzy logic." It's a great tool when you are not sure of the exact term to search on.

Concept searches find documents related to the idea of your search, and not just documents explicitly containing the search terms you enter. This method works best when you provide more than one search term. For example, searching on the words *hard rock* alone will get you everything from the home pages for Hard Rock Cafés around the world to references about hard rock mining. But if you use *hard rock* and *music*, Excite will find more suitable references. Excite's results list also offers an extremely useful feature: if you scan the results or hit list and find a reference that looks promising, you can click a button beside the URL marked **More Like This** to get more pages that are similar to the one you identified.

You may also use Excite to search Usenet newsgroups. Advanced features such as Boolean searching are supported. However, you may not control the appearance of the hit list into standard/summary/detailed formats, as you can with some other search engines.

Like AltaVista, Excite also lets you use the plus sign or minus sign in front of a word rather than use the Boolean operators AND or AND NOT.

Excite has recently added a new, very useful feature for researchers. It's called the News Tracker, and it searches hundreds of newspapers and magazines for news stories on any topic you choose. All you have to do is specify the topic in the appropriate box on the News Tracker Page, click on **View**, and within seconds you will be presented with a list of recent news stories on that topic. The list provides the first few words of the articles to help you assess them, along with the hotlinked URL should you want to read any of the articles in full. It's a great way to find up-to-date information on any subject in the news. You can get to the News Tracker service from Excite's home page, or by going directly to it at:

http://nt.excite.com

FYI If you are looking for information designed especially for teachers and students using the Web for research, you should find useful advice and good sites at the following Web site: **http://www.mbnet.mb.ca/~mstimson/**

HotBot

HotBot is another, newer search engine that is gaining attention these days. It is located at:

http://www.hotbot.com/

HotBot is up to date and incredibly fast. It offers a list of options to help you refine your searches, one of which allows you to use Boolean operators. HotBot's home page also includes a button called "Media," which allows you to search for Web sites using the most up-to-date technologies. For example, it allows you to limit searches to Web pages that contain specific technologies such as Java script or Shockwave.

Infoseek

Infoseek is located at:

http://www.infoseek.com/

Infoseek is a popular search engine because it is comprehensive and provides consistently relevant results. It allows for phrase searching. One of its other strengths is the way in which it allows you to search newsgroups for postings on the subject you are researching. It provides a hotlinked title, the name and e-mail address of the poster, the first few lines of the article, and a link to the newsgroup where the article was posted. That link allows you to jump directly to other articles in the newsgroup. Infoseek also allows you to search FAQs (lists of Frequently Asked Questions), which can be very helpful places to start researching a topic. (Chapter 6 explains how to find and use FAQs.) Lastly, you can use Infoseek to search e-mail addresses, current news, and company listings.

However, Infoseek does not allow you to refine your searches quite as extensively as some other search engines, and it requires all proper names to be capitalized.

Infoseek has recently added two new features — *Ultrasmart* and *Ultraseek*. Ultrasmart is something of a cross between a search engine and a directory. It searches, by keyword, a comprehensive subject tree, which Infoseek claims is the largest subject directory on the Web. Along with a list of hits, it also provides you with the opportunity to click on "Related Topics" for other areas that might be relevant, and "Related News" for news stories that apply to your search. If you prefer a search without all those extras, Ultraseek offers a fast, accurate, and comprehensive search in a streamlined form.

Lycos

Lycos is located at:

http://www.lycos.com/

Lycos was one of the first search engines available on the Web. Although better search engines have since appeared, it remains comprehensive, dependable, and easy to use, though it is a little slow.

Lycos does not index every word of every page it finds, but rather searches document titles, links, and keywords. It offers several options that allow you to search the entire Web, or the top five percent of Web sites as determined by Lycos, or to search for sounds and pictures rather than text.

You can also fine-tune your search by selecting the option to customize it. From there you can choose a short or long description of each link. You can also choose one of five types of matches — loose, fair, good, close, or strong. A loose match could get you a lot of what you don't want; a strong match could turn up virtually nothing that doesn't match the literal string you typed. The stronger the match, the fewer the sites returned. To expand a word with a wildcard, add the **$** symbol to the end of the word. For example, *Chin$* to get *China* and *Chinese*. You can use the period (**.**) after a word to prohibit its expansion: for example, *washing.* to avoid *Washington.*

Lycos's options for refining searches are not as elegant or as extensive as AltaVista's. For example, you can choose to use only AND or OR between your search terms. If you don't choose to use AND, the default is OR, which can be confusing. For example, if you search on *African Americans* you will get hits that include *either* African *or* Americans, and it may be difficult to sift through them all to find ones with references to both.

FYI Interested in finding out more about the top stories in the news this week? Check out a Web page called **Hot News/Hot Research**, put together by the Poynter Institute for Media Studies. It provides a solid collection of Web resource links, and is updated weekly. It's at: **http://www.poynter.org/hr/hr_intro.htm**

OpenText

OpenText is located at:

http://index.opentext.net/

An excellent search tool, OpenText catalogs every word on every page it finds, though its database is smaller than those of other search engines like AltaVista. It allows you to do simple searches or power searches that let you search for words in the document summaries, titles, or URLs.

WebCrawler

WebCrawler can be found at:

http://WebCrawler.com/

It is fast and easy to use, but not nearly as comprehensive as other search engines.

On the initial search screen, above the search field, you may select whether you want the results to list Web titles only, or titles and summaries for each hit. You may also select the number of hits per page: ten, twenty-five, or a hundred. By choosing the summary mode, you will get a brief abstract of the page and its URL. WebCrawler allows the use of the Boolean operators AND, OR, and NOT in the standard search field. For better results, items may also be grouped within parentheses: *Fonda AND NOT (Jane or Peter)*.

FYI For an easy-to-use description of search engines that will keep you up to date about the latest improvements and changes to search tools on the Net, check out: **http://www.monash.com/spidap.html**

WebCrawler's advanced features also allow you to use NEAR/n, where *n* is the number of words by which the two search terms should be separated: for example, *Hiroshima NEAR/5 atomic bomb* will avoid hits about modern-day Hiroshima. You can also click on the **Special** button at the top of the page to access the Surf the Web Backwards link-back feature. This lets you search a Web page address to find out which other sites link to it.

Metasearch tools

In addition to the individual search engines, there are sites where you submit your query to several search engines at the same time.

Cyber 411

One of the newest "metasearch" sites is called **Cyber 411** at:

http://www.cyber411.com/

Here, plugging in a search term activates fifteen major search engines simultaneously and returns results within seconds. The results are a list of links that indicate which search engine found them. You can search using words or phrases (though you cannot refine your search terms), and you can choose fast or hyperfast results.

SavvySearch

Another metasearch site is **SavvySearch** at:

http://guaraldi.cs.colostate.edu:2000/form

SavvySearch is an extraordinary search tool. It combines more than twenty of the search engines on the Web into one interface. You have a search key entry box along with a selection of check boxes that allow you to choose the type of indexes to search, the number of matches to return, and other options. Once you perform a search, you are shown all your matches on a new page.

Depending on your choices, you can see the page title, the search engine that found it, the URL of the page, the size of the page, and a description of the contents. The list of search engines that this site uses includes Lycos, OpenText, AltaVista, Excite, Inktomi, Yahoo, WebCrawler, DejaNews, Infoseek, Galaxy, AliWeb, Yellow Pages, OKRA, and PointSearch. If you need to find something, this might well be the place to find it using the least amount of time and effort.

MetaCrawler

A third popular metasearch site is **MetaCrawler** at:

http://www.metacrawler.com/index.html

MetaCrawler is another site that could save you time and effort when looking for information on the Internet. It sends your queries to several different search engines at the same time. These include OpenText, Lycos, WebCrawler, Infoseek, Excite, Inktomi, Yahoo, and Galaxy. It may not be as fast as Cyber 411, but it collates the results and eliminates all redundant URLs.

Dogpile

This site is remarkable for more than just its tacky name. Its speed and flexibility set it apart as a very powerful metasearch site. **Dogpile** is located at:

http://www.dogpile.com/

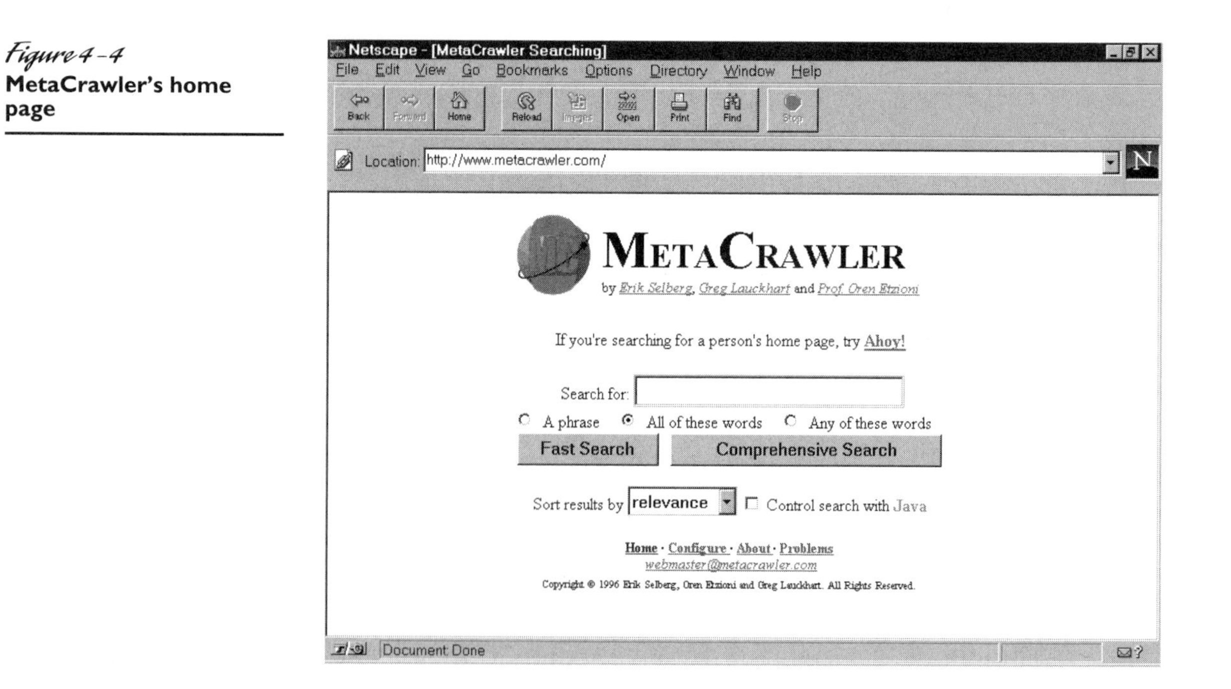

Figure 4-4
MetaCrawler's home page

FYI To sample all the ways you can search the Internet, access the **All-In-One Search Page** at:
http://www.albany.net/allinone
This page compiles various Internet search tools, including Web pages and software archives.

Dogpile allows you to choose which of up to twenty-three search engines you want to conduct your search and the order in which you want the results presented to you (e.g., the findings from Yahoo, then AltaVista, then Excite, etc.). It was developed by a guy named Aaron Flin who says he got tired of using Yahoo and finding almost no results, then turning to AltaVista and getting 30,000 hits. Unlike other metasearch sites, Dogpile also allows you to refine your search terms using Boolean operators. What's more, it's incredibly fast!

The biggest disadvantage of metasearch engines is the time it takes to complete the searches. The slowest search engine will determine how fast your results are displayed. As well, your ability to refine your searches is often limited.

> "In larger and larger numbers, journalists are exploring, writing about and pondering the meaning of the Internet. We and a few of our more enlightened bosses are cooking in an unsettling stew of awe, hunger, and fear. We wonder how we can best take advantage of this astonishing collection of resources ... Every reporter who has any kind of specialty — any reporter who's just curious, for that matter — should be on the Internet.
>
> — Dan Gillmor, *Internet World*, June, 1994

Comparing search tools

> "Knowledge is of two kinds. We know a subject ourselves, or we know where we can find information upon it."
>
> — Dr. Samuel Johnson

Which is the best search tool? It depends. If you are just browsing, start at Yahoo, or one of the other subject catalogs. If you are looking for the best of the Web — and your interests are popular — use Magellan. If you are doing serious research, start with AltaVista or Infoseek, but be prepared to use other good search engines, too. If you can't refine your keyword search enough to get manageable results, try concept searching with Excite. And, if you want to be as thorough as possible, try one of the metasearch sites, such as Dogpile.

Keep in mind, however, that if you are after news coverage of an issue, many news organizations such as the *Washington Post* and CNN have archives online that can be searched by going to the sites directly and using the built-in search engines there. And if you want to listen to the latest news on a breaking story around the world (and your computer is equipped with a sound card and speakers), you can use RealAudio to listen to radio stations from around the world. (See Chapter 3.)

Remember that search engines vary according to such factors as the size of their index, their search options, their speed of returning results, and their overall ease of use.

Find out more about RealAudio, and download a free version to try, from RealAudio's Web site at:
http://www.realaudio.com/

Subject Trees	URL	Comments
Magellan	http://magellan.mckinley.com/	Great general index of popular sites, with reviews and ratings of lots of sites.
Yahoo	http://www.yahoo.com/	Most popular and extensive subject catalog. It can be searched by keyword and provides links to search engines.
Search Engines	**URL**	**Comments**
AltaVista	http://www.altavista.digital.com/	Popular and comprehensive search engine on the Web. It's powerful, fast, and allows a variety of ways to refine searches. It returns many hits – often, too many.
Excite	http://www.excite.com/	Fast and comprehensive; allows unique concept searching. Its results list allows you to search for "More Like This."
Infoseek	http://www.infoseek.com/	Popular and fast. Difficult to refine searches, but includes other popular features like custom news service.
Lycos	http://www.lycos.com/	Reliable, easy to use. Best for simple searches. Sometimes slow. Includes site reviews.
HotBot	http://www.hotbot.com/	Very fast; easy to use.
OpenText	http://index.opentext.net/	Fast, but its index is not as comprehensive as others.
WebCrawler	http://WebCrawler.com/	Fast, easy to use; not very comprehensive.
Metasearch Engines	**URL**	**Comments**
Cyber 411	http://www.cyber411.com/	Very fast; uses 15 search engines at once. Good for simple searches.
Dogpile	http://www.dogpile.com/	Very fast, flexible; uses up to 23 search engines.
MetaCrawler	http://www.metacrawler.com/index.html	Solid, easy-to-read summaries. It can be slow.
SavvySearch	http://guaraldi.cs.colostate.edu:2000/form	Slower; uses several search engines, allows refinement of searches.

Table 4-1
Search tools at a glance

For example, AltaVista and OpenText index every word of a Web page, while the Lycos index is built with only selected words, such as the title, the headings, and the most significant one hundred words. These differences contribute to the very different results sets that are returned by different search engines for the same query.

When using search engines you will have to be persistent and creative for the best results. Different search engines are better for some searches than for others. Each search engine also presents and

FYI For a list of resources of articles and sites comparing search engines, see: **http://www.hamline.edu/library/bush/handouts/comparisons.html**

FYI To perfect your searching skills, try a great online tutorial, "Internet Search Tools & Techniques," at: **http://oksw01.okanagan.bc.ca/libr/connect96/search.htm**

10 tips and tricks for better searching

1. **Pick your search site and learn to use it.** All of them have search fields, but each site works a bit differently. Read the help menu, at least as far as necessary to determine how to search on phrases. Some sites require the words to be in quotes; others require the word AND between the search terms.
2. **Choose your keywords carefully.** Choose unusual words. Be specific. Use as many search terms or phrases that identify precisely the subject in which you are interested. The more precise you can be, the better the results. You want to avoid wading through a flood of irrelevant or inconsequential sites to get to the jewels.
3. **Use capital letters with care.** Search terms entered in lowercase letters are generally case insensitive, but those entered with capital letters will generally make the search case sensitive. Searching for *Rose* may find everything from the famous Kennedy matriarch to the popular comedienne Roseanne, but searching for *rose* will also turn up a lot about the flower, too.
4. **Use singular rather than plural words.** Most search engines will search on substrings: for example, if the search term is *bomb*, they will return hits on *bombs*, but searching on *bombs* might miss relevant information on the Oklahoma bomb.
5. **Use wildcards.** The symbols for these can vary depending on the search engine you are using. For example, when using AltaVista to search for information about immigration, you can search on *immigran** to cover *immigrant, immigrants, immigration.*
6. **Broaden or narrow your searches by using Boolean operators.** With AltaVista and some other engines you can use symbols in place of words: + (AND), | (OR), ~ (NEAR), – (AND NOT). However, most search engines require you to use words. If you want information about Sonny Bono's political career and you are using AltaVista, you could search on *"Sonny Bono" – Cher.* Or, if you are using another search engine, you would specify *Sonny AND Bono AND NOT Cher.* When using search engines other than AltaVista, remember that when you want to exclude something you must use the two words AND NOT. For example, you might search on *"John Lennon" AND NOT Beatles.*
7. **Use accented letters in your keyword when searching in a language other than English.** For example, if you want information about Quebec in French, by including the accent in *Québec*, you will greatly improve your chances of getting hits in French.
8. **Enter multiple spellings where appropriate.** For example, try *Khaddafi Quadafy Kaddafi Qadaffi.* If you are interested in rock climbing, try *rockclimbing* and *rock-climbing.*
9. **Try synonyms.** If you are looking for hiking trails, search on *hiking, trekking, backpacking,* and *camping.*
10. **If at first you don't succeed, try again.** Be persistent and creative. Don't get stuck using only one search engine. Search tools are wonderful, but their usefulness depends on your ingenuity and skill at using them.

CARL UnCover

CARL is a computerized network of library services developed by the Colorado Alliance of Research Libraries. CARL UnCover is the Alliance's ever-growing index to journals and magazines.

Of special interest to the professional and academic researcher, this service indexes more than 17,000 English-language journals and magazines, enabling you to find bibliographic references to more than seven million articles. UnCover includes periodicals from all subject areas, but concentrates heavily on the sciences and social sciences. It is also very up to date, adding five thousand citations daily. It includes the periodical collections of some of the major university and public libraries in the United States, as well as those in Europe and Australia.

You can reach CARL UnCover on the World Wide Web at:

http://uncweb.carl.org/

or by telnetting to:

database.carl.org

From the main Web page, you can select various options to find out more about CARL UnCover, its databases and pricing policies. But it's the first selection — the one that reads, "Search the UnCover Database" — that you will want to try. First, you will be asked to fill in some basic information and be given a profile number which you can save and use for subsequent visits. Even if you don't fill in all the information, you will get a profile number. It's your free ticket to search this incredible database.

You can search by keyword or author's name, or you can browse by journal title. If UnCover finds any matches for your search words or names, it will provide a list of articles, showing titles, the name of the periodical, the author's name, and the date of publication. If you want more information, you can request the full citation, which includes a summary and more bibliographic information.

The good news is that you can search the UnCover database for free. But, if you find something you want, you must pay to have the full text sent to you by fax or mail. This costs US$10 per article plus copyright fees, and it will be faxed within twenty-four hours. Of course, if you don't wish to pay, you can try retrieving the article at your local library.

CARL provides many services besides UnCover. However, most require additional subscriptions, and restrict access by ID or password.

ranks its findings differently. You should scan the list of links before going to any of them, because the links at the top of the list may not necessarily be the best ones.

When you are using search engines, don't settle for making simple queries. Read the help menu; try some advanced search techniques; follow some of the tips and tricks below. The time you spend mastering a few search techniques will be well worth the time you save sifting through useless results.

> "The Internet has become as vital to the way I work as the telephone and library. In addition to staying plugged into my areas of interest (science/medicine/technology), I routinely use the Net to research new stories, make contacts and gather resources."
>
> — Michael O'Reilly, freelance journalist, London, Ontario, January, 1995

Further reading

Leonard, Andrew. "Search Engines: Where to Find Anything on the Net." *CNET.COM*, 1996.
http://www.cnet.com/Content/Reviews/Compare/Search/

Liu, Jian. "Understanding WWW Search Tools."
http://www.indiana.edu/~librcsd/search/

Pfaffenberger, Bryan. *Web Search Strategies*. New York: MIS Press, 1996.

Rowland, Robin, and Kinnaman, Dave. *Researching on the Internet*. Rocklin, CA: Prima Publishing, 1995.

Scoville, Richard. "Special Report: Find It on the Net!" *PC World* (January, 1996), pp. 125–130.
http://www.pcworld.com/reprints/lycos.htm

Webster, Kathleen, and Paul, Kathryn. "Beyond Surfing: Tools and Techniques for Searching the Web." *Feliciter*, January 1996, pp. 48–54.

Chapter 5

Libraries, Databases, Media, and Government

"The fact that TV Guide *has been known to make larger profits than all four networks combined suggests that the value of information about information can be greater than the value of the information itself."*

— Nicholas Negroponte, *Being Digital*. New York: Alfred A. Knopf, 1995.

When many folks first start using the Internet, they are astonished at the amount of information that is available. And chances are, what they've found is only the tip of the iceberg.

The World Wide Web may seem to hold an unprecedented wealth of sources. But the business of information storage and retrieval is not a new phenomenon — after all, the ancient Mesopotamians maintained libraries of clay tablets from about 3500 BCE!

Today, newspapers and magazines are a chief source of both news and information: visit any large library and you will see shelves of microfiche for back issues of the *New York Times*, the *International Herald Tribune*, and other major newspapers. As well, online searching of research databases, statistical information sources, libraries, and government archives has been a reality for over a quarter of a century.

Since the advent of the Web, most of the traditional agencies involved in collecting and organizing data have established a presence on the Internet. As a researcher, you will certainly want to know how to access these sources.

The last chapter gave the "big picture" of how to find your way around the Net. In this chapter, we take a closer look at some valuable research sources, including a number of traditional ones now found on the Internet.

Chapter highlights

- **Subject guides**
- **Libraries on the Net**
- **Databases**
- **Media on the Web**
- **Government information on the Net**

Subject guides

One of the best ways to find out about the resources available in your area of interest is to visit the Argus Clearinghouse (which we suggested in Chapter 4 as a good general starting point). Since this is a particularly valuable subject tree, let's take a closer look at what's available there.

Argus Clearinghouse

You'll find the **Argus Clearinghouse** at:

http://www.clearinghouse.net

Formerly known as the Clearinghouse for Subject-Oriented Internet Resource Guides, Argus is a repository of over 400 guides to the Internet — many of which have been developed by experts in their field. These sources differ from starting pages (described in Chapter 4) in that they are *in-depth* guides to selected resources on specific subjects, such as English literature or animal rights.

Argus guides are donated, and each is the work of an individual author or group. As a result, they vary considerably in terms of format and the sorts of references that are included. A guide to environmental law developed by the Indiana University School of Law at Bloomington will differ considerably from a guide developed by an environmental activist.

The advantage of the Argus Clearinghouse guides is that the best ones provide you with a narrative overview of a topic, rather than just a set of links. Another plus is that Argus quickly points you in the direction of some of the best sources on your topic.

Argus guides typically list Web sites, but may also include Gophers, FTP sites, Usenet newsgroups, and electronic mailing lists for a specific topic or set of related topics. You'll also find *trailblazer pages* (aka "subject pages"), which point you to other important sources. Trailblazers can be found elsewhere on the Net, and you will undoubtedly discover some using the search engines. But the Argus Clearinghouse is one place to find these resources quickly.

There are a number of other locations on the Net where you can find well-researched subject guides to resources for particular topics — for example, Yahoo indices (see Chapter 4) can be used this way. Another good jumping-off point is Infomine.

Infomine

You'll find **Infomine** at:

http://lib-www.ucr.edu/

This virtual reference tool is intended specifically for university-level researchers. Developed by the University of California at Riverside, this site offers guides to the Internet for most disciplines, as well as access to useful databases, textbooks, conference proceedings, and journals.

Figure 5-1
The Argus Clearinghouse

Infomine lists virtual collections according to broad disciplines, for example: Biological, Agricultural, and Medical Resources, Government Information, Physical Sciences, Social Sciences, and Humanities. There are also components devoted to Maps and Geographic Information Systems, Visual and Performing Arts, and Internet Enabling Tools.

Libraries on the Net

Like many businesses and agencies, libraries are adapting to the electronic environment. Some libraries have made their catalogs searchable over the Internet, and others are developing digital archives, so that existing print resources — such as photographic collections or academic journals — can be accessed electronically. Further, some of the most useful Web resources have been developed by librarians — most often in an effort to organize Internet materials for a particular client group, such as a university community or business library. If you long for the Net to be organized more along the lines of the traditional library, where you know exactly where they keep the dictionaries or the psychology books, spend some time exploring the various library resources on the Internet.

The Internet Public Library

A fun place to experience an online library is **The Internet Public Library** at:

http://www.ipl.org/

Figure 5-2
Internet Public Library Reference Center

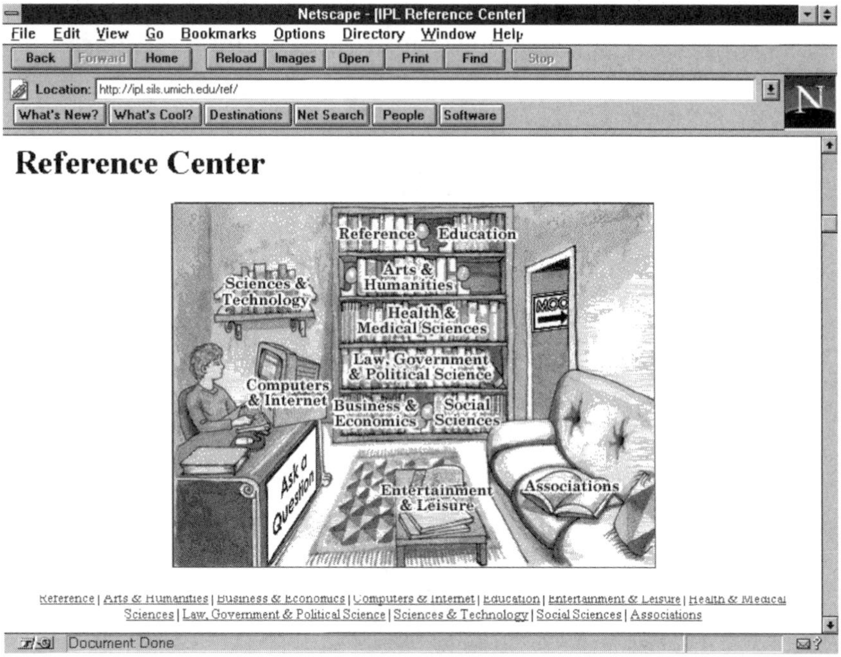

This library is set up like a real building, with a Reading Room, a Reference Center, and even an Exhibit Hall that displays virtual art. You'll also find services for youth, and a classroom where you can access introductory tutorials on how to use the Internet.

Of particular value to researchers is the Reference Center, which points to a selection of Internet reference sources. You can access the general reference area for dictionaries and similar tools, or you can go to a specific subject area, such as Arts and Humanities or Business and Economics, where you will find works targeted to specific subjects. The IPL provides a detailed overview of each of the sources they have selected to include in the library. The references are not extensive, but they are carefully selected and can point you toward some useful trailblazer pages.

If you visit the general reference collection (called Ready Reference), you will find many full-text books, such as almanacs, dictionaries, and encyclopedias. There are also telephone books, a currency converter, atlases, and Bartlett's *Familiar Quotations*. In the Reading Room there are books, newspapers, and magazines. You can use this area as a gateway to the many online books and periodicals available on the Internet: there are pointers to more than 2,600 books, 800 magazines, and 1,100 newspapers. And if one of the things you miss most (as traditional library services move onto the Net) is a helpful librarian, the IPL even provides an Ask a Question service. You can submit a question by filling in an online form, or via electronic mail. These are forwarded to a librarian or library student, who will either return an answer or point you in the direction of (mostly Internet) sources that you can use to research the topic.

Library of Congress

Another important Internet library source is the **Library of Congress**, located at:

http://www.loc.gov

The many valuable research sources here include a series of detailed background studies for seventy-one countries around the world; the American Memory Collection, a digital library of historical documents and photographs; a database of bibliographies for research in science and technology and social sciences; and records describing over 13,000 research organizations willing to provide information to anyone. Be forewarned that many of the resources here (including the library's book catalog) are accessible through LOCIS, which is a particularly arcane online catalog. But there are lots of help screens available, and you can even access help via electronic mail:

lconline@loc.gov

At the Library of Congress you will also find something called the *Z39.50 gateway*. This is a resource that lets you search a variety of library catalogs and databases directly from the Web. (Of particular interest is GILS, the database for Government Information Locator Service.) With the Z39.50 gateway, you fill in a simple onscreen form — so you don't have to figure out the exact commands usually required by a catalog or database.

The Library of Congress offers a further set of subject links to the Internet, called Explore the Internet. This service includes pointers to search engines, a number of Internet learning resources, and a particularly good set of links to U.S. government information.

FYI Be sure to visit your local public or university library on the Internet. Many libraries provide information about local resources and events. At a university, research agency, or newspaper, the librarians may have developed a Web resource that points to some of the best resources for persons in that organization, and some libraries actually offer an online reference service to their local users. You can find libraries at Yahoo and at **LibWeb**: **http://sunsite.berkeley.edu/LibWeb/**

Other Internet library sources

You can locate an extensive set of links to libraries on the World Wide Web at **WebCATS: Library Catalogs on the World Wide Web:**

http://library.usask.ca/hywebcat/

and at **Hytelnet:**

http://library.usask.ca/hytelnet/

Hytelnet includes instructions on how to search various library catalogs using telnet. (Many library catalogs still require the use of telnet for searching.)

Also, check out the resources below.

Berkeley Public Library's Index to the Internet

http://www.ci.berkeley.ca.us/bpl/bkmk/

This extremely useful resource includes, in addition to carefully selected subject resources, an Internet Search section with the BPL's choice of search engines, virtual reference links to business and other information, and a What's New? feature.

The Michigan Electronic Library (MEL)

http://mel.lib.mi.us/main-index.html

MEL offers a reference section and an exceptionally well-organized set of subject links. The links included here are selected by content specialists for quality, reliability, and relevance. The site covers many areas of general interest.

National Library of Canada

http://www.nlc-bnc.ca/

This resource is similar to the Library of Congress's online service. In addition to the library's own collection, the NAC provides access to a collection of Canadian online books and journals. Special services focus on Canadian labor history, children's literature, genealogy, and access to Canadian Federal Government Information. The NAC lists Canadian information by subjects according to the Dewey Decimal System, then provides links to Web sites with more information. For these links, access:

http://www.nlc-bnc.ca/caninfo/ecaninfo.htm

Databases

There are thousands of databases offering Internet access to information on hundreds of specialized topics. Examples include the ERIC database for educational research (http://ericir.syr.edu) and QPAT-US (http://www.qpat.com), which stores the full text of all U.S. patents issued since 1974. Many databases were established long before the Web came into being, but increasingly, organizations are attempting to make their databases available for searching over the World Wide Web. There are several good sources for locating searchable databases on the World Wide Web.

Internet Sleuth

One of the best resources is **The Internet Sleuth** at:

http://www.isleuth.com/

The Internet Sleuth provides access to over 1,500 databases on the Web and allows you to search these directly. The databases available include business directories, science databases, and job listings. This is also a useful resource for government and health information, and for finding people on the Net.

Searchable media information sources include Newsletter Access, a directory of over 5,000 newsletters; The Monster Magazine List, which links to over 2,000 magazines on the Web;

Telnet

Telnet is the application that lets you connect to another computer on the Internet, log on, and actually use the remote computer directly — rather than simply view the information, as is usually the case with a Web page. Although telnet is not used as often as it once was, there remain some resources (such as some commercial databases) that are not available any other way.

One common use for telnet is to log on to a computer where you have a second Internet account. For example, you may have a university account, and you may have a second account with a service provider or a local freenet. If you are at a conference and away from your home computer, you may be able to telnet to your home account and not have to dial long distance.

To use telnet, you will need some type of telnet software; your service provider should be able to supply this. In a Macintosh environment you can use NCSA Telnet or Nifty Telnet; in Windows you may use Ewan, NetTerm, QVTTerm, or another. If your service provider has not given you telnet software, you can obtain telnet clients for both Macintosh and Windows from **Tucows** at:

http://www.tucows.com/

A telnet client enables your smart computer to pretend it's a dumb terminal. Large mainframe computers usually require you to "dumb down" your personal computer before they will recognize you. If you configured your own communications software, you may recall setting the *terminal emulation.* Some common terminal emulation types are VT100, VT102, ANSI, and TTY. On the Internet, VT100 is the most frequently used terminal emulation, so you will probably want to set this as a default on your telnet software. With any telnet program, you need to use the software's menu choices to configure the software and access a site. Frequently, the default settings do not need to be adjusted. Remember that you will need to be logged on to your Internet account for the telnet software to be able to access other Internet computers.

It is possible to telnet using a Web browser, but only if you have set up your browser to use telnet software as a helper application. (See Chapter 3 to find out more about helper applications.) In this case, when you type in the URL for a telnet site (or click on a telnet link), your telnet software will automatically be activated. A telnet connection almost always requires you to log on to the remote computer you are accessing. Many systems allow you to log on as a guest.

You need two pieces of information for a telnet session:

- the address for the site that you want to connect to — for example, *lex.meaddata.com* to telnet to a Lexis-Nexis account. In this case, from within your Web browser, you would type in the URL field:

  telnet://lex.meaddata.com

- the logon information for the site. This could be your name and password for a personal account, or it could be a public logon, such as *guest*, on a telnet site that has been set up for public access.

Once you arrive at a telnet location, follow whatever onscreen instructions appear for using the system. You will not find telnet sites as easy to navigate as the World Wide Web, and some of the sites

Figure 5-3

Use your Netscape preferences or other set-up options to locate your telnet application from within your Netscape (or other) browser

can be confusing, but help screens are almost always available.

Be prepared to take time to familiarize yourself with a telnet site in order to use it efficiently. Watch carefully for logging off instructions when you are telnetting to a site. On many systems, typing the **Control C** key combination or **Control**] (Control plus right bracket) may break the connection. You can also just exit from your telnet software, though it is preferable to log off from a site before doing so.

If you are dialing in to a Unix computer, you can call up telnet simply by typing *telnet* at the system prompt. You can view the basic telnet commands by typing *help* at this point. The two basic commands used in Unix-based telnet are *open* followed by the address of the site you wish to go to, and *quit* to exit telnet.

and specific magazines, such as *Scientific American* and *U.S. News Online*. You can search these resources directly from The Internet Sleuth's home page. Further, the site provides a brief description of each database and hyperlinks to listed sites. You might want to bookmark this site.

Webtaxi

Another excellent tool for easy navigation of many different databases is **Webtaxi** at:

http://www.Webtaxi.com

Webtaxi provides a streamlined interface for quick access to search engines, newsfeeds, and over 1,800 databases arranged by subject. A "supersearch" feature will let you search three or four databases at one time. You can access and use Webtaxi as a normal Web page, or you can click on the Webtaxi **Remote** selection. This will place a Webtaxi toolbar in the upper left corner of your browser.

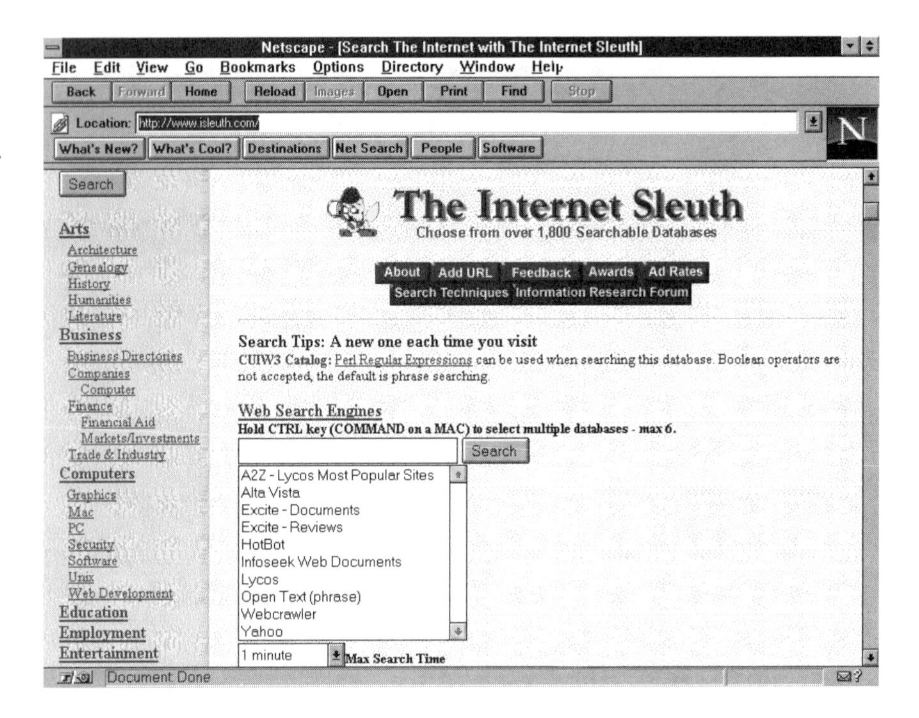

Figure 5-4
The Internet Sleuth is a popular database resource

The Cornell Gateway Catalog

Here's another substantial resource for locating databases. You'll find **The Cornell Gateway Catalog** at:

http://www.mannlib.cornell.edu/catalog/

Some of the databases listed are proprietary, meaning that you must be affiliated with Cornell University to gain access to these. But there are hundreds of other databases here, many of which can be searched for free: for example, many U.S. government databases; the Journalism Periodicals Database, which references professional and academic publications for journalism and mass communication; the Economic Research Service publications database; and *Psyche: An Interdisciplinary Journal of Research on Consciousness.*

The biggest disadvantage to the Cornell Gateway is the number of "Cornell Only" databases. Still, it's worth checking out to determine what resources might be available in your area.

Hytelnet

We have already mentioned Hytelnet (http://library.usask.ca/hytelnet/) as a good place to locate library catalogs on the Internet. This resource also provides a gateway to databases as well as bibliographies, freenets, and bulletin boards.

Some of the databases accessible from Hytelnet are the National Distance Learning Center database, which lists courses in distance education; World Bank socioeconomic data; the Social Sciences

Data Archive; an AIDS information database; Teacher Pages (full-text information) from the Pennsylvania Department of Education; NASA Spacelink, for space-related information; and the High Energy Astrophysics Science Archive Research Center. A number of fee-based services are also listed here.

The best way to get a sense of the many databases available through telnet is to browse through the offerings on Hytelnet.

Healthgate

You will find **Healthgate** at:

http://www.healthgate.com/HealthGate/home.html

This resource lists extensive health information databases and services. While access to most of these requires a subscription, Healthgate offers free access to the National Library of Medicine's biomedical database, Medline.

Medline is a primary medical research database that offers over eight million references to journal articles in medicine and related disciplines. Many of these references include abstracts. The Medline database can also be accessed from Medscape at:

http://www5.medscape.com/default.mhtml

InterNIC

InterNIC is a network information resource and registry located at:

http://www.internic.net/dod

Researchers should be aware of the site's Directory and Database Services. When they list themselves with InterNIC, agencies are encouraged to submit a brief description of their resource. InterNIC posts these descriptions and enables you to search them by keyword. You can either browse the resources referenced by InterNIC, or you can run a search to find out what's available in your area. With the advent of very powerful search engines, InterNIC's directory is not as valuable as it once was, but it remains a good place to browse, particularly for non-Web resources.

InterNIC is the home of the Scout Report and Net Happenings, two important sources for tracking new sites on the Internet.

FYI You can find a directory with contact information for U.S. businesses at **The Central Source Yellow Pages** at: **http://www.telephonebook.com/**
This resource is organized by region and category. A similar resource is the **NYNEX Interactive Yellow Pages** at: **http://www.niyp.com/**
For more comprehensive business information resources (some at a cost), visit **Hoovers Online** at: **http:// www.hoovers.com/**

Nice — for a price

As the material on the Net improves in quality, so do the costs. Commercial information services offer access to thousands of databases and provide much more in-depth coverage than is available from free sources on the Net. Here are some database resources that you will have to pay for, but which may be worth purchasing, depending upon your research needs.

N2K Telebase

http://www.telebase.com

This resource offers telnet and Web access to hundreds of commercial databases, including Dialog, DataStar, Dun & Bradstreet, and NewsNet. There is a cost, but much of the information is not available elsewhere. Professional researchers will appreciate the fact that this highly specialized information is made available from a single source.

NlightN

http://www.nlightn.com

NlightN is a quick way to acquire citations for materials that can be obtained from a library or document delivery service. Although this is not a full-text service, it can still be a useful resource for researchers. Databases include Academic Abstracts, ABI (American Business Information), PsychINFO from the American Psychological Association, Canadian Research Index, CNN News and Features, Education Index, Reader's Guide to Periodical Literature, Sociological Abstracts, Index to Legal Periodicals, and scores of others.

Dialog (Knight-Ridder's Dialog service)

http://www.krinfo.com

Lexis-Nexis

http://www.lexis-nexis.com

Both of these are well-established database services used for research in newsrooms and university libraries. Like many similar commercial information services, they are accessible via telnet. Unfortunately, many researchers may find the subscription costs prohibitive.

Media on the Web

> "What was once a trickle of international source material available in full text is now almost a rapid stream. The scenario is parallel to what literary historian Patrick Parrinder described happening around the turn of the 19th century, when an explosion of published books resulted in proto-information overload. 'The stream of books is felt as at once a promise and a threat,' he wrote. 'There is the promise of intellectual progress and cultural improvement ... by keeping up with the new. But there is also the threat of losing one's bearings, of being carried along in the cultural torrent with no sense of fixed standards.'"
>
> — "Browsing the Global Newsstand," *Database Magazine*, October 1994.

The Internet is transforming traditional media sources. There are now hundreds of newspapers, magazines, and books available on the Internet. Currently, access to many of these is free.

The advantage in using the Web for culling news stories is that you can access articles quickly and from many different sources. Further, online sources provide up-to-the-minute coverage, back-

Trawling the Net for news

ground information, feedback, and sometimes forums for public discussion.

Newspapers on the Web include specialized news sources such as *UniSci* (http://unisci.com), a science news publication, and weeklies, such as the *Village Voice* (http://www.villagevoice.com/), along with hundreds of dailies. Magazine sources include traditional general interest publications and trade journals, as well as "e-zines."

E-zines are online magazines, often the work of one individual. They cover a wide range of topics, from science fiction and fantasy to politics. While it is easy to dismiss e-zines as a variation on the "vanity presses" of an earlier era, some enjoy wide readership and are published by writers who are well informed about their topic. E-zines are an excellent source for story ideas for journalists and writers.

Figure 5-5
Many traditional news media, such as the *Washington Post*, **can now be found on the Web**

INFO*nugget*

"What's an 'e-zine,' anyway?

"For those of you not acquainted with the zine world, 'zine' is short for either 'fanzine' or 'magazine,' depending on your point of view. Zines are generally produced by one person or a small group of people, done often for fun or personal reasons, and tend to be irreverent, bizarre, and/or esoteric. Zines are not 'mainstream' publications — they generally do not contain advertisements (except, sometimes, advertisements for other zines), are not targeted towards a mass audience, and are generally not produced to make a profit."

— John Labovitz, E-Zine List
http://www.meer.net/~johnl/e-zine-list/

Hard-copy consumer magazines are understandably reluctant to put every article from every issue on the Web: they'd lose subscriptions. But many magazines have enough content online to justify visiting their sites. Academic journals are more likely to have full-text, complete issues online — although even some of these provide only abstracts, as a teaser to get you to subscribe or to order back issues.

Newswire services on the Net are an additional source of news. These services publish full-text bulletins, articles, and even scripts of speeches and debates online. Reuters, Associated Press, and United Press International all provide hourly updates on world events.

Journalists and researchers preparing background reports can tap into these online resources for in-depth coverage of an issue that may comprise different perspectives. Online articles often include an electronic mail address for the author. If you're a journalist writing an article and find an academic paper on your topic, you might contact the expert author for an interview.

The best way to find out about newspapers online is to sample what's available. The following sites make good starting points. Additional media resources are included in Appendix B.

FYI Many academic and scholarly journals are now available through the Internet. Also, libraries, museums, and universities are organizing massive resources (manuscripts, artifacts, research archives, etc.) for Internet access. For a truly amazing collection of computer technical reports (27,000 at last count), visit the **New Zealand Digital Library** at: **http://www.cs.waikato.ac.nz/~nzdl/**
To get an overview of some other projects that are underway, try **Digital Libraries Resource Page** at: **http://www.ece.uwaterloo.ca/%7Ektrgovac/digital/digital.html**

Electronic Newsstand
http://www.enews.com/

It's open 24 hours a day, and you can flip through every magazine in the place! These samples aren't merely links; they're actual articles from consumer magazines, and are obtainable from their own server. The best are kept in the Need to Read archive — so you can search through older articles. If you need still more stuff, check out the Monster Links pages, which cover a variety of fields and list a mind-boggling number of sites for online publications.

Ecola Newsstand
http://ecola.com/

This is another mega-site that provides separate indexes for newspapers, magazines, and computer publications. Here you can also search for a publication by name.

On-line Journals List
http://bioc02.uthscsa.edu/journal/journal.html

Compiled by the University of Texas Health Science Center, this list links you to online sites of journals publishing in science, news, business, art, and entertainment. The science list, for example, includes everything from the *Journal of Molecular Biology* to *Physics World*.

CMPA Reading Room
http://www.cmpa.ca/maghome.html

Sponsored by the Canadian Magazine Publishers Association, this is an important site for links to Canadian magazines online.

Editor & Publisher Interactive Online Newspaper Database
http://www.mediainfo.com/ephome/npaper/nphtm/online.htm

With links to more than 1,500 online newspapers, this resource is one of the most comprehensive. A good source for journalists.

Ultimate Collection of Newslinks
http://pppp.net/links/news/

Here you can browse through more than 3,700 links to newspapers around the world. The directory is organized geographically. Clicking on a link to a particular newspaper opens a new browser window with that paper's home page. This allows the user either to continue searching from the Ultimate Newslinks site, or to read the highlighted newspaper.

Best News on the Net
http://www.NovPapyrus.com/news/

In addition to some excellent newspapers, this resource includes links to wire services and broadcast news sources.

My Virtual Newspaper
http://www.refdesk.com/paper.html

This site offers up-to-date links to newspapers around the world.

NewsLink
http://www.newslink.org

This is another massive set of links to news sources. Broadcast news sources are included.

Newsroom
http://www.auburn.edu/~vestmon/news.html

The focus here is on the best sources for today's news.

Omnivore
http://way.net/omnivore/index.html

Global coverage of today's news. Use this source for access to current stories from world sources.

Top news sources on the Web

ABC News (http://www.abcradionet.com)
RealAudio news broadcasts — hourly updates.

Boston Globe (http://www.boston.com/globe/glohome.htm)
Opportunities to discuss the news and access to GlobeWire, which scrolls headlines to let you monitor breaking news stories while you work.

CANOE/Canadian Online Explorer (http://www.canoe.ca/Canoe/ home.html)
First-rate Canadian source for news — events, politics, sports, culture.

Chicago Sun-Times (http://www.suntimes.com)
Includes a searchable database of Roger Ebert movie reviews.

CNN (http://www.cnn.com/index.html)
Top stories and program transcripts.

The Globe and Mail (http://www.theglobeandmail.com)
Many articles from each section of Canada's national newspaper.

Los Angeles Times (http://www.latimes.com/)
HOME Search Post and AP stories. Home of the PointCast desktop news service.

Nando Times (http://www.nando.net/)
Well-established and respected online news source.

The New York Times (http://www.nytimes.com/)
Full-text articles from the entire paper are online, but for a price: US$35 per month. Free 30-day trial. (Bargain hunters can find the current version of the *New York Times Book Review* at the Amazon Bookstore, http://www.amazon.com).

The Times (http://www.the-times.co.uk)
Several full-text articles from the daily edition are available for free, as is the complete text from the London-based *Sunday Times*.

U.S. News Online (http://www.usnews.com/usnews)
Breaking news and background stories developed by *U.S. News*. "News You Can Use" reports on popular topics — health, computers, travel — and provides links to useful sources on the Net.

Time Daily (http://www.pathfinder.com/time/daily/)
Top stories and a news search for additional information.

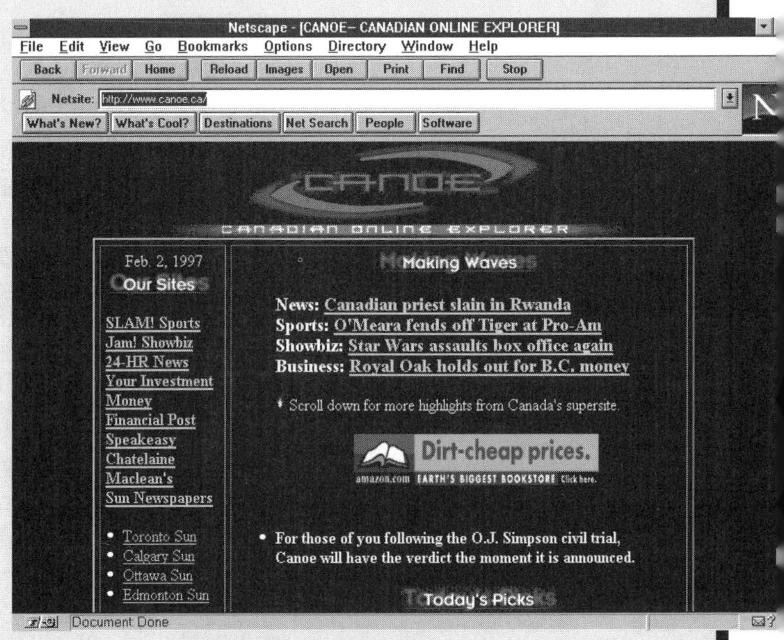

Figure 5-6
CANOE: Canadian Online Explorer

USA Today (http://www.usatoday.com)
Regularly updated news, plus a number of useful archives for research.

Washington Post (http://www.washingtonpost.com/)
Value-added service with its Search the World database. Lists resources for news, reference materials, and Internet sites for more than 220 countries and territories.

FYI Many Web sites of broadcasters focus more on entertainment and headlines than in-depth features and analysis. Further, some sites require you to download a RealAudio player. If you're a researcher looking for background information, this extra effort may not be worth the time involved — unless you're a die-hard audiophile!

INFO*nugget*

"By the year 2001, television and print newspapers will lose significant portions of their most valuable customers to online news and special-interest computer programming, according to a new study by Forrester Research. Based on current consumer computer purchase-and-use patterns, the study predicts that print newspapers could lose as much as 14 percent of their readership over the next five years."

— Hoag Levins, "Newspapers May Lose 14% to Internet." Editor & Publisher Interactive, November 1, 1996.
http://www.mediainfo.com/ephome/news/newshtm/recent/110196n1.htm

Web Times International/Web Times Canada
http://www.canadas.net/WebTimes/main.html
"The 24 Hour Guide to Live Audio and Video on the Internet."

Other news sources

For magazines that are not online, you can get full-text articles from **The Electric Library** at:

http://www.elibrary.com

This is a full-text service, meaning that entire magazine and newspaper articles and encyclopedia entries are displayed onscreen. You simply type in a keyword, and the screen displays up to thirty items containing that word. Beside each entry is an icon showing whether the item is from a magazine, newspaper, book, newswire service, or TV or radio transcript. There are also photos available online. Click on the title to display the whole text. It's free to search the library, which gives you the periodical name and date of publication — so you can find it at your local public library. Subscribers can download text at a monthly cost of US$9.95 for unlimited access. You can choose a free two-week trial.

Another full-text service is the **Encarta Online Library** at:

http://encarta.msn.com/library/intro.asp

Encarta offers access to tens of thousands of encyclopedia articles, pamphlets, reference books, and magazines, including *Editor & Publisher, Psychology Today,* and *Science News*. Their service costs US$6.95 per month, and trial subscriptions are available.

FYI It can be annoying when sites such as online newspapers require registration before you can access the material, but you only have to do it once. To help remember your ID name and password, try using the same ones whenever you register for anything. You could also try bookmarking the page that appears immediately after the prompt for your login information, so you can skip over that step every time — then you won't need to remember the codes. (This won't always work, but it's worth a try!)

Government information on the Net

Knowing how to access government information is a vital skill for any researcher or journalist, and this is an area where the Internet is playing a major role. Access to government information is increasingly streamlined; you can now retrieve documents in a fraction of the time it would once have taken. Most national and many regional governments have established a presence on the Web, and you can contact them by e-mail.

FYI Some institutions, such as governments and universities, may still have some information available at a Gopher site. Organizations that went online more recently have largely skipped over the old technology and put their information straight onto the Web, which is easier to use and can support graphics. You can use your Web browser to access both Gopher and FTP sites (see Chapter 3).

As well, the Web is an important communication vehicle for political parties of every stripe. This means that the proverbial man-or-woman-in-the-street is less dependent upon the traditional news media for information about politics: with very little effort, anyone can now obtain information on party platforms, policy statements, and campaign contributions. These matters become particularly timely in an election year.

The vast range of government material available via the Internet includes bureaucratic and legislative information, guidelines and applications for grants, and consumer publications far too numerous to list here. Through the Congressional Record (the official record of what goes on in the U.S. Congress), researchers can get full-text newspaper articles related to current bills (when the articles are read into the record as addenda called "Extensions to Remarks"). Because governments play a significant role in fostering social and economic development, you will find useful government publications dealing with the environment, education, health care, and small business.

The *Washington Post* publishes **A Guide to Government Information Online**, which includes links to popular U.S. government sources, including the Departments of Education; Energy; Health and Human Services; and Housing and Urban Development. The Guide highlights the most popular offerings, such as student financial assistance information from the Department of Education. Access the Guide at:

http://wp1.washingtonpost.com/wp-srv/national/longterm/fedcom/guide/guide.htm

One of the best ways to start hunting for government information on the Internet is to use one of the guides available from the **Argus Clearinghouse**. Here are three good ones:

Canadian Government Information on the Internet by Anita Cannon
http://www.lib.uwaterloo.ca/discipline/Government/CanGuide/

LSU Libraries' U.S. Federal Government Agencies Page compiled by David Atkins
http://www.lib.lsu.edu/gov/fedgov.html

Government Internet Publications by Maryann Readal
http://www.nhmccd.cc.tx.us/lrc/gov/gov.html

For information on access to regional, European, and other non-North American governments, check the government listings at **Yahoo**:

http://www.yahoo.com

If your research requires access to government information, spend time exploring each of these resources, as well as the additional sources included in Appendix B of this book.

A last word

When you need specialized information, such as government statistics, an all-purpose search engine may not yield the best results.

Government information sources on the Web

Champlain (http://info.ic.gc.ca/champlain/)
This searches all online information from federal and provincial government departments in Canada and allows you to download full-text documents.

Federal Web Locator (http://www.law.vill.edu/fed-agency/fedWebloc.html)
Operated by the Villanova Center for Information Law and Policy, this site aims "to be the one-stop shopping point for [U.S.] federal government information on the World Wide Web." It offers well-organized links to home pages for government branches, agencies, departments, and corporations. You can also type in a keyword to find a link to a specific agency or organization.

GovBot (http://www.business.gov/Search_Online.html)
Search for government information sources using the GovBot Database of Government Web Sites.

Government of Canada (http://canada.gc.ca/)
This is the Canadian government's official central site. Click on "About Canada" for geographical facts, a list of prime ministers, and more. The Federal Institutions section links Web sites of dozens of ministries, departments, agencies, and Crown corporations.

Government Resources on the Web (http://www.lib.umich.edu/libhome/Documents.center/federal.html)
Developed at the University of Michigan, this is another comprehensive and well-organized reference site for U.S. government information. It includes pointers to international organizations and governments around the world.

GPO Access (http://www.access.gpo.gov/su_docs/aces/aaces001.html)
This site is a gateway to many full-text databases of U.S. government information. Databases currently available include the Federal Register, the Congressional Record, the Budget of the United States, and the Economic Report of the President. The GPO also links to GILS (Government Information Locator Service), which identifies and describes publicly available federal information resources, including electronic information.

Infomine (http://lib-www.ucr.edu/govpub/)
Subtitled "The Comprehensive Government Information Internet Resource Collection," this site can be browsed using the Table of Contents' alphabetical list of subjects. You can also search by subject, keyword, or title for a resource.

Library of Congress: Federal Government: General Information Resources (http://lcWeb.loc.gov/global/executive/general_resources.html)
The LOC is a gateway to much U.S. government information, including facts and figures, speeches, reports, news releases, and legislative documents. From the Library of Congress you can also access a Z39.50 gateway specifically devoted to federal or to regional government sources.

Thomas Legislative Information (http://thomas.loc.gov)
Named after former U.S. President Thomas Jefferson, this site summarizes recent U.S. government activities: major bills (arranged by topic, title, and number), the Congressional Record, committee information, historical documents (such as the Declaration of Independence), and much more. There is even a primer describing how a bill becomes law. ▶

United Nations Web Site Locator (http://www.unsystem.org/)
Navigating the quagmire of U.N. information can be a researcher's nightmare. This site makes your search systematic. It links home pages of U.N. departments and agencies, indexing them according to subject. Documents from the World Trade Organization, UNICEF, World Health Organization, and others are at your fingertips. Check the listing of other international organizations.

The White House (http//www.whitehouse.gov)
As the name implies, this site features information from the executive branch of the U.S. government. An Interactive Citizens' Handbook offers press releases, speeches, and full text from presidential press conferences.

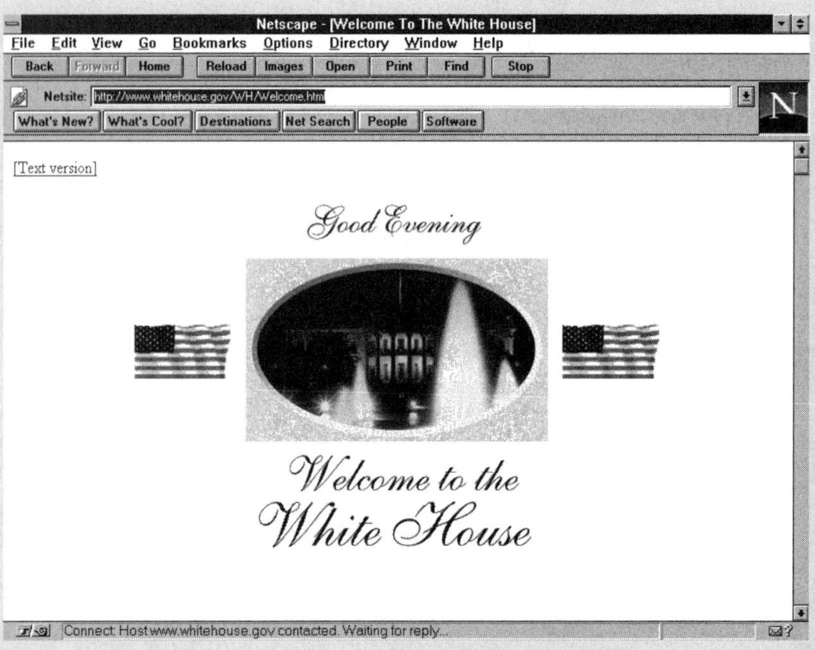

Figure 5-6
The White House site provides information from the executive branch of the U.S. government

This chapter has highlighted library, database, media, and government sources on the Web. Knowing some of the specialized databases now available on the Internet will help you to refine your search techniques and increase your efficiency online. If you invest a little time exploring the resources introduced in this chapter, you'll find you have many new and valuable research tools at your fingertips.

Further reading

"Databases" (Canada and U.S.)
Investigative Journalism on the Internet
http://www.vir.com/~sher/data.htm

Directory of Database Services. St. Petersburg, FL: Poynter Institute for Media Studies.
http://www.poynter.org/car/cg_cardirec.htm

Gale Guide to Internet Databases. Detroit: Gale Research. (Annual.)

"Internet Research — McFarlin Library Research Guide"
http://www.lib.utulsa.edu/guides/rsrch3.htm

"Library/Information Gateways"
Megasources (a database of links from the School of Journalism, Ryerson Polytechnic University)
http://www.acs.ryerson.ca/~journal/megasources.html#02

Maxwell, Bruce. *How to Access the Federal Government on the Internet*. Available from Congressional Quarterly, 1414—22nd Street NW, Washington, DC 20037; (tel.) 202 887-8500.

"Star-Spangled Net." *Internet World*, Vol. 6, No. 8 (August 1995), pp. 28–78.

Chapter 6

Beyond the Web: More E-Mail; Listservs, Newsgroups, and FAQs

"Like the telephone, electronic mail expands the reach of reporters, enabling you to obtain quotable information from around the world efficiently and at low cost. ... E-mail is having and will have a tremendous impact on reporting. Few people can imagine reporting today without access to a telephone. E-mail is destined to play a similarly integral role in journalism."

— Randy Reddick and Elliot King, *The Online Journalist*. Orlando, Florida: Harcourt Brace, 1995, p. 76.

The Internet's value to writers, researchers, editors, and journalists goes well beyond the information available on the World Wide Web. There are many other online resources that are useful for finding people (along with their phone numbers or e-mail addresses!), as well as information in every conceivable field.

For example, online discussion groups are great places to find interesting people sharing opinions and knowledge. Here you can pick up tips, locate experts, and make other contacts for breaking news and original story ideas. There are also online groups that allow you to network with other writers and researchers.

This chapter takes you beyond the Web to explore other electronic resources that are especially valuable to writers, researchers, editors, and journalists.

Chapter highlights

- **Electronic mail as a research tool**
- **How to use Eudora Mail and Pine Mail**
- **Using Netscape Mail or Internet Explorer Mail**
- **Finding people on the Net**
- **Listservs and newsgroups**
- **Is there an expert in the house?**
- **Conducting interviews online**
- **Getting the FAQs: Frequently Asked Questions**

Electronic mail as a research tool

Electronic mail is the most widely used feature of the Internet. It's estimated that more than fifty million people worldwide use e-mail, and the number grows every day. E-mail is usually the means by which people are introduced to cyberspace. It's a good way to get comfortable online, because you can start by using it to contact friends and family members around the world. But it is also a tool you can use to reach experts and make other contacts relevant to issues you are researching. For example, you can send messages to people you may not know in order to introduce yourself and request information, to ask for an interview, to determine whether someone is worth interviewing, to verify quotes, or even to conduct an interview online.

There are even some advantages in using electronic mail over the old-fashioned ways of contacting people. E-mail is generally free; or at least, with most Internet service providers (ISPs), you don't pay for individual messages the way you would long distance telephone calls. You can reach people around the world with ease. You can send a message when it is convenient for you, knowing the person to whom you send it will read it only when it is convenient for them. E-mail is more efficient than playing telephone tag with hard-to-reach individuals, or trying to catch people during business hours in a different time zone. It also allows you to send a single message to many people at the same time. For example, you could send a simple request for information about a topic you are researching to a discussion group devoted to that topic, and get lots of replies.

There are disadvantages to using electronic mail for research, too. Just because e-mail arrives with a name attached to it doesn't mean that's the name of the person who wrote the message. Lots of people use other people's e-mail accounts to send messages. Others use pseudonyms. Still others may be playing a hoax. If you plan to quote an e-mail message, you should contact the sender directly to confirm that they are, indeed, the author and to verify their credentials.

Like a postal address, an e-mail address directs computers on the network to deliver the message to the right mail slot. An e-mail address consists of four parts, and you can often determine something about a person's e-mail account by following the clues in the address. For example, let's break down the e-mail address:

jsmith@harvard.edu

- **jsmith** is the *user name*. The first letter is probably the initial of the person's first name; "Smith" is probably the account holder's last name.
- @ is the symbol for "at," which separates the user name from the rest of the address.
- **harvard** is the name of the *host computer*, where the user has his or her e-mail box.
- **edu** is the *domain name*, which identifies the type of institution where the address is located ("edu" for university, "org" for

non-commercial organization, "gov" for government, "com" for commercial organization, "net" for network). Sometimes the country may also be indicated by a two-letter code ("jp" for Japan, "ca" for Canada, "uk" for United Kingdom, etc.).

Domain

A comparison of e-mail programs

All e-mail programs allow you to receive messages, display the messages, reply to messages, compose and send new messages, and store messages. The ease with which you can do each of those things depends on the particular electronic mail package you are using.

FYI For a detailed review of several popular mail programs, check out **C|Net: The Computer Network's Review** at: **http://www.cnet.com/Content/Reviews/Compare/Email2/ss01.html** or its more extensive review at: **http://www.cnet.com/Content/Reviews/Compare/Email/index.html**

In a Windows or Macintosh environment, you can choose among several user-friendly mail programs, such as Eudora Mail or Pegasus. With a non-graphical account on a Unix machine, the software will be less "intuitive," but will provide you with many of the same features. A commonly used non-graphical e-mail package is Pine, which presents you with a menu of all the basic electronic mail functions.

If you are using a Web browser such as Netscape or Microsoft Internet Explorer, you can also choose the browser's built-in mail program to avoid having to use a separate one.

Let's look first at how two different mail programs work — one that is available for both Windows and Macintosh environments, and another for Unix-based machines. Then we'll consider the mail features of two popular browsers.

How to use Eudora Mail

Sending an e-mail message

1. Click on the **Message** menu and select **New Message.**
2. Complete the **To:** field with the electronic mail address from the person to whom you are sending the message. The **From:** field will already include your own address as established in your configuration file. Use the **tab** key to move to additional fields in the header.
3. Type your message in the space provided.
4. Click on the **Send** button to send the message immediately.

Receiving messages

1. Check for incoming messages by clicking on the **File** menu. Select **Check Mail.** Note that the system will check for mail when you first log on. It will also check for mail at regular intervals if you set up your configuration file to do that.

Figure 6-1
Eudora's start-up screen displays each sender's name, time of posting, and a brief subject line

Eudora Light - [In]

File Edit Mailbox Message Transfer Special Tools Window Help Eudora Pro

	Sender	Date	Size	Subject
	E.W. Brody	03:00 PM 8/24/95	3	graduate journalism programs
	Robin Rowland	02:01 AM 3/23/96	16	My CAR course and seminars
	Lynne Van Luven	09:52 AM 4/4/96	9	Computerization (fwd)
	Kevin Thom	11:28 AM 4/15/96	2	CAR
	Dean Tudor	05:15 PM 8/11/96	3	Write Better (fwd)
	Hal Doran	01:18 PM 8/26/96	3	Re: Fave web sites
	Hal Doran	07:43 AM 8/27/96	3	Re: Fave web sites
	George Frajkor	11:45 PM 9/13/96	11	Re: MULTIMEDIA
	Dan Pottier	07:42 AM 9/14/96	4	Re: MULTIMEDIA
	Kevin Thom	09:25 AM 9/16/96	4	Re: Hello!
	Lionel Lumb	10:11 AM 9/16/96	13	Re: MULTIMEDIA
	Ross_Mutton	10:43 AM 9/16/96	4	RE: MULTIMEDIA
•	Mary McGuire	10:01 PM 9/25/96	4	(fwd) Fwd: NYT, NPR create interactive electi
•	John Crump	09:54 AM 9/30/96	4	[Fwd: INFO: Public Listserver for Internet Se
	Dave Smillie	09:34 AM 9/30/96	7	Handy Quotes
	Smith, Kirsten	09:47 AM 10/3/96	2	fun websites
	ALEXANDRA SPEROU	07:02 PM 10/10/9	3	hello from Cardiff!
	Mary McGuire	02:15 PM 10/10/9	3	(fwd) Fwd: Reporter's Internet Survival Guide
	Saul Schwartz	01:18 PM 10/13/9	2	Internet Policy seminar
	Donna Fox	04:36 PM 10/14/9	2	Re: Hello from CA
	Dave Sutherland	03:43 PM 10/15/9	10	FW: WEB conference on WEB delivery of distanc
	John M. McGuire	11:38 AM 10/26/9	4	Re: your mail
•	Mary McGuire	10:45 AM 10/29/9	3	(fwd) Fwd: Meta-link to research sources
	MSFH@angonet.gn.	05:42 PM 10/29/9	2	Message for Sheri Lecker

25/110K/561K

For Help, press F1 NUM

FYI An upgraded version of Eudora, called Eudora Pro, is also available. This version is relatively inexpensive and comes with a number of slick enhancements, such as the ability to click on a Web site reference to bring the Web page into your browser automatically. Find out more from the Eudora home page at: **http://www.eudora.com/**

2. The POP (Post Office Protocol) mail server will request your password the first time you request mail after logging on to the system. Type in your password and click **OK.** (You can also configure Eudora to remember your password.)
3. Incoming messages are downloaded into your **In Mailbox.** You can read your incoming messages by double-clicking on the message listed in the message summary.
4. When you have received a message, you have the option of forwarding it or replying to it. In either case, use the icon buttons on the summary screen. When the message is displayed, you can choose these options from the **Message** menu.

Saving messages

Save a current message to a file by selecting **Transfer.** Next, click on the name of the folder in which you wish to save the item. If you have not already established a folder in which to save your message, you can do so by selecting **New.** You will be prompted for a new filename. Creating a folder allows you to establish a series of subdirectories, so that you can group together related messages without having to file them in the same file.

Deleting messages

You can delete a message from any folder by highlighting it in the summary screen and then clicking on the **Trash** icon. You can also delete a message by clicking on **Message** and then clicking on

FYI: Download new messages and disconnect from your server before taking time to read your mail. Reading and replying to mail offline helps reduce costs.

Delete. Items are not removed from the Trash until you exit (if you have Eudora configured to Empty Trash on Exit), or until you click on **Special** and select **Empty Trash**.

Nicknames

Nicknames allow you to avoid having to type in a complete address each time you send a message. Instead, you can simply type the nickname you have assigned that person, and the program will fill in the correct address. It's a bit like using the speed-dial button on your phone.

1. Select **Window** and click on **Nicknames**. To add a new nickname, click on **New**. You will be prompted for the nickname. Putting a name on the recipients list (address book) will let you bring up the name in a window for quick selection when mailing.
2. Once you have typed in a nickname, click on **OK**. Next, place your cursor in the address field and type in the address of the person (or persons, if establishing a group address) to whom you are assigning the nickname. Multiple addresses must be separated by commas.
3. When you have finished adding address information, close the window by double-clicking on the upper left-hand box. At the prompt, you can choose to save or discard the changes to the nickname list. If you are reading a message from someone you would like to have on your nicknames list, it's even easier. Just click on **Special**, then select **Add to Nicknames**, and the address will be added to the folder automatically.

FYI: There's a Web site that helps you convert lists of nicknames or address lists from one e-mail program to another. You will find it at: **http://www.interguru.com/mailconv.htm**

Signature files

Signature files, which can be automatically appended to outgoing messages, lend a personal touch to your e-mail. Many people use humorous or thought-provoking quotes as part of their signatures. Some people also provide their phone number, address, and fax number.

1. Click on **Window**. Then select **Signature**.
2. Type in whatever information you wish to include as a signature.
3. Close the file by double-clicking on the upper left-hand box. Save any changes.
4. You can choose to exclude the signature on a specific message by manipulating the signature window (middle window just above the new message header) when a new message is being generated.

Signatures lend a distinctive touch to messages and tell something about the sender

Mary Lam, Flautist (marylam@aol.com)

__O______((__o_o_o__(__o_o_o__(__()_

Attachments

This feature enables you to send files that have been prepared earlier with a word processor. However, you must remember not to attach files that contain word processing codes, unless you are certain the recipient uses the same word processing software that you do, or uses software that is capable of converting your file.

If you want to attach a file, you must first save it — not in the usual way you save files in your word processing program, but rather as a text file (bearing the file extension *.txt*; also known as an ASCII file). Look under the **Save** or **Save As** options and choose **Text File**. With the text file format, you don't have to worry that the recipients will be unable to read your message because they don't use the same software as you.

FYI You can learn more about Eudora from **Peter's Eudora Page** at: **http://www.gildea.com/eudora**

1. Once the file is saved as a text file you can attach it to an outgoing message by clicking on **Message**, then clicking on **Attach Document**.
2. From the Windows **File** listing, highlight the document you wish to attach. Then click **OK**. The filenames are automatically listed with attachments.
3. If you have not saved your file as a text file and wish to send the binary file (i.e., with all the word processing codes), then you must code it before sending it as part of an electronic mail message. Eudora offers BinHex and MIME (some versions also include Uuencode) as format options for sending files. If the receiver is using Eudora also, you can send the file using BinHex. Otherwise, choose MIME or Uuencode. To select BinHex or other formats, use the third window across the top of the outgoing message.

How to use Pine Mail

In a non-graphical environment, there are various software programs that are used to read and send electronic messages. One of the most user-friendly is Pine. Pine was originally developed for novice e-mail users in an attempt to improve on another commonly available mail package called Elm. (*Pine* stands for *Pine Is Not Elm*.) There are two key advantages to using Pine in a non-graphical setting:

- Pine uses a menu-based interface, which makes it relatively easy to learn.
- Pine can also be used to read newsgroups (discussed below), whereas most systems require a separate newsreader package.

If Pine is not available on your local system, ask your access provider about the possibility of obtaining it. If Pine is already on your system, you can access it by typing **pine** from your system prompt. (Do this after you have connected to your Internet service provider.)

FYI If you send an electronic message and it "bounces" (i.e., is returned to you from the Mailer-Daemon or Postmaster), look carefully at the header information — it may tell you why the message bounced. **Host Unknown** means that the computer address cannot be located. Often that's just because of a simple typo. **User Unknown** could mean a typo, but it might also indicate that the intended recipient is no longer at that location.

Figure 6-3 shows Pine's main menu, or the first screen you will see once you have activated the program. You can highlight the menu item of your choice or simply type the single-letter command for that option.

A rule of thumb for using Pine is to read carefully the list of commands displayed at the bottom of the screen. These commands indicate the choices available for any given function. Also, users should be aware that Pine Help is context-sensitive. This means that each Pine screen you use will have its own Help text explaining the choices available for that screen. Many first-time Pine users quickly learn to send and receive messages just by following the screen commands.

Sending attachments

With Pine, you will need first to upload the file you want to attach from your computer to your ISP's computer. Your provider may have set up a process for doing this. The manual for your communications software should give additional information. (You may wish to ask a knowledgeable colleague or friend for help the first time you attempt this.) Once you have uploaded the file, you can specify the filename (including the correct directory specification) following the **Attachments** prompt in the header.

Using Netscape Mail or Internet Explorer Mail

Rather than use separate mail programs, these days many people are using the mail programs built into their browsers — Netscape or Internet Explorer.

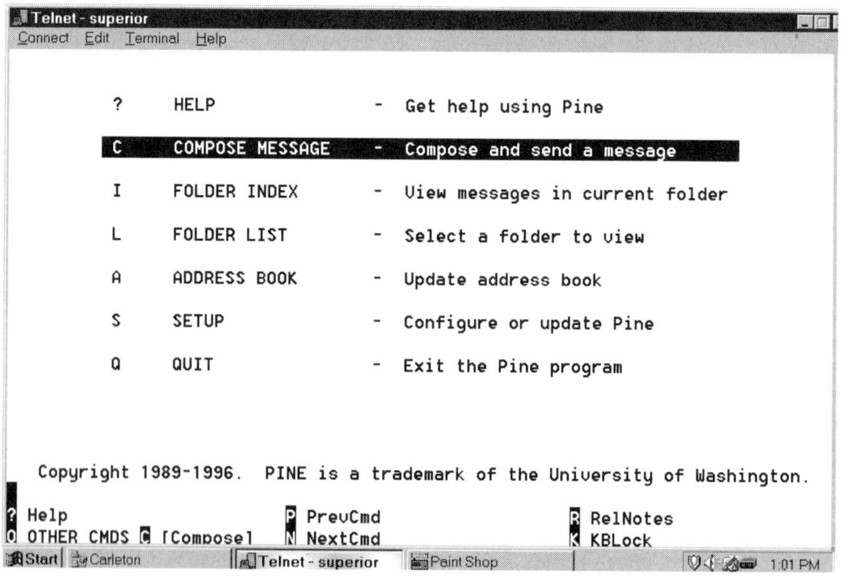

Figure 6-3
Pine's simple start-up menu makes it a good program for "newbies"

```
Telnet - superior
Connect  Edit  Terminal  Help

    ?     HELP              -  Get help using Pine

    C     COMPOSE MESSAGE   -  Compose and send a message

    I     FOLDER INDEX      -  View messages in current folder

    L     FOLDER LIST       -  Select a folder to view

    A     ADDRESS BOOK      -  Update address book

    S     SETUP             -  Configure or update Pine

    Q     QUIT              -  Exit the Pine program

  Copyright 1989-1996.  PINE is a trademark of the University of Washington.

? Help                      P PrevCmd                  R RelNotes
O OTHER CMDS C [Compose]    N NextCmd                  K KBLock
Start | Carleton | Telnet - superior | Paint Shop |  1:01 PM
```

FYI To learn more about Netscape's **Drag and Drop** editing feature, see the FYI in Chapter 7 on page 119.

When you log onto Netscape Mail you will be shown your organizational folders, the message headers, and the message contents. You can drag and drop your messages between folders to keep your mail organized. Unfortunately, you cannot direct Netscape to sort the messages automatically into folders. But as with other mail programs, you can attach files to a message and sort messages by date, subject, or sender. And Netscape Mail allows you to send full Web pages within your e-mail messages, complete with live links and full images.

Internet Mail works similarly if you are using Internet Explorer. It's easy to set up and operate. When you log on, you are shown message headers and a preview of the selected message. You can organize folders through the toolbar. You can also set up elementary rules for filtering incoming mail into particular folders.

> "My number one purpose for the Internet is e-mail because I exchange notes with very learned people in areas I'm interested in. Once you find those people they become sources for life. I find when you make a phone call there's a 50 percent chance it will come back but when you send e-mail for some reason it's like you're on a level playing field and everyone sends messages back. It's a different culture. You're never put on hold. The answers are always relevant. There's no chat; no small talk."
>
> — Alana Kainz, former high-technology writer for the *Ottawa Citizen*.

Finding people on the Net

Before you can contact someone via electronic mail, you have to get the e-mail address. The best way to do that used to be to phone and

Figure 6-4
Using Netscape Mail

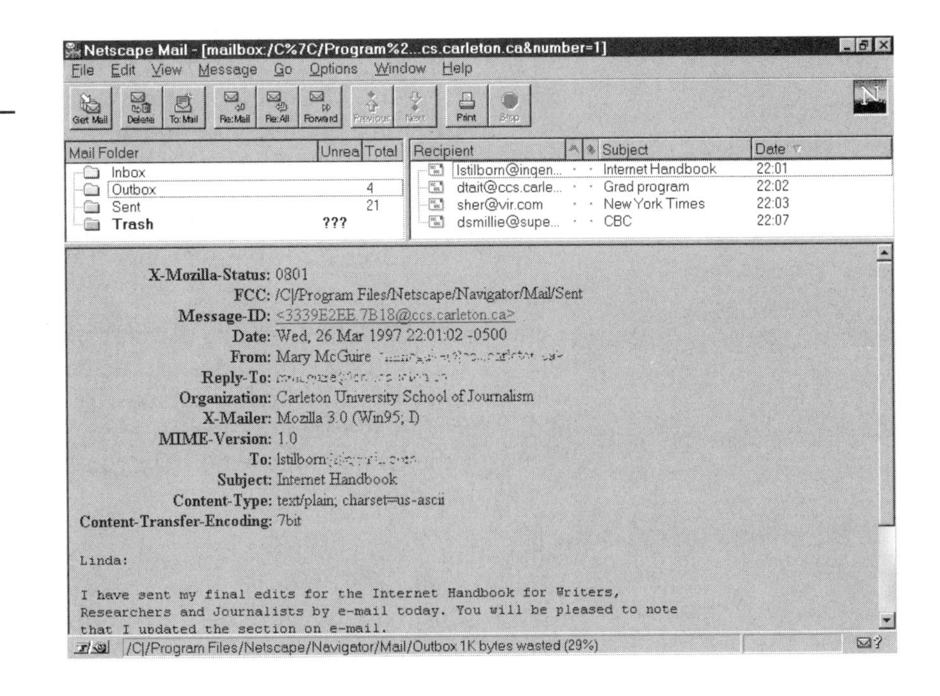

ask for it, assuming you knew the person's phone number or how to find it. But several new resources on the Web are making it easier to find e-mail addresses, as well as people's phone numbers, online.

There are now electronic databases of millions of e-mail addresses. There are also electronic versions of most of the world's phone books — White Pages, Yellow Pages, and even fax directories. Some give you more information than you can get from most directory assistance operators. For example, many of the online phone directories also give you a person's postal ("snail mail") address, including zip code or postal code. Some let you search by city and category, for example, all the dentists, restaurants, or car rental agencies in that city.

But while the databases are massive, they are still far from comprehensive. Even the largest can't claim to list more than a quarter of the people using e-mail these days. So, while databases are useful, it may still be more efficient to phone someone and ask for his or her e-mail address. If that's not possible or desirable, but you know where someone works, try going to that organization's Web site first and looking for a directory of employees, which might list e-mail addresses. If none of that works, you can try one of the Internet directories described below.

Infospace

One of the most useful directories on the Net is **Infospace**, located at:

http://www.infospaceinc.com/

Infospace claims to be the most comprehensive and innovative directory on the Net. You can use it to search for people, businesses, Yellow Pages, or fax directories in the United States and Canada. It has more than 112 million listings of people, government offices, and businesses, including fax and toll-free numbers. It also has a large e-mail directory. A special section, called "My Town," allows you to search any city in North America for lists of everything from art galleries to video stores. It provides addresses and telephone numbers, and even allows you to view the location on a street map!

Four11

Some directories allow you to search primarily for e-mail addresses. One of the biggest and best organized is the Four11 directory, which allows you to search a database of more than seven million e-mail addresses worldwide. It also lets you search a massive White Pages for the United States. **Four 11** can be found at:

http://www.Four11.com/

Whowhere

Another well-organized database, this one allows you to search for e-mail addresses worldwide and phone numbers in the United States. **Whowhere** is located at:

http://www.whowhere.com/

The Internet Address Finder
This is a popular Web site, used primarily for searching e-mail addresses. Look for it at:

http://www.iaf.net/

Since none of these databases is comprehensive, it's best to try several rather than just one. It's also a good idea to try variations on people's names. If your first attempts are unsuccessful, modify your search by using only the person's first initial. For example, some Internet directories will return only exact matches — so if "Jane Gates" is listed as "J. Gates" in the phone book, some online directories will not find her unless you type in only "J. Gates."

FYI Another way to search for people who may have posted messages on the Internet is to use search engines such as AltaVista and HotBot and search on variations of the person's name. (See Chapter 4.)

Let your fingers do the walking
There are also Yellow Pages on the Net. These can provide a lot more information than print versions of Yellow Pages.

BigBook (**http://www.bigbook.com/**) allows you to search for businesses by category in each city and provides you with the business address, phone number, and even a street map indicating the company's location. A similar resource is **BigYellow** (**http://s16.bigyellow.com/**).

If you are looking for someone overseas, there's the **International Telephone Directory** (**http://www.infobel.be/infobel/infobelworld.html**), a searchable database that includes Yellow Pages, White Pages, and fax directories for dozens of countries around the world.

If you're looking for Canadians, you can try **Canada 411** (**http://canada411.sympatico.ca/**). This service gives you Yellow Pages and White Pages listings for all the provinces and territories except Alberta and Saskatchewan. Another great resource for researchers and journalists in Canada is a directory of all the employees of the federal government at:

http://direct.srv.gc.ca/cgi-bin/wgweng

Listservs and newsgroups

There are two kinds of electronic discussion groups: listservs and Usenet newsgroups. Although both have a similar format, listservs are generally more valuable to researchers.

"Usenet" is short for "*Use*r *Net*work" — an array of computer discussion groups that can be visited by anyone with Internet access. Don't let the term "newsgroups" fool you — these are not sources of breaking news. Newsgroups are the online equivalent of the call-in radio show, where anyone can call and share an opinion, no matter how uninformed.

On the other hand, listservs (or listservers, or mailing lists, as they are also called) are more like television panel discussions where experts are invited to share their views. Sometimes, however, participants in a listserv may be more opinionated than informed.

There are also some differences in the way you participate in these online discussion groups. For newsgroups, once you log on you must go to the newsgroup area, generally by clicking on your newsreader software. There you can read messages which are posted for all to see, just as you might browse at the bulletin board of a grocery store or community center. Listservs are less public. To read messages posted to them, you must subscribe to the list; then, the messages are sent directly to your e-mail box.

Serious researchers and journalists may not find much value in monitoring or participating in newsgroups. But many find listservs the most consistently valuable resource on the Net for finding information, making contacts, and seeking out experts. Let's take a closer look at both.

Listservs: Where experts share information

> "The operative word in thinking about mailing lists is 'community.' Lists, much more so than Web threaded discussions or Usenet newsgroups, create a deep sense of community among their members. I can attest to that with my own lists; on online-news and online-newspapers, many of us 'know' each other well through the online experience and meet for drinks or dinner when we show up at the same conferences."
>
> — Steve Outing, "The Lowly Mailing List: A New Start?" *Editor and Publisher*, October 14, 1996.

To participate in a mailing list or listserv, or even just to monitor the list's discussions, you must subscribe. It's free, but you must send a specially composed message to the list owner's computer saying you wish to subscribe. The list owner usually responds with a welcome message that confirms your subscription and outlines rules for membership. Thereafter, any and all messages posted by list members come directly to your e-mail box. You can read them and delete them, or respond — either by sending an e-mail message to the entire group, or by replying privately to the original sender.

Although anyone can subscribe to most listservs, the subscription process — not to mention the heavy volume of electronic mail these lists can generate — tends to weed out all but those with a genuine, ongoing interest in the subject. Instead of the noisy chatter you find in newsgroups, you get a higher quality of discussion on mailing lists. Also, unlike newsgroups, most listservs are moderated or screened by their owners or administrators and prohibit abusive language and hate mail.

Listservs can be very useful to researchers and journalists. For example, if you are asked to prepare a report or write a story about multiple sclerosis, you could search for and subscribe to a mailing list devoted to the disease. Many of the messages posted to the list will come from people who live with multiple sclerosis and use the online group to network with one another, compare symptoms and treatments, and share advice. Some messages may come from doctors or researchers interested in helping people with the disease.

After "lurking" (monitoring the discussion) for awhile, you might post a message asking for information or leads to experts in the field. Then you might continue to correspond (perhaps via private e-mail) with people whom you meet in the group. When you have finished your report or story, you can unsubscribe — and perhaps go on to find another group more suited to your next assignment.

There are also some mailing lists that offer just a regular newsletter on a specific subject. For example, if you are interested in news from India (or some other countries that get very little coverage in the North American media), you can subscribe to a mailing list that will send you a brief summary of news events in the country for that day or week.

Beat reporters or researchers on special topics should consider subscribing to at least one listserv on that topic to find out what the experts are saying, make contacts, and request information.

There are thousands of mailing lists on the Net. One of the best places to search for ones you might be interested in is **Liszt**. It's at:

http://www.liszt.com/

When the Liszt welcome screen appears, just type in a single word that best describes the topic you're interested in. For example, if you were doing research on the Holocaust, you would type in *holocaust*. Liszt would respond with a list of at least twelve groups, including one devoted to the children and grandchildren of survivors and another for historians of that period.

You can subscribe to any listserv directly from the Liszt search results page. Just click on the link to that group, and follow the instructions. But be careful: you are sending a message to a robot computer — so you must fill in the information exactly as specified. Some commands require your name, others your e-mail address.

If you do it right, you should immediately get a reply confirming your subscription. *Be sure to keep that message.* It tells you how to post messages and, more importantly, how to unsubscribe when you need to do that. The most common and aggravating mistake people make on mailing lists is to post a message to everyone on the list asking how to unsubscribe. (People who do that tend to receive a lot of "flames" — angry e-mail messages — from other list members!)

You must remember that every mailing list has two separate addresses: one for contributing to the group's discussions, and the other for handling administrative matters, such as searching the archives or unsubscribing. The first address usually includes the

Figure 6-5
Liszt, the searchable directory of e-mail discussion groups

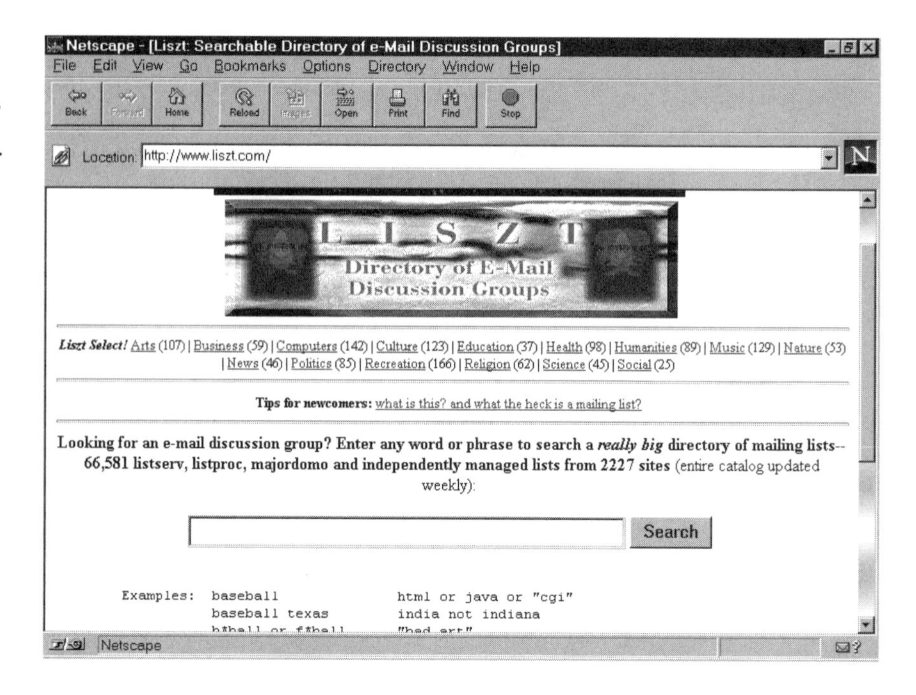

name of the list (for example, Writer-L for the list for writers, or NewsLib for news librarians); the latter usually starts with "listserv," "listproc," or "majordomo." Don't confuse the two, or your experience with mailing lists may be an unpleasant one.

The list owner's welcome message usually explains such procedures as how to initiate a search of the list's archives of previous postings, and how to change your subscription options. For example, if you find the list generates too many messages each day that clutter up your mailbox, you can subscribe to a digest — one long message a day which includes the full text of all the messages posted that day. Or, you can simply request a daily index, which lists all the subject headings posted that day. If there are any that interest you, you can order them sent to your mailbox. Finally, the welcome message also explains how to suspend delivery of messages while you are on vacation, so that you don't come home to a mailbox overflowing with mail.

FYI Inter-Links is a site that lets you search a master list of more than 6,000 discussion groups, including scholarly listservs. It also provides subscription information. Look for **Inter-Links** at: **http://www.nova.edu/Inter-Links/listserv.html**

If you want to subscribe to a list without going to the Liszt page, you must send an e-mail message to the listserv's administrative address. Leave the subject line blank. In the body of the message, type:

subscribe (listname) (your first name) (your last name).

Don't include your signature.

For example, if Peter Jennings wants to subscribe to the list for people interested in Computer-Assisted Reporting and Research,

FYI For a step-by-step guide especially for reporters and writers who want to find and use Internet mailing lists, check out:
http://www.daily.umn.edu/~broeker/guide.html

which is called CARR-L, he would send a message to the listserv address for that group that says only:

Subscribe CARR-L Peter Jennings

A welcome message outlining how to post messages, how to unsubscribe, and other important instructions should arrive in his mailbox shortly thereafter.

Another place (besides Liszt) to find scholarly and academic mailing lists is located at:

http://n2h2.com/KOVACS/

A third helpful site to find mailing lists by topic or country is at:

http://tile.net/lists/

Newsgroups: Where people share opinions

Unlike listservs, newsgroups don't require you to subscribe. Many newsreader programs will ask you to "subscribe," but that simply means choosing which newsgroups you want to read on a regular basis.

To join a newsgroup, first find out how to access your newsreader program from your Internet provider. Then, once you log on, you can use your newsreader to select any one of thousands of newsgroups.

The newsgroup's messages will not come to your electronic mailbox. Instead, your newsreader allows you to get a list of subject headings for all recent messages posted to a given newsgroup. If you see a subject that interests you, you can select the message and read the full text. If you wish to reply, you can respond by posting a message to the whole group, or you can send a private e-mail message to the person who originally posted.

There are newsgroups on every topic imaginable, from *alt.sex* (the busiest newsgroup on the Internet) to *sci.zebrafish*. You could probably find a newsgroup on virtually any topic you might be researching. You can search for newsgroups at:

http://www.dejanews.com/toplevel.html

While the quality of the discussion in newsgroups may not be as high as in listservs, newsgroups can be useful to writers, researchers, and journalists. For example, journalists might monitor newsgroups for new story ideas. They may also find newsgroups useful for locating people who are knowledgeable about a specific topic.

Like listservs, newsgroups usually have archives that you can search. One place where you will find newsgroup archives is at:

http://starbase.neosoft.com/~claird/news.lists/newsgroup_archives.html

(continued on page 108)

FOCUS ON...

Listservs for knowledge networking

Listservs can be a great way to keep in touch with colleagues. Whether you are a writer, researcher, editor, or journalist, there is a special mailing list for others like you where you can share ideas, problems, solutions, and experiences. If you are a researcher or a journalist with a regular beat, such as science or high technology, it is also a great way to network with a community of sources and people who share your interest.

CAJ-L
This is a list for members of the Canadian Association of Journalists. Here many of Canada's online journalists participate in wide-ranging discussions on everything from their frustrations with editors and publishers to tips on using software on the job.

Subscription address:
majordomo@eagle.ca

CARR-L (Computer-Assisted Reporting and Research List)
The best list around for journalists. Although its focus is computer-assisted research and reporting (how to find data, software programs, and use of data in stories), it covers many journalism topics. The list owner, Elliott Parker, an American university professor, feeds the list with wonderful tips and posts about Internet resources for researchers and journalists. Be warned, though: it's an active list, so if you subscribe, expect dozens of messages a day!

Subscription address:
listserv@ulkyvm.louisville.edu

CANCAR-L (Canadian Computer-Assisted Reporting List)
A list with a similar focus to CARR-L, but more specifically for Canadians. Participants include the most computer- and Net-savvy Canadian journalists. The list is run by Dean Tudor, a journalism professor at Ryerson University's School of Journalism. Unlike CARR-L, this list is not very active; you don't need to worry about a mailbox overflowing with messages if you subscribe.

Subscription address:
majordomo@acs.ryerson.ca

COPYEDITING-L
A list for copy editors that includes lots of helpful tips on grammar and sentence construction.

Subscription address:
listproc@cornell.edu

EAC-ACR-L
A list for members of the Editors' Association of Canada that discusses the craft of editing and other related issues.

Subscription address:
listserv@ netserver.web.net

FOI-L
A list for journalists and others interested in freedom-of-information issues, access to meetings, and the public's right to know. A project of the National Freedom of Information Coalition, this discussion group operates from the S.I. Newhouse School at Syracuse University.

Subscription address:
listserv@listserv.syr.edu

FREELANCE
This list covers evolving ways for freelance journalists to market content electronically.

Subscription address:
owner-freelance@newshare.com

INTCAR-L
Here's where you'll find out all about investigative reporting internationally. Covers journalism and computer-assisted reporting outside the U.S. Run by Professor Chris Simpson at American University.

Subscription address:
listserv@american.edu

IRE-L
General discussion about investigative reporting. Frequented by members of the professional organization, Investigative Reporters and Editors (IRE). A great resource.

Subscription address:
listserv@mizzou1.missouri.edu

JHISTORY
Discussions about academic and professional issues related to the history of journalism, as well as info on job placements and research topics.

Subscription address:
listserv@acfcluster.nyu.edu

JOURNET
This is a must for journalism educators. It covers information and discussion about course content, resources, teaching strategies, ethics, and current news events. It's an active group run by Carleton University journalism professor, George Frajkor.

Subscription address:
listserv@qucdn.Queensu.Ca

NEWSLIB
All about researching news stories. Members of this list are predominantly news librarians, but some are journalists and researchers. It provides many helpful pointers to great sites on the Internet and tips on where to find information.

Subscription address:
listproc@ripken.oit.unc.edu

NICAR-L
Information on computer-assisted reporting run by the National Institute for Computer-Assisted Reporting in Missouri. It is very helpful for trading detailed information about CAR techniques and software programs.

Subscription address:
listserv@mizzou1.missouri.edu

RTVJ-L
Radio and TV journalism and other issues of interest to professors and radio and television students. It's run by the Radio and Television Journalism Division of the Association of Educators in Journalism and Mass Communications, under the guidance of Prof. Bill Knowles of the University of Montana.

Subscription address:
listproc@listserv.umt.edu

SPJ-L
An active list run by the Society of Professional Journalists, the oldest journalistic organization in the U.S. It covers a wide range of topics and current events in news.

Subscription address:
listserv@psuvm.psu.edu

STUMEDIA
A fairly active list for student journalists run by a U.S. school of journalism.

Subscription address:
LISTSERV@UABDPO.DPO.UAB.EDU

WRITER-L
Discussions of feature writing, explanatory journalism, literary journalism, and book journalism. Includes info on techniques, markets, jobs, agents, and editors. The list is moderated by Pulitzer-prize winner Jon Franklin, coordinator of the University of Oregon's creative nonfiction program. He requests that each subscriber send a short bio and contribute $20 to cover costs ($5 for students).

Subscription address:
JonFrank@nicar.org

To subscribe to a mailing list: If the subscription address is a "listserv" or a "listproc" address — send a message to the address leaving the subject line blank. In the body of the message type:

Subscribe (listname) (your first name) (your last name)

Do not include your signature.

If the subscription address is a "majordomo" address — send a message, leaving the subject line blank. In the body of the message type:

Subscribe (listname) (your e-mail address)

Do not include your signature.

Save your welcome message for instructions about how to unsubscribe.

One terrific resource that journalists and researchers can use to search newsgroups for interesting topics is **DejaNews**, located at:

http://www.dejanews.com/

Let's imagine you want to find an online debate on the regulation of firearms. You might go to DejaNews and type in the word *firearms*. DejaNews will then search out newsgroup postings containing the word "firearms," and return a list of the messages and the groups to which they were posted. To read a particular message, simply click on it. Further, a quick glance at the list will determine that the majority of such messages are posted to a group called *rec.guns*. You can then begin monitoring that group for information, opinions, and sources, search its archives, and even look for its FAQ. (A FAQ is a list of Frequently Asked Questions; we discuss these in detail later in this chapter.)

A little-known feature of DejaNews makes it especially valuable for checking out people. When you click on a message to read it, you will also see the sender's e-mail address. Click on this, and you'll get a list of other messages that person has posted to other newsgroups over the last several years. It can be very revealing!

Is there an expert in the house?

> "ProfNet is an example of how the global web of computer networks known as the Internet is changing the way information is gathered, by eliminating boundaries of time and geography."
>
> — Nathaniel Sheppard, Jr., *Chicago Tribune*, January 1995.

FYI For more ideas about using newsgroups and listservs, check out an online publication called, "Computer-Assisted Research: A Guide to Tapping Online Information," by Nora Paul, chief librarian at the Poynter Institute for Media Studies, at: **http://www.nando.net/prof/poynter/chome.html**

ProfNet

One great resource for finding experts online is ProfNet (for Professors' Network). Instead of picking up the phone and trying to find an expert at your local university, you can ask ProfNet to search out the most knowledgeable academics at universities and other institutions across North America.

ProfNet is an international cooperative of public information officers linked by the Internet to give journalists and authors conve-

7 tips for using listservs and newsgroups

- **Don't** send messages to a mailing list until you have "lurked" for awhile to get a feeling for the tone of the discussion on that list.
- **Don't** post questions before searching the group's archives to determine if the question has been asked and answered before.
- **Don't** post messages or questions that are not appropriate to the group's topic. Stick to the subject of the discussion list, or you risk being flamed.
- **Do** identify yourself. Sign your messages and include your e-mail address so that people can reach you privately, if necessary.
- **Do** choose your words carefully. Typing and sending a brief message may seem like the online equivalent of small talk. But your message can "live" for a long time in cyberspace, to be passed around or dug out by people searching the archives months, even years, later. You never know who might find it and read it long after you have forgotten it. So, post with caution.
- **Don't** ask for things you can easily find out elsewhere. People who ask about things they could easily look up at the library are often flamed for being lazy, or are simply ignored.
- **Don't** send messages to a mailing list asking how to unsubscribe. You will be flamed for not knowing basic list procedures.

Flame

nient access to expert sources. Most of those experts are affiliated with colleges and universities, but some come from medical centers, non-profit organizations, corporations, and government agencies.

Journalists and authors can send their query in a message to **ProfNet** at:

profnet@vyne.com

The message will be forwarded to universities and foundations across North America. It is the same as being able to post queries directly to the e-mail boxes of public information officers representing 800 institutions in seventeen countries. You can even specify whether you need an expert in your region. Within twenty-four hours you will receive a message back containing the names of people you might want to interview and ways to reach them.

ProfNet also has an excellent database that lists thousands of experts by name and specialty. You will find it at:

http://www.vyne.com/profnet/index.html

You will find guidelines for using ProfNet and making queries at:
http://www.vyne.com/profnet/profforpress.html

Figure 6-6
ProfNet, the Professors' Network

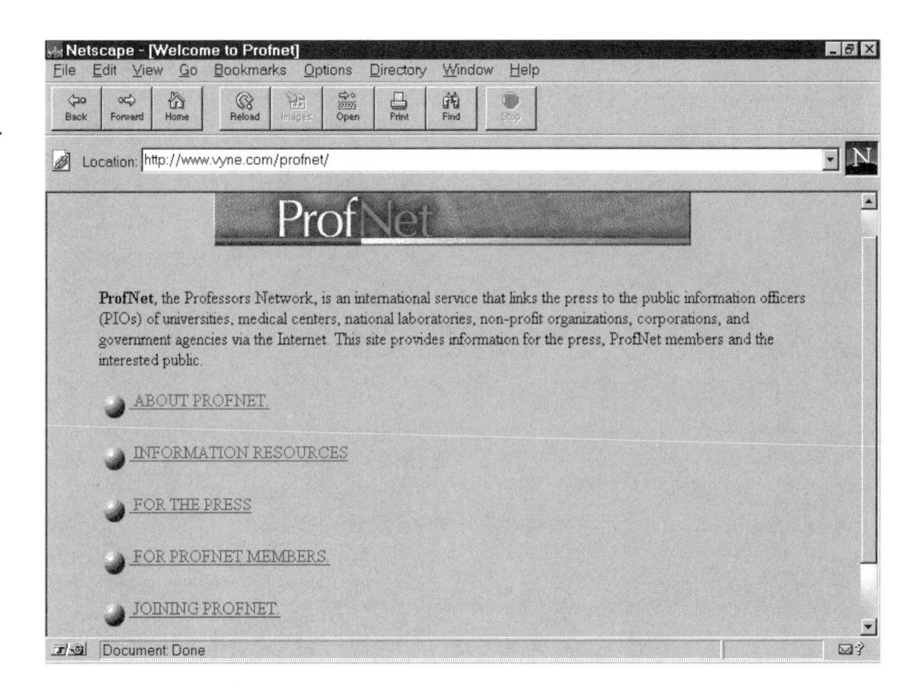

Other expert sources

Other places to look for experts, particularly in the United States, is the **Yearbook of Authorities, Experts and Spokespersons** at:

http://www.yearbooknews.com/

There's also an excellent list of contacts by story subject at the **Beat Page** at:

http://www.reporter.org/beat/

For people seeking Canadian sources, there's Julian Sher's site, **Investigative Journalism on the Internet**, at:

http://www.vir.com/~sher/topics.htm

Also for Canadian researchers, there is now an online version of the old reliable **Sources** magazine that is easy to search. It's at:

http://www.sources.com/

For British sources, there's also **ExpertNet** at:

http://www.cvcp.ac.uk/expertnet.html

Another source for finding experts is **FACSNet**, a site put together by the Foundation for American Communications (FACS). It's located at:

http://www.facsnet.org/sources_online/facs_source/main.html

FACSNet will provide the names, areas of expertise, short curricula vitae, and contact information for experts in economics, science,

FYI For an extensive list of discussion groups for people interested in the media, check out the site for **Syracuse University's Newhouse School of Public Communication** at: **http://web.syr.edu/~bcfought/nnl.html**

law, and public policy. The news sources are drawn from the academic community, research institutes, and the private sector. The name of the organization submitting the name to the database is also given. The sources provided are people known personally to FACS as articulate experts dedicated to helping journalists understand issues rather than promoting a particular agenda.

Conducting interviews online

It's easy to use e-mail, listservs, and newsgroups to request interviews, check facts, and verify quotes, or when you're trying to determine whether someone is appropriate to interview. Some researchers and journalists even conduct interviews online, by sending a long list of questions to the interviewee.

This method can be effective, but it poses some risks. Sending a list of questions via e-mail gives people a chance to polish their answers, perhaps with the aid of assistants or public relations experts who are never identified. In any case, their answers will not be the same as they would in a face-to-face interview, because very few people write the way they speak.

Online interviews also force interviewers to reveal their entire strategy up front. This makes it impossible, for example, to recover from a poor first question or an incorrect assumption, or to spring a tough question at the end. It also makes it impossible to ask questions that follow directly from the subject's answers. In short, an online interview may get you a usable quote, but it's unlikely to produce a revealing interview. Most journalists prefer to do their interviews the old-fashioned way.

FYI A helpful computer system programmer in Florida has put together a detailed guide to Netiquette. Look for it at: **http://www.fau.edu/rinaldi/net/**

Netiquette

The rules are still being written on how writers and journalists can use information they find on the Net. Some news organizations have developed detailed and elaborate policies about how quotes from e-mail messages or postings to newsgroups can be used in published stories. Others have not yet come to terms with such issues.

In the absence of guidelines from your editors and publishers, it's important to use common sense if you want to use online resources.

- **Behave yourself as you would at a public meeting.** There's nothing very private about the Internet — your messages and postings go out to hundreds or thousands of people. Messages can also "live" for a long time, be passed around among people, and dug out of archives years after you wrote them.
- **Identify yourself just you would in person or over the phone.** Disclose who you are, something about why you are looking for comments, and the source of any information you are passing on.
- **Verify whatever you read in a newsgroup or mailing list.** Just as you wouldn't put something you overheard on the street in print without verifying it, check anything you read online before publishing or broadcasting it.

For an example of one organization's policy on online newsgathering, see Appendix F.

Getting the FAQs

FAQ is an acronym for *Frequently Asked Questions*. These are compilations of questions (and, more importantly, answers) that are constantly being posted in a newsgroup or mailing list. Finding and reading FAQs can be a productive way to begin researching a topic.

One place you can search for FAQs by topic is the **FAQ Finder** at:

http://ps.superb.net/FAQ/

Another resource that lists all the Usenet FAQs found in a particular newsgroup is called **news.answers**. It is alphabetized by topic, and can be found at:

http://www.cis.ohio-state.edu/hypertext/faq/usenet/FAQ-List.html

Another way you can find FAQs that have been posted on the Web is to use the search engine **Infoseek** at:

http://www2.infoseek.com/

When Infoseek's home page comes up, the search field says, "World Wide Web," but beside the search field is an arrow you can click on that will give you a list of other things you can search, including FAQs.

A last word

Finding information at Web sites may be easy — but all you get is the information someone chooses to give you. For researchers and journalists, finding people and groups on the Internet who can answer specific questions is likely to be a much more valuable activity. This takes more effort: you have to learn how to use e-mail programs, newsgroups, mailing lists, and one or more online directories. We hope the advice in this chapter will help you get started. You will find the effort worth the results — because so much of what's valuable on the Internet lies beyond the Web.

Further reading

Garrison, Bruce. *Computer-Assisted Reporting*. Hillsdale, NJ: Lawrence Erlbaum Associates, 1995.

Huston, Brant. *Computer-Assisted Reporting: A Practical Guide*. New York: St. Martin's Press, 1996.

Notess, Greg R. "E-mail Address Databases." *Database*, October, 1996.
http://www.onlineinc.com/online/online/database/OctDB/nets10.html

Reddick, Randy, and King, Elliot. *The Online Journalist*. Orlando, FL: Harcourt Brace, 1995.

Sher, Julian. "Mailing Lists — A Journalist's Best Friend." *Media Magazine*, Summer 1996.
http://www.vir.com/~sher/mail.htm

Chapter 7

Managing the World of Online Information

“People have to understand that the WWW is like a huge shopping mall; there are lots of stores and merchandise, but it’s all in a size 5. There is a ton of ‘stuff’ out there, but so little actually fits one’s needs.”

— NANCY SCHAADT, FREELANCE WRITER, DALLAS, TEXAS

“Newbies” to the Internet often act like kids at Halloween: collecting all those goodies is so much fun, you don’t want to stop. But eating them all will only make you sick.

As you begin to find your way around the Net, you’ll likely collect a great deal of information that is useful, interesting, or simply entertaining. Before you know it, your list of bookmarks will be overflowing, like a child’s Halloween bag, with far more resources than you need. This is a problem for all Net users, but those most at risk are information junkies like writers, researchers, journalists, and editors. We need to develop special strategies to cope with the Internet’s vast resources, and refine our techniques for sorting treasure from junk.

This chapter will explore some of the strategies that information professionals have developed to evaluate and manage online resources.

Chapter highlights

- **Evaluating information resources**
- **Managing information overload**
- **How to organize a hotlist**
- **News filters**
- **Managing e-mail overload**
- **Personal information managers**
- **Keeping up to date**

Evaluating information resources

“It’s becoming more difficult to distinguish ‘official’ sites from ‘wanna-bes.’ If you’re looking for the text of the speech President Clinton made to a group of American veterans last week, you might find versions on half a dozen sites. Which can you trust? Which sites are corporate, government, or personal ones?

Official-looking documents might still be bogus. Last year the Associated Press had to officially debunk a document circulating on the Net as an AP dispatch indicating Microsoft Corp. had bought the Roman Catholic Church. Incredible, but enough people believed it to create a problem."

— James Derk, "Net Sites for Journalists," *Online User*, 1996.
http://www.onlineinc.com/oluser/JulyOU/derk7.html

Evaluating the information you find on the Web can be the biggest challenge facing writers, researchers, and journalists who use the Internet for their work. The quality of the information varies tremendously, just as it does among books, magazines, and newspapers. Sarah Ferguson's autobiography gives a very different picture of her fall from grace than the British tabloids do!

When it comes to Web sites, it's probably wise to view them with the same degree of skepticism you would an infomercial. But since many sites do contain valuable information, here are a few guidelines to apply when you're trying to determine which are reliable sources.

- **Check the authority of the person or institution that published the material.** Who sponsors the site? Look for a phone number or an address that you might use to verify the sponsor's legitimacy. If the author is an individual, what are his or her credentials? Often it's difficult to tell who wrote the material, let alone their qualifications. But because the Web can be used as a soapbox by people who are biased about the subjects they're writing about, it's important to try to determine something about the author of any material you wish to use as research. If the site is sponsored by an institution or organization, you should be able to verify the material through that organization, as well as get further information from their home page. In the case of personal home pages, it's virtually impossible to determine an author's legitimacy; for that reason, personal Web pages should be used only as a source of opinion, not a source of fact.
- **Check the accuracy of the material.** Does the material appear to have been edited? Would the facts have been checked by someone other than the author? The problem with the World Wide Web, for information professionals, is the same characteristic that makes it attractive to so many others — its egalitarianism. Almost anyone can publish on the Web. Thus, the systems that exist at newspapers, magazines, and book publishers to ensure accuracy don't exist on the Web. If you find spelling, grammatical, and typographical errors, it is probably safe to assume the material has not been edited. You should take this as a clue that the information still needs to be verified. But even in the absence of any such mistakes, you must verify, verify, verify. Any reputable site should include links or references to other sources that you can use to corroborate the information on the page.

FYI For more guidelines on using resources from the World Wide Web, check out the document, "Evaluating World Wide Web Information" at Purdue University Libraries: **http://thorplus.lib.purdue.edu/research/classes/gs175/3gs175/evaluation.html**

- **Check the currency of the material.** Many sites indicate the date when something was posted and when it was last revised. If not, do not assume the material is up to date.
- **Check the context of the material.** Bear in mind that search engines locate Web pages out of context. When you find a page that looks interesting, try to link back to the site's home page to determine more about the source of the information and whether it is valid to your research.
- **Beware of hackers.** Remember that Web pages can be altered deliberately by hackers, or even sometimes accidentally by users. This is another reason to verify, verify, verify.

Managing information overload

> "As a person who is very thorough and wants to have all the information before making a decision, I'm finding that I'm spending more time collecting and organizing information than I am reading and using it. ... Some of the factors contributing to this include a compulsion about wanting to use the best resources available and make the best choices, and a fear of 'what if I need it and it isn't there?' ... I am attempting now to acquire only information that I can reasonably be certain I will use within the next few weeks."
>
> —Tracy Marks, software and Internet trainer, Cambridge Center for Adult Education

The World Wide Web is a seductive place, especially for curious people. It's all too easy to follow one link after another, reading fascinating material from sources all over the world. But before you know it, hours have passed, and you have gleaned very little about the subject you set out to research.

As an information professional, your time is at a premium. Make the most of it by acquiring a few simple strategies for online research.

- **Follow a map.** Stay focused. Especially when you're navigating the Web, always remember where you are going and why, and discipline yourself to resist distractions. Just as you wouldn't spend time at work reading a comic book, you must avoid doing the online equivalent just because you came across an amusing link.
- **Bookmark with care.** If you bookmark everything you think might be useful someday, your bookmark list will quickly become unmanageable. (In the next section, we give some tips for organizing a bookmark list.) Bookmark only those sites you know you will return to over and over again. Subject catalogs and search engines like AltaVista should be at the top of your bookmark list. Beyond that, be selective. Developing good

search techniques is a better strategy than simply bookmarking everything.

- **Don't waste hard-disk space.** Be selective about what you keep. Much of the information you need is only a few clicks away on the World Wide Web. Just as you wouldn't collect and store the phone numbers of everyone you've ever met in your life, don't try to collect and store all the interesting information you find online. The phone book will always be there where you need it; so will the search engines.
- **Keep one eye on the clock.** Taking the "scenic route" may be OK when you're on vacation. But when you're under the pressure of a deadline, you can't afford to get lost wandering among Web sites — even if they have spectacular graphics and live sound. You can always come back to explore when you have more time.

How to organize a hotlist

> "I used to carefully catalog useful or nifty sites, and even organized them into a Web launcher, but I gave it up in a fit of common sense. The Web was just growing too fast. Now I treat the Net as any other information resource. I keep a short list of key addresses — sort of like my phone Rolodex — that will lead me either to sites I visit repeatedly or to broader sources of information. Search engines, led by AltaVista, are vital."
>
> — Mike Christenson, defense and foreign policy editor of *Congressional Quarterly*; former Washington correspondent for the *Atlanta Journal and Constitution*

A *hotlist* is the online equivalent of a journalist's notebook of contacts. It's your personal collection of important Web addresses — ones you have found useful and may want to use again. But there's no need to keep a separate notebook for writing down all those long URLs. Instead, you can simply bookmark them. Then when you want to return to those sites, you need only to log on, load Netscape (or another browser), and click on the bookmark. (To review how to bookmark sites, see Chapter 3.)

That's the easy part. The challenge is what to do when your list of bookmarks becomes so long you can no longer find things easily.

When you first start making bookmarks, you will probably just click on **Bookmarks | Add Bookmark**, and the Web address for the page you are viewing will automatically be added to the bottom of your bookmark list. As long as you have only a few bookmarks, that method will work well. But as the number of items begins to grow, you'll need to take steps to ensure that your hotlist stays useful. For example, you may alphabetize your bookmarks. Or, you may wish to organize them in folders, by subject.

If you are using Netscape, the way in which you organize your bookmark list will vary slightly depending on which version you are using. If you are using Netscape 3.0, the following guidelines apply.

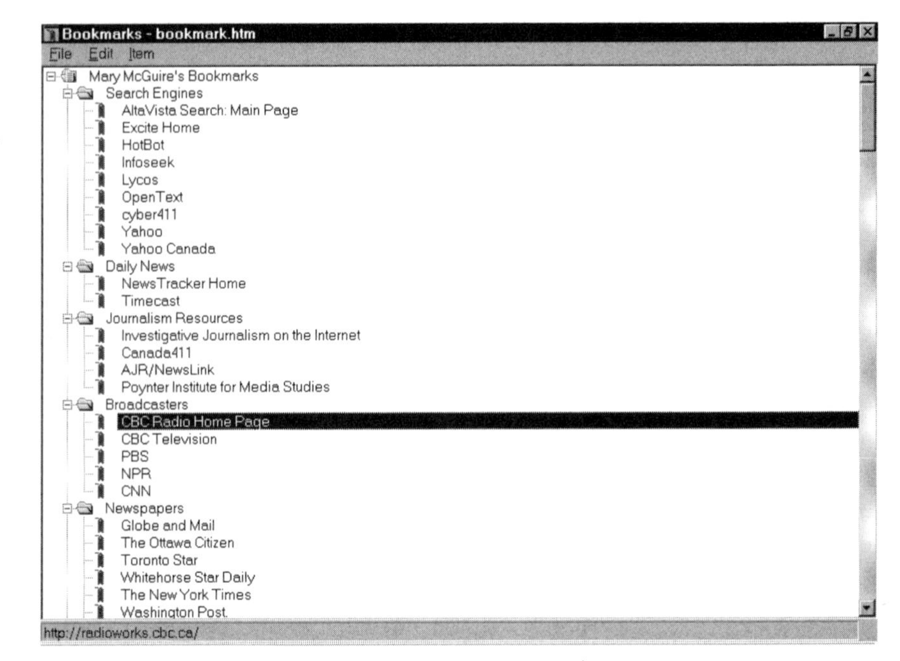

Figure 7-1
Netscape 3.0 offers several options for organizing bookmarks

If you are not using that version, it's worth upgrading to Netscape 3.0 because it offers many improvements in bookmark organization.

To organize your bookmarks alphabetically

- Click on **Bookmarks** at the top of the Netscape screen
- Choose **Go to Bookmarks**
- Choose **Edit** at the top of the screen
- Click on **Select All**
- Choose **Item** at the top of the screen
- Click on **Sort Bookmarks.**

To give a bookmark a meaningful name

- Click on **Bookmarks** at the top of the Netscape screen
- Choose **Go to Bookmarks**
- Click on the bookmark you wish to rename
- Choose **Item** at the top of the screen
- Choose **Properties**
- Replace the name of the bookmark in the appropriate box.

To insert a bookmark at a specific point on your list

- Click on **Bookmarks** at the top of the Netscape screen
- Select the bookmark above the place where you want to insert the new one
- Choose **Item** from the top of the screen
- Click on **Insert Bookmark.**

FYI

To use Netscape's **Drag and Drop** editing feature, place your cursor on the item you wish to move. Click and hold down the left mouse button as you drag the item to wherever you want. You can reposition both bookmarks and folder entries this way. (If you drag and drop a folder, the items inside it will move as well.)

To move bookmarks around on your list

- Click on **Bookmarks** at the top of the Netscape screen
- Click on **Edit** and use the **Cut** and **Paste** functions to move bookmarks around; or
- Use your mouse to click on a bookmark and "drag and drop" it to another place on the list.

To create folders for related bookmarks

- Click on **Bookmarks** at the top of the Netscape screen
- Choose **Go to Bookmarks**
- Click on **Item** at the top of the bookmark screen
- Choose **Insert Folder**
- Give the folder a name — e.g., Search Engines
- Put all your bookmarks for search engines in this folder by cutting and pasting them on top of the folder, or by dragging and dropping them on top of the folder.

To place new bookmarks into a temporary folder

Here's an alternative to accumulating new bookmarks at the bottom of your bookmark list.

- Click on **Bookmarks** at the top of the Netscape screen
- Choose **Go to Bookmarks**
- Click on **Item** at the top of the bookmark screen
- Choose **Insert Folder**
- Name folder **New Bookmark Folder**
- Choose **Item** at the top of the screen
- Click on **Set to New Bookmarks Folder**. All new bookmarks will automatically be added to that folder, from which you can move them to the appropriate folder.

Bookmark backups

It's a good idea to save backup copies of your bookmarks on a regular basis. Bookmarks can become corrupted or be deleted accidentally, and regenerating them can mean a lot of work.

To back up your bookmark file, go to your bookmark list and choose **File**. From there, click on **Save As** and give your backup copy another name, or save it to a floppy disk.

You can also set your browser to open with your bookmark list rather than the usual home page. Netscape maintains an HTML version of your bookmarks. It's a file called *Bookmarks.html* and can be found in the Netscape folder. Click on **File | Open File**, then copy the file's location from the location field. From the Netscape home page, choose **Options | General Preferences**. Now copy the location of your bookmark file into the field that indicates where you want your browser to start. This makes your bookmark file your default home page!

FYI

There are software products you can buy to help organize your bookmarks and keep track of changes to your favorite sites. One is called **Smart Bookmarks**, which you can read about and download at:

http://www.firstfloor.com

Another is called **BookIt! Pro** at: **http://www.igsnet.com/igs/bookit.html**
There are also programs that allow you to use the same set of bookmarks, whether you are using Netscape Navigator or Internet Explorer. **SiteMarks** is available at:

http://www.sitetech.com/

Bookmark Magician is available at:

http://www.q-d.com/index.html

Another bookmark manager is **Quiklink**, which saves URL collections from different browsers and allows you to sort and organize them quickly and easily. It's at:

http://quiklinks.com/products.html

If you want to be able to access your bookmarks from any computer (and not just the one on which the bookmarks are saved), or if you want to make them accessible to other people, you can also make your bookmark list — which is simply an HTML file — a Web page. (We explain how to do this in Chapter 8.)

If you do set up your bookmark page as a Web page, you can then use it as your start-up page. From the main Netscape page, choose **Options | General Preferences**. Copy the URL of your Web page into the field that indicates where you want your browser to start.

News filters

If you want breaking news, but don't have time to read all the online news sources, there's a type of filter that writers, researchers, editors, and journalists can use to help manage online information.

News filters help you avoid having to scan all the newsgroups or wire services on the Internet for messages on a specific topic. These are software programs running at various places on the Internet. They cost money, and each filter operates a little differently, but all allow you to specify topics of interest. The program stores your interest profile and checks for stories or messages that contain those topics. When it finds them, the news filter posts them to your e-mail box.

For example, if you are engaged in a major investigation of capital punishment, you can use a filter to find wire service stories on that topic. You will then get stories from around the world for background information. You can also use a message news filter to get messages posted by individuals to newsgroups such as *alt.activism.death-penalty*, and you can use your results to contact people through e-mail for more information.

Figure 7-2
Infoseek Personal search topics

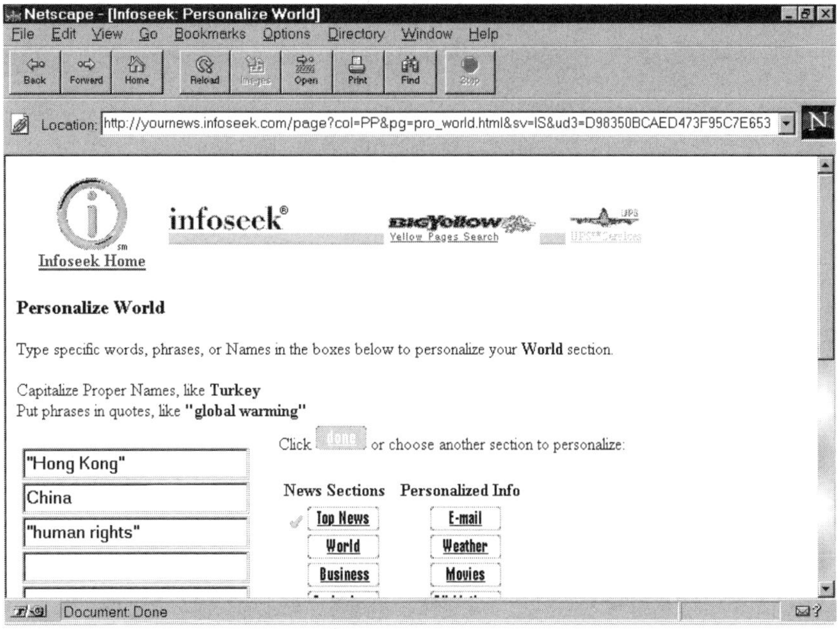

Netscape - [Infoseek: Personalize World]

File Edit View Go Bookmarks Options Directory Window Help

Back Forward Home Reload Images Open Print Find Stop

Location: http://yournews.infoseek.com/page?col=PP&pg=pro_world.html&sv=IS&ud3=D98350BCAED473F95C7E653

infoseek® BigYellow Yellow Pages Search UPS Services

Infoseek Home

Personalize World

Type specific words, phrases, or Names in the boxes below to personalize your **World** section.

Capitalize Proper Names, like **Turkey**
Put phrases in quotes, like **"global warming"**

Click done or choose another section to personalize:

"Hong Kong"
China
"human rights"

News Sections: Top News, World, Business
Personalized Info: E-mail, Weather, Movies

Document: Done

Figure 7-2A
Infoseek Personal search results

Netscape - [Infoseek News Center]

File Edit View Go Bookmarks Options Directory Window Help

Back Forward Home Reload Images Open Print Find Stop

Location: http://yournews.infoseek.com/page?col=PP&pg=pworld.html&sv=IS&ud3=D98350BCAED473F95C7E653127

infoseek® BigYellow Yellow Pages Search UPS Services

Infoseek Home

Want to boost your SEX APPEAL? Click here for details...

To Find Out the Secret to Real Sex Appeal, Click Here

news center
Use Login ID

Personalized World News personalize

News Flash: Is DVD the next must-have technology -- or not?

Personalized News
Top News
>World
Stocks

General News
Top News

Gingrich taps views of a divided Hong Kong Wed 26 Mar 7:28
HK's Chan to meet Chinese premier Li Peng Wed 26 Mar 8:14
Gore talks fundraising and human rights in China Wed 26 Mar 10:37
Gore Assures China in Funds Row Wed 26 Mar 10:46
Gore raises human rights issues with China Wed 26 Mar 6:13
HK passport holders welcome after handover-Manila Wed 26 Mar 9:28

Netscape

FYI Every news filter has a FAQ (list of Frequently Asked Questions). Read it to find out how the filter works, how often files are searched, and how you can modify it for better results. To find out more about news filters in general, check out the **Poynter Institute for Media Studies**' "Guide to Tapping Online Information" at: **http://www.poynter.org/car/cg_carfilte.htm** For a comprehensive list of information filtering resources, check out the one maintained by Doug Oard at: **http://www.ee.umd.edu/medlab/filter/**

News filters are available from most commercial ISPs for a price. There is also one available, free of charge, from Infoseek, called **Infoseek Personal**. It will search out news on subjects of your choice from Reuters, Business Wire, Newswire, and Usenet newsgroups, and is available at:

http://personal.infoseek.com

Managing e-mail overload

> "When I first got on the Internet, I was like a thirsty woman who hadn't had a drink in three days. Now I have to discipline myself and be very focused about what I'm looking for when I use this medium. I subscribe to only two or three select listservs that help me professionally, and even then I use the delete key a lot. I will scan the first one to two sentences of a message, and if it doesn't interest me, Zap! I also use the subject line as a filter. If I'm interested in a new listserv, I subject it to a 30-day trial period. During that time, it needs to meet specific criteria and filters."
>
> — Nancy Walsh, former editor/writer for The Research Foundation, State University of New York

For most people, the novelty of having electronic mail fades in direct proportion to the expanding volume of mail that arrives each day. As more of us use the Internet, we'll all be getting more, not less, e-mail — but we will never get more time to deal with it, unless someone finds a cure for sleep.

If you want to avoid spending the rest of your life answering e-mail (or sorting messages to decide which to delete and which to answer — presumably on that mythical slow day you know will come only after you retire), try some of the following strategies for making the best use of your time.

- **Decide which messages have priority.** For example, you may want to consider messages from colleagues, friends, and family as the most important; then messages from professional mailing lists, such as those for writers and journalists; finally, those from lists about gardening, parenting, or other personal interests. Rather than read your mail in the order in which the messages are received, read only the most important messages. Save the others to read when you have more time.
- **Don't read all your e-mail.** Some of it is bound to be irrelevant junk. Before reading anything, scan the list of messages first to determine which ones deserve to be read right away (see above). When you have time later, read the rest of the subject headings to decide which messages should be read, which can be filed away until later, and which can be deleted unread. You'll have to learn to be brutal with that delete key unless you really do want to spend the rest of your life reading e-mail.
- **Read and reply to important e-mail every day.** In the long run, it

saves time to attend to your mail regularly. This reduces the number of times you end up "handling" each message. Of course, keep your replies short!

- **Request mail digests from mailing lists.** A digest is a collection of all the messages posted to the list that day (see section on listservs in Chapter 6). This way, you get only one message a day from that list. It is much easier to scroll through one long message than it is to read and delete each of the messages individually. The disadvantage, however, is that it is more difficult to reply to a single message from the digest, and it is easier to miss something.
- **Suspend your listserv subscriptions when you're away.** Whether you are going on vacation or simply need to avoid e-mail for a while, suspend your subscription. (The welcome message you received when you joined the list should tell you how to do this.) Otherwise, you will return to a mailbox overflowing with mail.
- **Create folders for messages.** Establish a few clearly labeled folders for messages that you want to save. For example, you might create folders for each story or issue you are researching, one for personal mail, one for each mailing list you belong to, and one for tips about using the Internet. (Don't try to save and file everything — just those items you are likely to use in the future.) Once your folders begin to fill up, finding things in them may not be easy. Most e-mail systems offer some way to search for particular information through all messages in a folder. Find out what that command is for your e-mail program.
- **Set automatic filters to sort your e-mail into different piles before you start reading it.** Instead of going into your mailbox and manually sorting your messages into folders, there are programs that will do this for you automatically. In addition to suitable software, you need a bit of technical skill (including the ability to give precise commands to your computer). For example, you can set up the program to file all mail that comes to you from professional mailing lists automatically into the special folders you have set up, as well as all the mail from personal interest lists. Then, the only mail that lands directly in your inbox is mail you have decided deserves highest priority. The rest will be in folders waiting for you when you get the chance to read it.

FYI For details on how to use e-mail filters with two of the most popular programs, Qualcomm's Eudora Pro and Claris's Emailer, check out: **http://www.cnet.com/Content/Features/Howto/Email/ss1b.html**

Personal Information Managers

There are programs specifically designed to help you organize your personal information, and many of them are now Internet compatible. *Personal Information Managers* (PIMs) are essentially electronic day-timers: they include computerized address books, appointment calendars, to-do lists, autodialers, and notepads. The newer PIMs

Figure 7-3
By setting filters in your mail program, you can save time that would otherwise be spent sorting e-mail messages

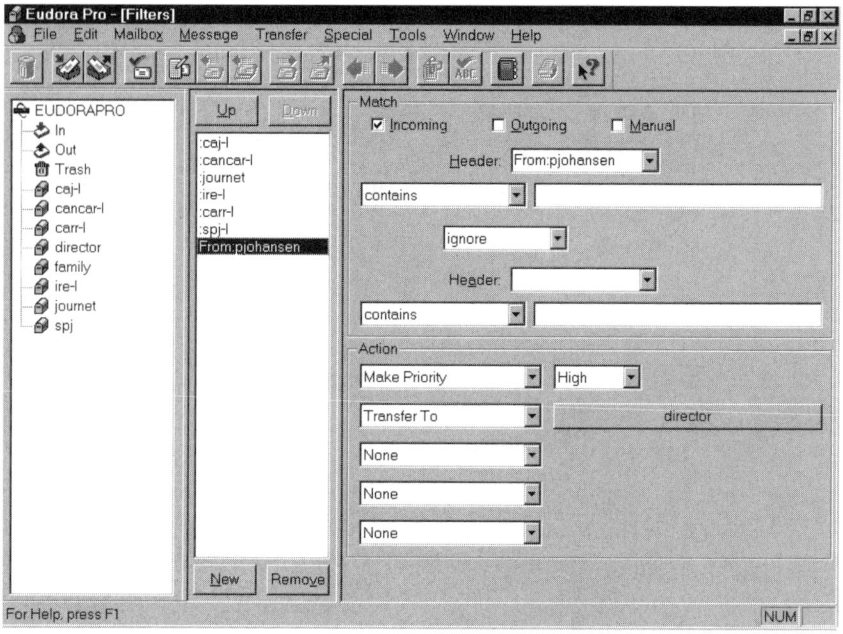

also allow you to enter your contacts' e-mail addresses and Web sites on the address book entry form and make them live links. So, by clicking on your contact's URL from your address file, you automatically load Netscape and dial up your contact's Web site. Some PIMs also make it just as easy to send e-mail: by clicking on your contact's e-mail address, you are automatically presented with a mail form that has your contact's address and your return address already filled in.

As PIMs become more sophisticated they will not only help you keep in touch with others, but may also let others keep in contact with you. Some are being upgraded to allow users to post a daily schedule on the Web, so that colleagues can get in touch with you at critical times. They will also allow you to move your databases of names and phone numbers online so that others can use them, too. (However, considering how guarded some reporters are with their contact lists, this might not be a feature that journalists will use!)

FYI For details on various Personal Information Management programs, go to: **http://www.cnet.com/Content/Reviews/Compare/Pim/**

Keeping up to date

> "If you are receiving too much e-mail and end up deleting half of your incoming messages before reading them, sign off from your least important e-mail discussion groups. If you can't keep up surfing around for the new, useful Web sites, then don't — let someone else do the work for you by reading 'best of the Web' magazines or visiting 'best of the Web' Web sites."
>
> — Steve Cramer, Reference Librarian, Davenport College of Business, Holland, Michigan

Net search assistant software

For people who spend a serious amount of time conducting in-depth, complex searches online, or those who conduct the same searches over and over again looking for new information, there are several products on the market designed to help you update, sort, organize, and keep track of your searches.

One of the most sophisticated is Quarterdeck's WebCompass. It allows you to define a topic and then connects to multiple search sites on the Web to search on that topic. It provides results that include a text summary of every link it retrieves, based on information it finds at the site's home page. You can then sort your hits visually according to any one of a number of criteria, and save your query returns by topic. The program also allows you to monitor Web pages of your choice with "agents" that run your queries for you at regular intervals and notify you of any changes. It also includes a comprehensive set of search terms. To find out more about **WebCompass** and give it a try, check out:

http://www.qdeck.com/qdeck/products/webcompass/

A simpler, less powerful program for Web searches is Symantec Internet FastFind. It allows you to do text searches on the Web that return accurate hits in a minute or two on a single page, which you can then sort. A special feature automatically checks your favorite Web sites for new information. To find out more or to download a trial copy of **FastFind**, check out:

http://www.symantec.com/iff02.html

Another search assistant is called More Like This. It consists of a simple toolbar that sits at the top of your screen while you are on the Web. With it, you can run sophisticated queries quickly and easily by clicking on the "More Like This" button and entering the subject you're looking for. The program submits your query to the search engine of your choice, and you don't even have to know the guidelines for that search engine — the program will translate your query into intelligible commands. To download a free trial copy of **More Like This**, go to:

http://www.morelikethis.com/

Other search tools include **Iconovex EchoSearch** at:

http://www.iconovex.com/ECHO/DESCRIBE.HTM

and **Vironex Software NetFerret** at:

http://www.vironix.com/netferret/netferret.htm

There's also a handy shareware program that allows you to index Web pages whether you bookmark them or not, and search for them later by topic. It's called **Webdex**, and you'll find it at:

http://www.netcom.com/~alcohen/

Keeping up to date with the phenomenal proliferation of Web sites and new software is a challenge. Rather than try to do it alone, it is sometimes best to rely on others to do it for you. There are several resources that offer tips and advice about sites you shouldn't miss.

One of the best resources for writers, researchers, and journalists is the mailing list for **Computer-Assisted Reporting and Research**

(CARR-L; see Chapter 6 on listservs). The list owner regularly passes on messages of interest to those doing online research from other groups that monitor the Net for new Web sites and software.

Another is the Scout Report. It filters over 130 sources of new Internet sites and news stories each week and provides an annotated report offering the best new and newly discovered sites for people in the research and education community. "Surf smarter, not longer" is its slogan. You can subscribe to the **Scout Report** and receive it each week by e-mail, or you can access it and past editions on the Web at:

http://www.cs.wisc.edu/scout/

At the same Web site, you can access current and past versions of Net Happenings, a similar service that is more comprehensive and less selective.

A last word

Managing information overload has become a bigger challenge than ever, thanks to the Internet. It's not a skill you can learn by taking a course but instead something you must learn the hard way, by trial and error.

This chapter has offered some tips and tricks from information professionals. As the Internet grows and becomes more sophisticated, it's a good idea to continue seeking the advice of experienced users: online discussion groups and online publications for researchers are good sources of valuable advice and will help you keep up to date with this ever-changing technology.

Further reading

Alexander, Jan, and Tate, Marsha. "Teaching Critical Evaluation Skills for World Wide Web Resources."
http://www.science.widener.edu/~withers/webeval.htm

Crittendon, John. "Information Overload." Pacific Byte, 1996.
http://www.pacificbyte.com/_stories/1infovr.html

Grassian, Esther. "Thinking Critically about World Wide Web Resources."
http://www.library.ucla.edu/libraries/college/instruct/critical.htm

Chapter 8 Writing for the Web

"We can perhaps assume that the use of a medium of communication over a long period will to some extent determine the character of knowledge to be communicated and suggest that its pervasive influence will eventually create a civilization in which life and flexibility will become exceedingly difficult to maintain and that the advantages of a new medium will become such as to lead to the emergence of a new civilization."

— HAROLD A. INNIS, *THE BIAS OF COMMUNICATION*. TORONTO: UNIVERSITY OF TORONTO PRESS, 1951, P. 34.

The Internet is changing communication, and the future of work for writers, editors, journalists, researchers, and all other wordsmiths must change as well. This chapter explains how you can become a participant in — and not just a user of — this new medium.

You don't have to be a programmer or an artist to create Web pages. You probably don't even need any software that you don't already have. Word processing documents can easily be converted to Web pages.

Any writer can now put his or her work up on the Web for others to read. You can broadcast your résumé, start a newsletter, or just supply a list of your favorite online resources for others to share. There are no paper or printing costs, and the potential audience is in the millions.

This chapter introduces Hypertext Markup Language (HTML), the foundation of all Web pages: what it is, and how to write it with a simple text editor. We'll give you enough of the "vocabulary" of this language to create your own Web pages — starting today. You'll see illustrated examples of HTML codes and the actual Web pages they produce. If learning HTML isn't your cup of tea, you can try one of several software programs (described later in this chapter) that make a Web page as easy to craft as an ordinary business letter.

You'll also learn the basics of Web graphics, find recommended software to help you add visual elements to your Web pages, and discover the ground rules for designing Web content.

All that's left is for you to put your Web pages online and publicize them. Further sources of information listed at the end of the chapter will enable you to build on the foundation skills you'll gain here.

Chapter highlights

- What is HTML?
- Basic HTML tags
- Make a Web page
- Web graphics
- HTML editor software
- Designing Web content
- Putting your Web pages online
- How to publicize your Web site

What is HTML?

Changing a regular document into a Web page means using Hypertext Markup Language. HTML gives us a simple way to format a document so that it can be viewed with any Web browser. Hypertext also makes it possible to link documents together.

HTML is not programming. It's more like a set of labels that identify the structure of a document. These labels are the HTML "tags." One kind of tag says, "Start a new paragraph here." Another kind of tag comes as a pair; the first tag says, "Start a heading here," and the second tag says, "End that heading over here." These tags are created by using combinations of familiar characters from your keyboard.

You can use a word processing program to put HTML tags into any plain text file, thereby turning it into a Web-ready document.

FYI You can turn any word processor document into a plain text file. Just open the document in your usual word processing program and select **Save As ...** from the **File** menu. A dialog box will open, and near the bottom you'll see options for saving the file. Look for the option **Text Only** or **ASCII Text**.

INFO*nugget*

Today, HTML allows all kinds of complex and wonderful things to happen on the World Wide Web. But its original purpose was very simple: in 1990, physicist Tim Berners-Lee wanted to enable scientists around the world to share their research papers quickly. He came up with a system that would make the papers readable on any kind of computer and that would allow the scientists to cite other research papers, not with a mere footnote but by actually connecting the papers to one another. These connections (called *hypertext links*) could cross borders and oceans in seconds via the Internet. So, this system of tags was created for writers and researchers — not for programmers!

To find out more about Tim Berners-Lee and the beginnings of the World Wide Web, visit:

http://www.w3.org/pub/WWW/People/Berners-Lee-Bio.html

Some word processing programs, notably recent versions of Microsoft Word, handle an HTML document differently from a plain text file. These programs may hide the HTML tags, acting somewhat like a Web browser instead of like a word processor. Automatic formatting can wreak havoc with the tags. It's not advisable to use these overly clever word processing programs for your own HTML editing. Instead, you can use a low-end text editor such as Notepad (not WordPad) in Windows 3.1 and Windows 95, or SimpleText on the Macintosh. (If you're using Notepad, remember to select **Word Wrap** in the **Edit** menu.) You might also acquire an HTML editor program (described later in this chapter).

It's only when you open the file with a Web browser that it looks like a Web page.

Figure 8-1 (page 130) shows one page of a newsletter as it might appear on the Web. Compare this with the text file that produced it (Figure 8-1A).

FOCUS ON...

Using a text editor to create Web pages

1. Open a basic text editor program, such as Windows Notepad (not WordPad) or SimpleText on the Macintosh.
2. Open a plain text file in the text editor, or write a new one. (Keep it short for this first exercise.)
3. Type `<HTML>` at the very top of the document, before all other text.
4. Type `</HTML>` at the very bottom of the document, after all other text. (Note that the slash tilts to the right, unlike the DOS backslash.)
5. Save your document by selecting **File | Save As...** . Make sure the new filename ends with the extension *.htm* — or *.html* on the Mac (example: *mystory.htm*). This extension enables the Web browser software to recognize the file as an HTML document. In Notepad, be sure not to save with the *.txt* extension. Windows 95 users should stick to eight-letter filenames for these files.
6. Open your Web browser. (You do not have to be connected to the Internet to do this.) Keep the text editor program open, too.
7. Open your new document in the Web browser (it can be open in both programs at the same time, so long as you are using a basic text editor). To open it in Netscape, choose **File | Open File...** and then locate the file on your hard drive. To open it in Microsoft Internet Explorer, choose **File | Open**, click the **Browse** button, and then locate the file on your hard drive.

   You should see your document in the Web browser now. It won't have any paragraphs or other formatting yet, but it will appear in the screen font that your Web browser uses.
8. Editing your document will be much easier if you can arrange your Web browser window and your text editor window in a way that lets you toggle (click back and forth) between the two windows. Try dragging one window to the far left and the other window to the far right. Resize the two windows if necessary so that neither one entirely covers the other.
9. By clicking on the text editor window, go back to the editor program.
10. Just below the top tag `<HTML>`, type this:

    ```
    <H1>My First Web Page</H1>
    ```

    Be careful to get all the angle brackets and the slash correct. Also, be sure to type the numeral one after the two H's — do not type a lowercase L.
11. Save the document again. (Select **File | Save** from the menu in the text editor.) Do not change the filename.
12. By clicking on the Web browser window, go back to the Web browser.

13. Reload the Web page. In Netscape, click the button labeled **Reload.** In MS Internet Explorer, click the button labeled **Refresh.** (This button may be covered by the Address window. Slide the bar to the right to find it.)
14. You should see a large bold heading announcing your first Web page.

    Sample text file:

```
<HTML>
<H1>My First Web Page</H1>
Some text here it can say anything it doesn't
even need to have any punctuation or paragraphs
or anything like that just some text as a sample
for your first Web page exercise.
</HTML>
```

Congratulations! You're ready to learn more HTML. Using this method, you can easily fine-tune your work and test it in your Web browser. Just remember to save the file in the text editor after you have made changes, and then reload in the browser.

Figure 8-1
A Web page from a typical online newsletter

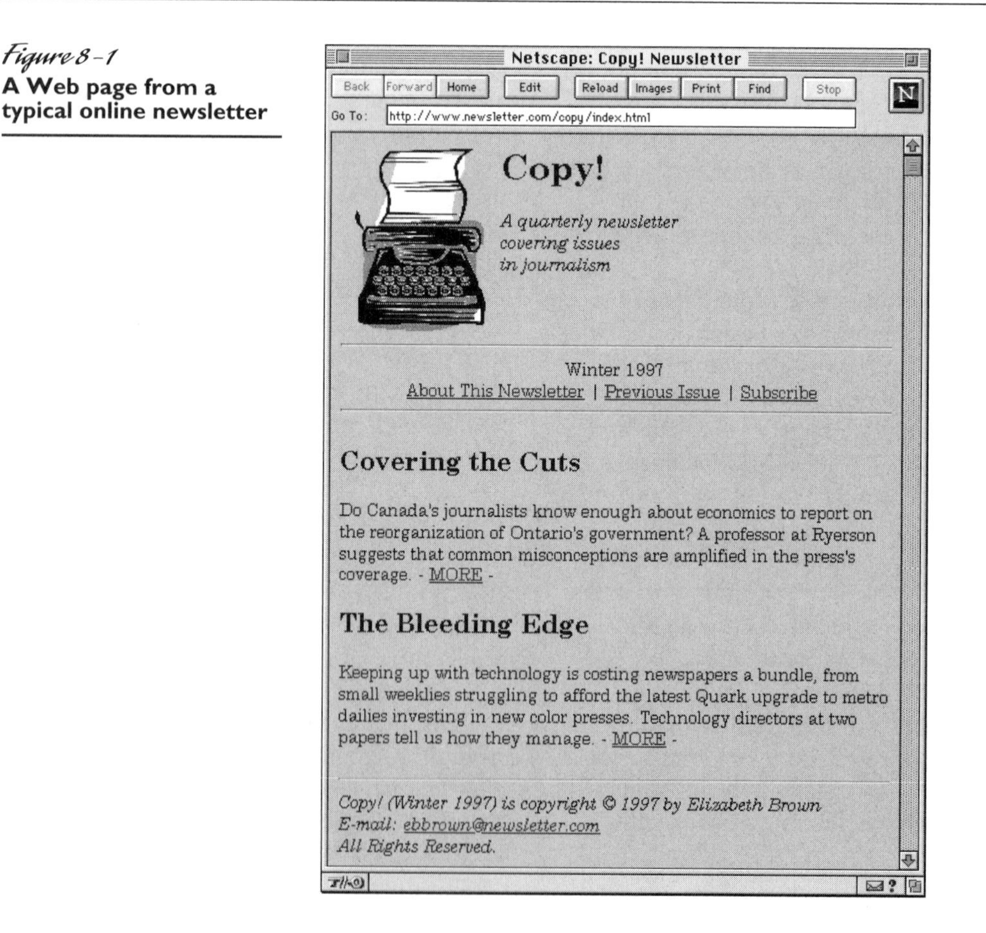

Figure 8-1A
Text file for newsletter (Figure 8-1)

```
<HTML>
<HEAD>
<TITLE>Copy! Newsletter</TITLE>
</HEAD>
<BODY>

<IMG SRC="typewriter.gif" ALIGN=left>

<H1>Copy!</H1>

<I>A quarterly newsletter<BR>
covering issues<BR>
in journalism</I><BR CLEAR=left>

<DIV ALIGN=center>
<HR>
Winter 1997<BR>
<A HREF="about.html">About This Newsletter</A> |
<A HREF="96dec/">Previous Issue</A> |
<A HREF="subscribe.html">Subscribe</A>
<HR>
</DIV>

<H2>Covering the Cuts</H2>
<P>
Do Canada's journalists know enough about economics to
report on the reorganization of Ontario's government?
A professor at Ryerson suggests that common
misconceptions are amplified in the press's coverage.
- <A HREF="97jan/cuts.html">MORE</A> -

<H2>The Bleeding Edge</H2>
<P>
Keeping up with technology is costing newspapers a bundle,
from small weeklies struggling to afford the latest Quark
upgrade to metro dailies investing in new color presses.
Technology directors at two papers tell us how they manage.
- <A HREF="97jan/edge.html">MORE</A> -

<P>
<HR>
```

▶

```
<ADDRESS>
Copy! (Winter 1997) is copyright  &copy;  1997 by
Elizabeth Brown<BR>
E-mail: <A HREF="mailto:ebbrown@newsletter.com">
ebbrown@newsletter.com</A><BR>
All Rights Reserved.
</ADDRESS>

</BODY>
</HTML>
```

The HTML tags, contained within angle brackets, cause headings, italics, and boldface to be displayed in the Web browser window. The Web browser program controls the typeface and size of the heading and the text.

Basic HTML tags

You can see the HTML code for any Web page by choosing **View | Document Source** in Netscape while the Web page is open in the browser. An excellent way to learn HTML is to print out Web pages you like (choose **File | Print** from the Web browser menu), then print out the source code for those pages, and compare the two side by side to see how the page was formatted.

HTML tags are always enclosed by angle brackets, which you can find on your keyboard above the comma and the period.

Many HTML tags come in pairs. The first tag in the pair goes just before the text you want to format, and the second tag in the pair goes immediately after that text. To format the phrase **Web browser** in boldface, frame the word between the `<B>` tag and the `</B>` tag:

```
<B>Web browser</B>
```

The only difference between the two tags in most pairs is that the second tag has a slash after the opening angle bracket. Note that the slash tilts to the right, unlike a DOS backslash. (Not all HTML tags come in pairs, as you'll see.)

Figure 8-2 shows a brief Web résumé. It uses no difficult coding or graphical elements, yet looks clean and attractive. The author has used hypertext links sparingly, probably because she hopes you will read the entire résumé!

Beginning on page 133 is the complete HTML document that produced the Web résumé shown in Figures 8-2 and 8-2A. Don't be put off by the tags! Look for the regular text (between the tags) and compare it with the Web pages in the two illustrations. You'll soon see the direct relationship between the HTML and the final product.

Figure 8-2

To see the lower half of the résumé (Figure 8-2A), which is below the bottom edge of the Web browser window, the user must scroll the page.

Figure 8-2A

The lower half of the résumé. Additional sections could easily be included, such as "Personal," "Other Projects," or "Awards," but if the Web page got much longer, the author might consider breaking some sections off onto separate Web pages.

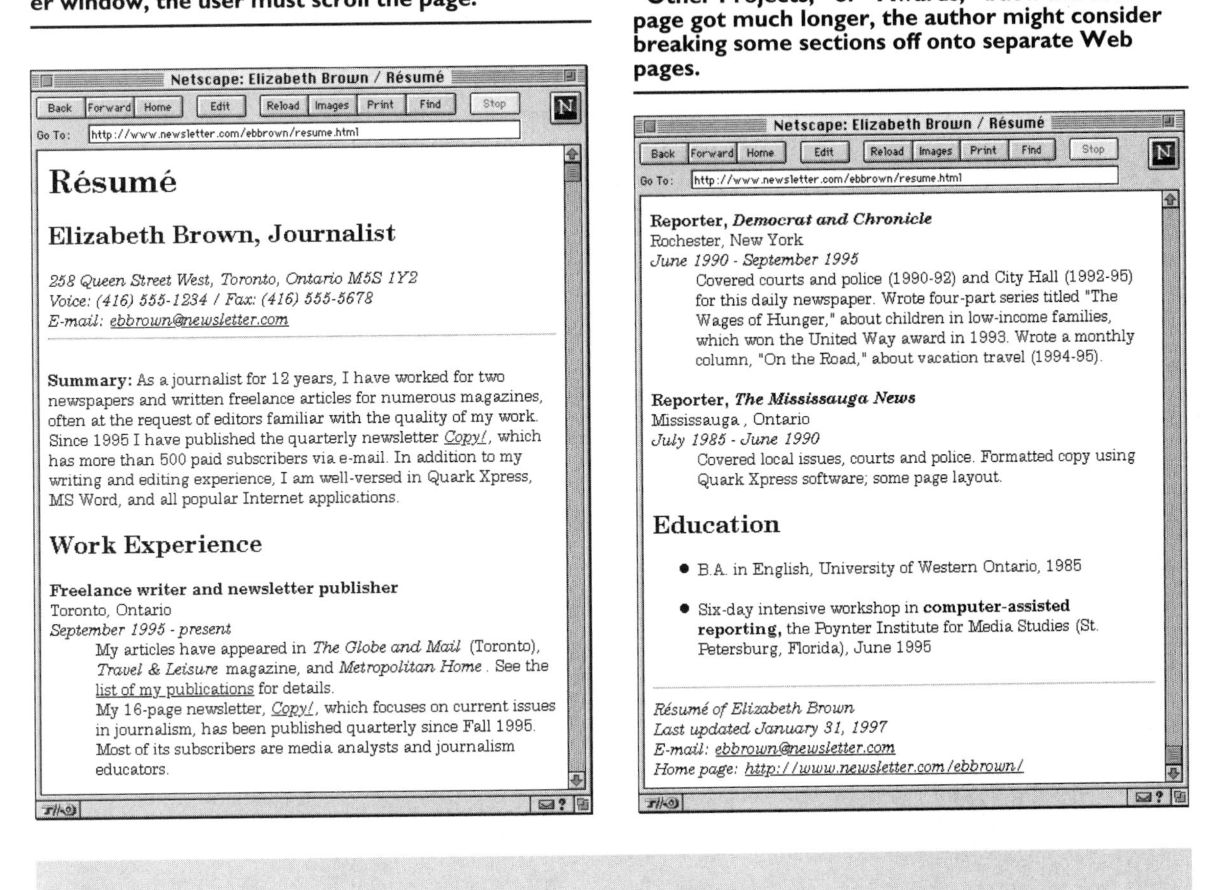

Netscape: Elizabeth Brown / Résumé

Back Forward Home Edit Reload Images Print Find Stop

Go To: http://www.newsletter.com/ebbrown/resume.html

Résumé

Elizabeth Brown, Journalist

258 Queen Street West, Toronto, Ontario M5S 1Y2
Voice: (416) 555-1234 / Fax: (416) 555-5678
E-mail: ebbrown@newsletter.com

Summary: As a journalist for 12 years, I have worked for two newspapers and written freelance articles for numerous magazines, often at the request of editors familiar with the quality of my work. Since 1995 I have published the quarterly newsletter *Copy!*, which has more than 500 paid subscribers via e-mail. In addition to my writing and editing experience, I am well-versed in Quark Xpress, MS Word, and all popular Internet applications.

Work Experience

Freelance writer and newsletter publisher
Toronto, Ontario
September 1995 - present
My articles have appeared in *The Globe and Mail* (Toronto), *Travel & Leisure* magazine, and *Metropolitan Home*. See the list of my publications for details.
My 16-page newsletter, *Copy!*, which focuses on current issues in journalism, has been published quarterly since Fall 1995. Most of its subscribers are media analysts and journalism educators.

Netscape: Elizabeth Brown / Résumé

Back Forward Home Edit Reload Images Print Find Stop

Go To: http://www.newsletter.com/ebbrown/resume.html

Reporter, *Democrat and Chronicle*
Rochester, New York
June 1990 - September 1995
Covered courts and police (1990-92) and City Hall (1992-95) for this daily newspaper. Wrote four-part series titled "The Wages of Hunger," about children in low-income families, which won the United Way award in 1993. Wrote a monthly column, "On the Road," about vacation travel (1994-95).

Reporter, *The Mississauga News*
Mississauga , Ontario
July 1985 - June 1990
Covered local issues, courts and police. Formatted copy using Quark Xpress software; some page layout.

Education

- B.A. in English, University of Western Ontario, 1985
- Six-day intensive workshop in **computer-assisted reporting,** the Poynter Institute for Media Studies (St. Petersburg, Florida), June 1995

Résumé of Elizabeth Brown
Last updated January 31, 1997
E-mail: ebbrown@newsletter.com
Home page: http://www.newsletter.com/ebbrown/

```
<HTML>
<HEAD>
<TITLE>Elizabeth Brown / R&eacute;sum&eacute;</TITLE>
</HEAD>

<BODY BGCOLOR=#FFFFFF TEXT=#000000 LINK=#000099
VLINK=#660066 ALINK=#CCCCCC>

<H1>R&eacute;sum&eacute;</H1>

<H2>Elizabeth Brown, Journalist</H2>

<I>258 Queen Street West, Toronto, Ontario M5S 1Y2<BR>
Voice: (416) 555-1234 / Fax: (416) 555-5678<BR>
E-mail: <A HREF="mailto:ebbrown@newsletter.com">
ebbrown@newsletter.com</A></I><BR>
```

```
<HR>

<P>
<B>Summary:</B> As a journalist for 12 years, I have
worked for two newspapers and written freelance
articles for numerous magazines, often at the
request of editors familiar with the quality of
my work. Since 1995 I have published the quarterly
newsletter <A HREF="http://www.newsletter.com/copy/">
<CITE>Copy!</CITE></A>, which has more than 500 paid
subscribers via e-mail. In addition to my writing and
editing experience, I am well-versed in Quark Xpress,
MS Word, and all popular Internet applications.

<H2>Work Experience</H2>

<DL>  <!— begin definition list —>

<DT>
<B>Freelance writer and newsletter publisher</B><BR>
Toronto, Ontario<BR>
<I>September 1995 - present</I><BR>
<DD>
My articles have appeared in <CITE>The Globe and
Mail</CITE> (Toronto), <CITE>Travel & Leisure</CITE>
magazine, and <CITE>Metropolitan Home</CITE>. See the
<A HREF="publications.html">list of my publications</A>
for details.<BR>
My 16-page newsletter,
<A HREF="http://www.newsletter.com/copy/">
<CITE>Copy!</CITE></A>, which focuses on current issues
in journalism, has been published quarterly since Fall
1995. Most of its subscribers are media analysts and
journalism educators.

<P><DT>
<B>Reporter,  <CITE>Democrat and Chronicle</CITE></B><BR>
Rochester, New York<BR>
<I>June 1990 - September 1995</I><BR>
<DD>
Covered courts and police (1990-92) and City Hall (1992-95)
for this daily newspaper. Wrote four-part series titled
"The Wages of Hunger," about children in low-income
families, which won the United Way award in 1993. Wrote
a monthly column, "On the Road," about vacation travel
(1994-95).
```

```
<P><DT>
<B>Reporter, <CITE>The Mississauga News</CITE></B><BR>
Mississauga , Ontario<BR>
<I>July 1985 - June 1990</I><BR>
<DD>
Covered local issues, courts and police. Formatted copy
using Quark Xpress software; some page layout.

</DL>  <!— end definition list —>


<H2>Education</H2>

<UL>  <!— begin bulleted list —>

<LI>B.A. in English, University of Western Ontario, 1985

<P>
<LI>Six-day intensive workshop in <B>computer-assisted
reporting,</B> the Poynter Institute for Media Studies
(St. Petersburg, Florida), June 1995

</UL>  <!— end bulleted list —>

<P>
<HR>

<ADDRESS>
R&eacute;sum&eacute; of Elizabeth Brown<BR>
Last updated January 31, 1997<BR>
E-mail: <A HREF="mailto:ebbrown@newsletter.com">
ebbrown@newsletter.com</A><BR>
Home page: <A HREF="http://www.newsletter.com/ebbrown/">
http://www.newsletter.com/ebbrown/</A>
</ADDRESS>

</BODY>
</HTML>
```

Feel free to copy this HTML formatting for your own online résumé. To add more sections, just copy and paste the formatting for Elizabeth's "Work Experience" or "Education" sections and write a different heading. (Note: Elizabeth Brown doesn't exist, and her résumé and newsletter are completely fictitious.)

The following guide is by no means a complete dictionary of HTML. However, you could create dozens of good Web pages without knowing any tags other than those described below. The aim here is to keep things simple so that you can get started. For more

The HTML specification, which describes the HTML tags and how they work, is continually changing. (This is typical of new technical specs.) In practical terms, this means two things:

- New capabilities are added to HTML frequently. If you feel an urgent need to be hip and snazzy, you will redesign your pages often. But it isn't necessary.
- Web browser software will change to keep up with the latest revisions to the HTML spec. If you use HTML tags in unconventional ways to achieve certain design effects, the next generation of browser software may wreck your design. New versions of HTML try to stay compatible with earlier versions, but they cannot stay compatible with nonstandard uses of the tags.

detailed information about HTML and other tags and options, see the resources listed at the end of this chapter.

Tags that should be in all HTML documents

`<HTML> </HTML>`
The first and last codes in your document; they frame the entire document.

`<HEAD> </HEAD>`
Frame the document's header, which includes the title, and which can also contain other information about the document that will not be displayed.

`<TITLE> </TITLE>`
Frame the actual title that will be searched on the Web and that users will see in the title bar of the browser window (or equivalent) and in the Go menu (this is not a heading).

`<BODY> </BODY>`
Frame the body of the document — everything after the header (but before the closing `</HTML>` tag).

Let's take a very simple example of a complete Web page:

```
<HTML>

<HEAD>
<TITLE>My Home Page</TITLE>
</HEAD>

<BODY>
<H1>Welcome!</H1>
This is the text of my home page. It is only
two sentences long.
</BODY>

</HTML>
```

Now compare the above text file with the Web page it produces (Figure 8-3). Notice where the title appears (in the bar at the top edge of the window). The Web browser program has determined the typeface and size of the heading and the text.

All HTML 3.2 documents must begin with a rather complex `<!DOCTYPE>` tag, in this format:

```
<!DOCTYPE HTML PUBLIC "-//W3C//DTD HTML
3.2//EN">
```

This tag precedes the `<HTML>` tag. You do not have to use this tag

Figure 8-3
A Web page Welcome!

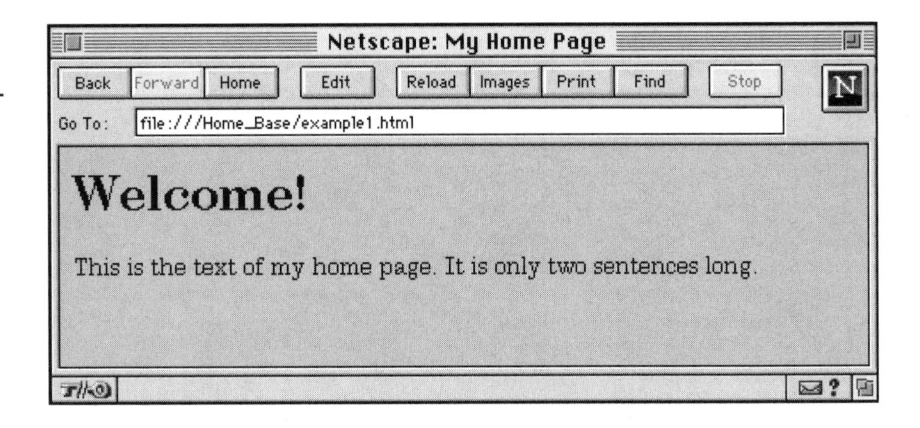

Common text-formatting tags

1. HEADINGS

<H1> </H1> Frame the largest heading (or headline)

<H2> </H2> Frame the second largest heading

<H6> </H6> Frame the sixth largest heading

(There are six heading levels, including H3, H4, and H5.)

2. TEXT-BREAKING TAGS (NO CLOSING TAG REQUIRED FOR THESE)

<P> Start paragraph (adds one line of space)

<HR> Insert a horizontal rule (dividing line)

 Break the line

3. TAGS FOR EMPHASIS

<B> </B> Boldface

<I> </I> Italics

<STRONG> </STRONG> Produces boldface or highlighting

<EM> </EM> Produces italics or highlighting (less than <STRONG>)

(In most cases it's fine to use <B> and not <STRONG>; <I> and not <EM>.)

4. LISTS

<OL> </OL> Frame an ordered (numbered) list

<UL> </UL> Frame an unordered (bulleted) list

<LI> Begin each new list item (no closing tag required)

<DL> </DL> Frame a definition list; instead of <LI>, use <DT> to precede the term to be defined and <DD> to precede the definition; no closing tag is required with <DT> or <DD>.

Figure 8-4
The Web browser interprets the HTML codes indicating a bulleted list

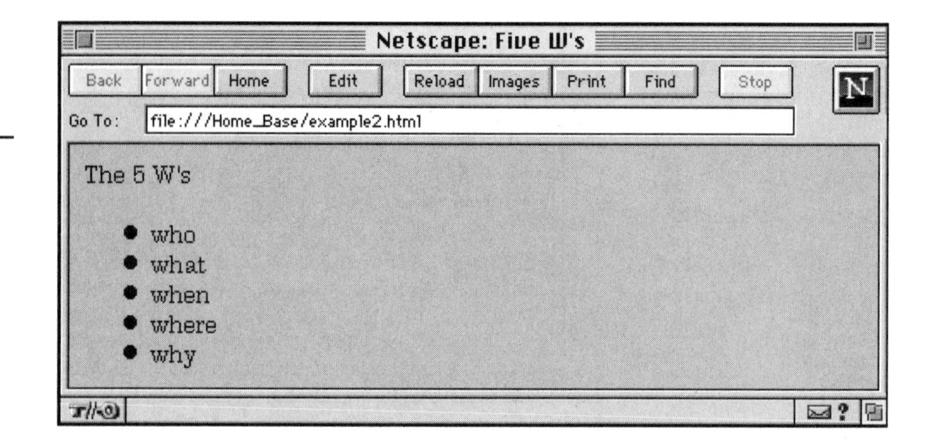

Example:

```
The 5 W's
<UL>
<LI>who  <LI>what <LI>when  <LI>where
<LI>why
</UL>
```

The tag `<LI>` creates a bullet and also starts a new line, even if your text document did not show a new line. In many browsers, a list is automatically indented (see Figure 8-4).

Hypertext links

1. TO A WEB PAGE ON ANOTHER SERVER

```
<A HREF="http://www.someplace.com/">
```

Leave the present document and open one with the URL *http://www.someplace.com/.*

```
</A>
```

End the descriptive name (that is, the link text) — this is the second tag in a pair.

Examples:

```
<A HREF="http://www.someplace.com/">The
Someplace Cafe</A>
```

The Someplace Cafe

Come to

```
<A HREF="http://www.books.com/writers/mystery.html">
the Mystery Writers' Den</A> for a clue.
```

Come to the Mystery Writers' Den for a clue.

FYI Typographical characters such as dashes, curved quotation marks, and apostrophes do not "translate" into text-only format. Use search-and-replace in your word processing program to change these characters to their typewriter-style equivalents before saving a document as plain text. If you use curved quotation marks inside an HTML <A HREF> tag, the link will not work.

2. TO A WEB PAGE ON THE SAME SERVER

```
<A HREF="home.htm">
```

Leave this document and open one that is in the same directory on the same server and that has the filename *home.htm*. (Note that *http://* is not used for local documents; also note that some filenames use the extension *.htm* and others use *.html*, which are equivalent to the Web browser.)

```
</A>
```

End the descriptive name (the link text) — this is the second tag in a pair.

Example:

```
Come to <A HREF="home.htm">my home page</A> today.
```

Come to <u>my home page</u> today.

3. TO A PLACE ELSEWHERE ON THIS SAME WEB PAGE

```
<A HREF="#hobbies">
```

Go to another part of this document where you have put the tag:

<A NAME="hobbies"> (see NAME anchor example, below).

```
</A>
```

End the descriptive name (the link text) — this is the second tag in a pair.

Example:

```
There is <A HREF="#hobbies">a list of other things
I like</A> below.
```

There is <u>a list of other things I like</u> below.

NAME anchor *Example:*

```
<A NAME="hobbies">My Other Interests</A>
```

My Other Interests
(This text will not be underlined or highlighted; the tags create an anchor location, not an active link.)

The NAME anchor marks a destination to which the HREF link above will take you. The text between the tags ("My Other Interests") could be any text at all, including a heading, or even

If you have only a few Web pages and images, it's fine (and simplest) to keep them all in one directory. If you have more than a dozen Web pages, you should learn how to create new directories on the server where your pages are stored. Say that *home.htm* is in your main (or top-level) directory, and you have a page named *italy.htm* in a subdirectory named *freelanc*. To put a working link to *italy.htm* on the page *home.htm*, you must include the name of the subdirectory where *italy.htm* can be found:

```
<A HREF="freelanc/italy.htm">Italian Art</A>
```

an image. Instead, you could set up the two tags with only a space between them, and the anchor would also work:

```
<A NAME="hobbies"> </A>
```

Note the function of the pound sign (#) here: use it with HREF, but do not use it with NAME.

This kind of in-document link works best on a Web page divided into sections. You can provide a preview of the sections at the top of the page by creating a small table of contents, with each section name linked to the start of a section below.

Example:

```
<A HREF="#current">My Current Project</A>
<A HREF="#history">Work History</A>
<A HREF="#edu">Education</A>
```

Farther down the page we would find `<A NAME="history"> </A>` followed, no doubt, by a list of jobs this person has held.

Adding images

```
<IMG SRC="globe.gif" ALIGN=top ALT=" ">
```

Insert an image (in this case, one that is contained in a file named *globe.gif*). No closing tag is required.

Obtaining images and using file formats are discussed later in this chapter. There are many options (attributes) that can be included within the `<IMG>` tag; they are far too numerous to list here. To learn more, consult the online graphics resources listed at the end of this chapter.

IMG TAG ATTRIBUTES

`ALIGN=top`

The options for the ALIGN attribute include *bottom, middle, left,* and *right*. These affect how the text before and after the image will be aligned.

`ALT=" "`

The ALT attribute spares text-only users from seeing an unhelpful label, such as [IMAGE] or [INLINE] (see Figure 8-5B, page 145). More important, it can be used to provide information for the many Web users who surf with graphics turned off. You can put text

FYI

Most Web browsers will automatically draw a rectangular border around a linked image. If you don't like the border, turn it off by adding `BORDER=0` within the `<IMG>` tag:

```
<IMG SRC="globe.gif" BORDER=0 ALT=" ">
```

You could also make the border thicker by specifying, for example, `BORDER=5`.

between the quotes if it would be useful. For example, if you have an art banner that says **Welcome**, you might use `ALT="Welcome"` so that the word "Welcome" would be printed for people who will not see the banner.

You can leave out the ALIGN and ALT attributes. This is an example of the simplest form of the `<IMG>` tag:

```
<IMG SRC="globe.gif">
```

USING AN IMAGE AS A LINK

When text is used as a link, it is framed by the two parts of the `<A>` tag; that is, it is preceded by `<A HREF="filename.html">` and followed by `</A>` (see "Hypertext Links," page 138). An image is handled the same way, but instead of framing a word or phrase with a pair of `<A>` tags, the complete `<IMG>` tag is framed.

Example:

```
<A HREF="home.html"><IMG SRC="globe.gif"></A>
```

This would show the *globe.gif* image, and the image would act as a link to the Web page *home.html*.

Other tags and codes

`<!– an invisible comment –>`
To note comments within your HTML code that will be visible when anyone views the source code but that will not appear on the Web page itself, frame the notation with `<!–` and `–>` (this can be useful for pages that will require maintenance).

`<CITE> </CITE>`
Frame a citation, such as a book title (usually rendered in italics).

`<ADDRESS> </ADDRESS>`
Frame your address information at the end of the document.

THE E-MAIL LINK

`<A HREF="mailto:mmcadams@well.com">`
Enable users to send an e-mail message to the address: *mmcadams@well.com*

`</A>`
End the description (the link text) of the e-mail destination — this is the second tag in a pair.

Examples:

```
<A HREF="mailto:mmcadams@well.com">Mindy
McAdams</A>
```

This will appear as:

Mindy McAdams

It's better style to make the e-mail address visible:

```
<A HREF="mailto:mmcadams@well.com">
mmcadams@well.com</A>
```

This will appear as:

mmcadams@well.com

Clicking either one of these links will cause an e-mail window to open so that someone can send a comment on the spot, without opening a separate e-mail program.

SYMBOLS AND ACCENTS

There are two ways to produce typographical symbols and accented letters, as illustrated below with the copyright symbol and the lowercase letter *e* with an acute accent (é).

Option 1. To produce a special character, find the ISO-Latin-1 numeric entity for the symbol or letter you want (see the list at *http://www.w3.org/pub/WWW/MarkUp/Wilbur/latin1.gif*), precede it with an ampersand and a pound sign, and follow it with a semicolon. The copyright symbol (©) is represented by *169* (`©`). An *e* with an acute accent (é) is represented by *233* (`é`).

Examples:

```
Copyright &#169; 1996
```

Copyright © 1996

```
r&#233;sum&#233;
```

résumé

Option 2. Many accented letters can be represented by a character entity instead. Find the character entity for the symbol or letter you want (see the list at *http://www.uni-passau.de/~ramsch/iso8859-1.html*), precede it with an ampersand, and follow it with a semicolon. The character entity for the copyright symbol is *copy* (`©`). For the acute-accented e the character entity is *eacute* (`é`).

Examples:

```
Copyright &copy; 1996
```

Copyright © 1996

```
r&eacute;sum&eacute;
```

résumé

Other HTML capabilities

HTML allows the creation of *tables*, both simple grids and complex layouts with cells of varying sizes. It also makes possible *interactive*

HTML tags, like programming languages, are completely unforgiving when it comes to typos. Whenever something doesn't work as expected when you open your page in a Web browser, go back to the HTML text document and check for errors, especially missing quotes, slashes, and angle brackets.

forms, which enable users to type in information that can be e-mailed to you or entered into a database, or that can be processed by the Web server to provide an immediate response. HTML forms require a *CGI script* (a kind of computer program) to work. Multimedia content can be added to Web pages via numerous *viewers, helper applications*, and *plug-ins* (see Chapter 3). Last but far from least, HTML 3.2 provides for the inclusion of *style sheets*, which let you specify fonts and font sizes, colors, and even leading (line spacing) for an entire set of Web pages. Some Web browsers support style sheets today, but most do not, and the results are not always predictable.

If you have created a few simple Web pages using the basic tags, you can certainly go on to master any or all of the other features of HTML. The additional resources listed at the end of this chapter will tell you all you need to know.

Make a Web page

You can now make a fully functioning Web page with headings, paragraphs, lists, images, and hypertext links. For guidance, compare the text document in Figure 8-5 (page 144) to Figure 8-5A opposite it.

Web graphics

> "If you really want to do some scientific testing, do the following: 1) Get a group of volunteers who are all interested in a common subject (say, cats); 2) Show them ten cats Web sites. Make five of those sites highly graphical and five highly informative; 3) 24 hours later, do a standard retention test and see which sites they remember most. I'll bet that the content sites stay in their minds better than the graphic-intensive sites. Ditto for people that are looking for something specific, and searching all over the Net for it."
>
> — Mary Morris, author, "What Is Good Design?"
> http://www.sun.com/950801/columns/MaryMorris.col9508.html

It's not necessary to put images on a Web page, but they do look nice — when used in moderation. There are two common ways to get images to use on your Web pages: make them yourself, or use clip art (ready-made images).

You can create a link to any site on the Web, but you will have to be connected to the Internet to make those external links work. If you want to test a link without connecting, create another Web page on your own hard drive and link to it. For example, create a text file named *test.htm* and link to it this way:

```
<A HREF="test.htm">my test page</A>
```

Clip art

It's very easy to copy images directly from a Web page:

1. Place your cursor on the image.
2. On the PC, click the right-hand mouse button once. On the Mac, hold down the mouse button. In either case, you will get a pop-up menu near your cursor.
3. Select the menu option **Save This Image As...**

(continued on page 146)

Figure 8-5
Notice the effects produced by the <P> tags, the <BR> tag, the two <HR> tags, and by the extra spaces in the last paragraph. There are two hypertext links and one image in this example.

```
<HTML>
<HEAD>
<TITLE>An HTML Example</TITLE>
</HEAD>

<BODY>

<H1>Hypertext Markup Language</H1>

<HR>

The text in an HTML document is plain text,
or ASCII.

<P>
Images are inserted <BR>
wherever there is a tag that gives the
filename <IMG SRC="monkey.gif"> of the image.

<P>
Hypertext links are also created with tags. The
filename of a local document or the complete URL
(Uniform Resource Locator) of an external document
precedes the link text, and a closing tag follows.
As an example of an external link, I offer
<A HREF="http://www.yahoo.com/">Yahoo!</A> As an
example of a local document, I offer
<A HREF="index.html">my home page</A>.

<P>
"Typographer's quotation marks" cannot be used in
HTML; neither can true dashes — or other marks that
do not appear on an old-style typewriter.

<P>
The number of spaces between               words or
between lines



of text has no effect on formatting in HTML.

<HR>

</BODY>
</HTML>
```

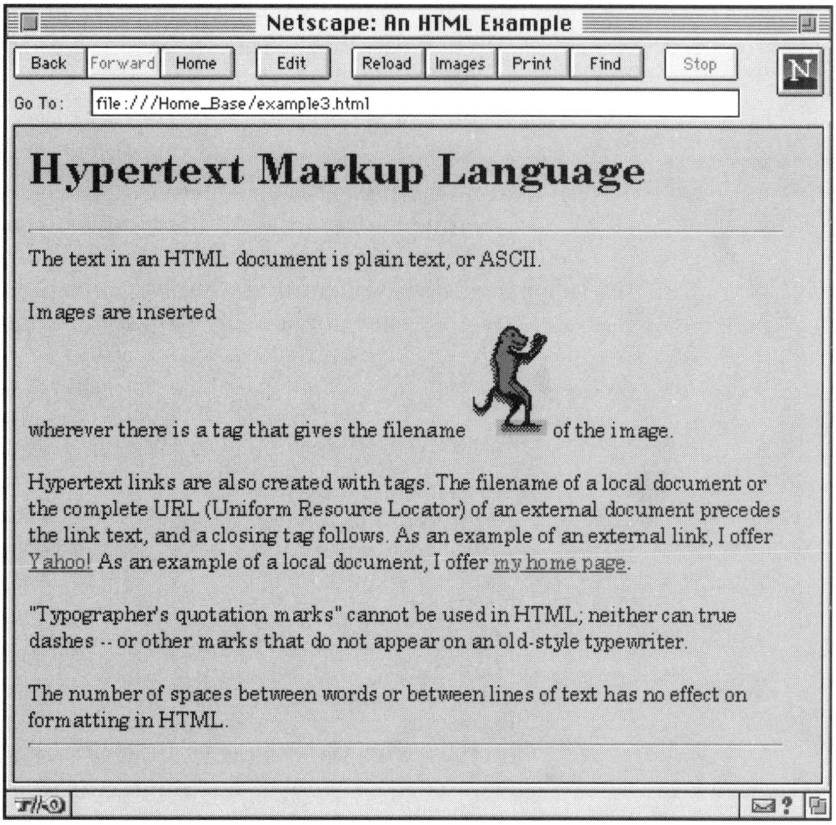

Figure 8-5A

The text file shown in Figure 8-5 was opened in Netscape. This is the result.

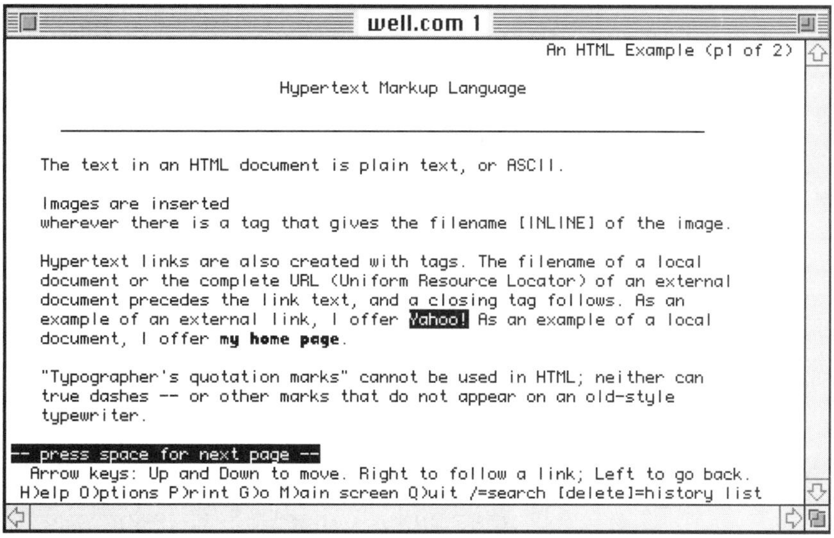

Netscape: An HTML Example

Back Forward Home Edit Reload Images Print Find Stop

Go To: file:///Home_Base/example3.html

Hypertext Markup Language

The text in an HTML document is plain text, or ASCII.

Images are inserted

wherever there is a tag that gives the filename of the image.

Hypertext links are also created with tags. The filename of a local document or the complete URL (Uniform Resource Locator) of an external document precedes the link text, and a closing tag follows. As an example of an external link, I offer Yahoo! As an example of a local document, I offer my home page.

"Typographer's quotation marks" cannot be used in HTML; neither can true dashes -- or other marks that do not appear on an old-style typewriter.

The number of spaces between words or between lines of text has no effect on formatting in HTML.

Figure 8-5B

The same file opened in Lynx. Lynx is a text-only Web browser that provides Web access to many people, including those using older computers with limited memory (see Appendix A). Note that everything in our file, including the two hypertext links, works adequately in Lynx — except the graphics. If we had used the ALT attribute in the `<IMG>` tag (see page 140), we could have prevented the word "[INLINE]" from appearing in the second paragraph.

well.com 1

```
                                          An HTML Example (p1 of 2)

                        Hypertext Markup Language

      ____________________________________________________________

   The text in an HTML document is plain text, or ASCII.

   Images are inserted
   wherever there is a tag that gives the filename [INLINE] of the image.

   Hypertext links are also created with tags. The filename of a local
   document or the complete URL (Uniform Resource Locator) of an external
   document precedes the link text, and a closing tag follows. As an
   example of an external link, I offer Yahoo! As an example of a local
   document, I offer my home page.

   "Typographer's quotation marks" cannot be used in HTML; neither can
   true dashes -- or other marks that do not appear on an old-style
   typewriter.

-- press space for next page --
  Arrow keys: Up and Down to move. Right to follow a link; Left to go back.
 H)elp O)ptions P)rint G)o M)ain screen Q)uit /=search [delete]=history list
```

4. You will get a dialog box that allows you to choose where (on your own hard drive) to save the image. Choose a directory or folder (such as *temp*) and click the **Save** button. (You may want to create a separate directory just for Web images.)

Never copy an image from the Web unless you have permission from the person who created the image. Otherwise, you would be violating copyright (see "Scanned Images," page 147).

There are a number of Web sites that provide free clip art. Such sites clearly identify themselves and plainly state that their images may be freely copied. Here are some of the better sites:

Ender Design: Realm Graphics
http://www.ender-design.com/rg/
A big collection of nice backgrounds, bullets, buttons, icons, lines.

Icon Bazaar
http://www.iconbazaar.com/
A vast site with hundreds of icons of all kinds.

Kira's Icon Library
http://www59.metronet.com/kicons/
High-quality original buttons, icons, lines, background textures.

Pixelsight
http://www.pixelsight.com/
An amazing array of beautiful graphics; registration required (but still free).

Texture Land
http://www.meat.com/textures/
A treasure trove of wild background textures.

Your own original images

To create your own images for the Web, you need a graphics program. Some of these cost hundreds of dollars (notably, Adobe Photoshop); some cost less than $100. You can get very good effects with an inexpensive program. If you have no artistic skills, even the most expensive program won't help you. If that's the case, you should rely on clip art (or hire an artist).

JASC Inc.'s **Paint Shop Pro (http://www.jasc.com/psp.html)** can do just about everything you will ever need. This full-featured Windows paint program saves in (and converts) many file formats, resizes beautifully, and has too many other features to name, for under US$75.

Fractal Design Corp.'s **Dabbler (http://www.fractal.com/products/dabbler/)**, for both Windows and Mac, is a very nice paint program for under US$75, and it's fun to use. Its options for saving

Draw programs create separate objects, such as boxes, circles, and blocks of text, that can be dragged around on the screen, scaled, copied, cut, and pasted. *Paint* programs provide more artistic effects, often including smoother lines (called anti-aliasing), but cut or copied selections can't be easily repositioned once they have been pasted.

in different file formats are limited, though, so you would also need GIF/JPEG conversion software (see below).

For Mac only, Adobe Systems' **SuperPaint Deluxe (http://www.adobe.com/prodindex/superpaint/)** provides a wide range of both draw and paint functions for about US$100. Its options for saving in different file formats are also limited, so you would also need conversion software (see "Web Graphics File Formats," page 148).

Scanned images

If you have access to a scanner, you may be tempted to scan photographs and artwork to add to your Web pages. There are two important concerns: copyright and image size.

Copyright. In most cases, you are within your legal rights only when you scan a photo you took or artwork you created. Even though no one may hold copyright on an ancient cave painting, the photograph of that painting is almost certainly copyrighted. The same is true of museum artworks, regardless of their age, and comic-strip characters. Even copyright-free clip art printed in a book may be protected from digital reproduction. If a permission statement regarding reproduction does not clearly include digital media, assume that they are excluded. (For more information on copyright, see Appendix D.)

Image file size. Scanned image files are usually large, often exceeding 100K. That is much too large a file for a Web page.

Image size

> "Every day my modem seems to get slower. No, it's not broken. Rather, more and more sites ... use the latest and greatest fancy graphics with frames and images that flash and move repeatedly, and Java applets that make new things happen non-stop. There seems to be some law of human nature on the Internet that everyone needs to push the limits of the technology, using all the graphics and multimedia effects that they possibly can, to prove to themselves and to the world that they can do it. I ask myself — what are they communicating? What's the content?"
>
> — Richard Seltzer, "Low-Tech Web-Page Design," B&R Samizdat Express
> http://www.samizdat.com/lowtech.html

The most important thing to know about Web images is this: the smaller, the better. By "small," we mean the file size, not how big the image looks on the screen. There are various ways to see how large a file is; often your graphics program can tell you. Image files are reduced in size when they are saved in GIF or JPEG format (see below). You can further reduce the file size by saving the image with fewer colors or by trimming the edges of the image.

Any image larger than 35K is questionable for use on the Web. Images larger than 50K can rarely be defended.

If you overtax a Web page with too many images that take too long to load, people visiting your page are likely to be annoyed. You may think it looks fantastic, but others will lose patience and go on to another, faster-loading page — without even reading yours.

Web graphics file formats

Images must be in a particular file format before a Web browser can display them.

A file format is a pattern for storing information. Word processing files, for example, can be stored in plain text format or in a special format such as MS Word or WordPerfect.

There are many different file formats for graphics files. Only two are commonly used for Web images: GIF and JPEG. As a rule of thumb, GIF is usually better for drawings, icons, and other simple images. JPEG is usually better for photographs, paintings, and other highly detailed images. If you copy an image from the Web, it will almost always be in one of these two formats.

If you have an image that is not in GIF or JPEG format, you must convert the image before you can display it on a Web page. To do so, open the image and then save it in the format you want. Many, but not all, graphics programs allow this. (You get a list of file format options when you choose **File | Save As...** within a graphics program.)

If your graphics program does not include these file formats, you can use graphics conversion software (usually free; see below) to open and save your file.

It's not always enough simply to save the file in the right format. Web browsers expect the filename of an image to have an extension (either *.gif* or *.jpg*). When you save a graphic as a GIF file in Windows, the filename will automatically end with *.gif* (and when you save a JPEG file, it will end with *.jpg*). Mac users may have to add the correct extension manually, depending on the graphics software they use.

Recommended graphics software

Below are some programs you may find useful for viewing, converting, or editing Web graphics.

WINDOWS 3.1 AND WINDOWS 95

GIF Construction Set
http://www.mindworkshop.com/alchemy/gifcon.html
A collection of tools for editing GIFs, creating animated GIFs, and creating transparent backgrounds.

LView Pro
http://world.std.com/~mmedia/lviewp.html
This viewer is excellent for creating transparent backgrounds. It also performs complex color-correction functions.

Map This!
http://www.ecaetc.ohio-state.edu/tc/mt/
Creates image maps (Windows 95 only); free.

MACINTOSH

Clip2GIF
http://iawww.epfl.ch/Staff/Yves.Piguet/clip2gif-home/clip2gif.html
Coverts PICT and GIF files to JPEGs, GIFs, or PICTs; adds interlacing and creates transparent backgrounds. Free.

GifBuilder
http://iawww.epfl.ch/Staff/Yves.Piguet/clip2gif-home/GifBuilder.html
From the same author as Clip2GIF, this program creates animated GIFs. Free.

JPEGview
(Download from **http://www.zdnet.com/macuser/software/ or http://www.shareware.com/**)
This viewer converts and resizes GIFs and JPEGs, and modifies color palettes. Free (postcard-ware).

WebMap
(Download from **http://www.zdnet.com/macuser/software/ or http://www.shareware.com/**)
Creates image maps.

Screen colors and Web browsers

Before you go wild with graphics on your Web pages, you should know that Web browsers display fewer than 256 colors. This can cause some very ugly effects if your computer is set to display millions of colors while you are creating images. What looks great on your screen may look appalling on someone else's. For a full explanation (and ways to compensate for this limited palette), see these two pages:

The Browser Safe Color Palette
http://www.lynda.com/hex.html

Victor Engel's No Dither Netscape Color Palette
http://www.onr.com/user/lights/netcol.html

Adding color to text and backgrounds

Apart from adding images to your Web pages, you can make your text, links, and page background just about any color you like (within the limited palette, that is). This is done by adding codes within the `<BODY>` tag of the HTML document. The codes — actually, hexadecimal numbers — represent a value of red plus

ColorMaker is a Web site that lets you try out different color combinations and supplies the necessary codes for you to use on your own pages, making color selection very easy. You'll find it at: **http://www.missouri.edu/~wwwtools/colormaker/**

green plus blue (RGB; the color model used by your computer monitor) by using three pairs of characters: 00, 33, 66, 99, CC, or FF. For example, 000000 is black, FFFFFF is white, FF0000 is bright red, 990099 is purple, and 00FF00 is a rather blinding shade of green.

In the following example, the body tag sets the page colors to a black background with white text and red links; the followed links (VLINK) are purple, and the activated link (ALINK), which you see for only a moment as you press the mouse button, is blinding green:

```
<BODY BGCOLOR=#000000 TEXT=#FFFFFF
LINK=#FF0000 VLINK=#990099 ALINK=#00FF00>
```

To learn more about using graphics on the Web, including how to superimpose text on a background image on a Web page, see the additional resources listed at the end of this chapter.

HTML editor software

Software can handle the HTML coding for you. Some HTML editor programs display the HTML tags; many hide them from you altogether.

The advantages to using an HTML editor program are:

- You may never need to learn any HTML.
- Because you don't type the tags yourself, you won't make typographical errors that affect the appearance of the Web page.

The drawbacks of using an HTML editor are:

- You have to learn how to use the software (when you could be learning HTML directly instead).
- Your ability to control how your Web pages look is somewhat reduced.
- You'll have to wait for the next version of the HTML editor program before you can incorporate new HTML features developed after the editor program was released.

Our view is that it's still better to learn HTML. In the future, when the editor software is better, that might not be true. However, many people like the existing HTML editors, so you may like them too. Also, some Web designers use an HTML editor to do the "first draft" of a Web page and then fine-tune it in a text editor.

You can download a demo or trial version of most programs, so try before you buy. Most of the HTML editors have a list price between US$100 and $150, unless otherwise noted below. Pricing details are available on the Web sites.

WINDOWS 3.1 AND WINDOWS 95

HotDog (Sausage Software)
http://www.sausage.com/

Widely used and well-liked; separate 32-bit version (Windows 95). Download a free 30-day evaluation copy.

HTML Assistant Pro (Brooklyn North Software Works)
http://www.brooknorth.com/
Well-regarded; there is a new version for Windows 95. Download a free copy.

HTMLed (shareware)
http://www.ist.ca/htmled/
Download a full copy of either 16-bit (Windows 3.1) or 32-bit (Windows 95) version.

InContext Spider (InContext Systems)
http://www.incontext.ca/products/spider1.html
Offers templates, ready-to-use graphics, sounds; discount price for online purchase. Download a free 30-day evaluation copy.

WebEdit (Nesbitt Software)
http://www.nesbitt.com/products.html
Many features; separate version for Windows 95. Download a free 30-day evaluation copy.

WINDOWS 95 ONLY

FrontPage 97 (Microsoft)
http://www.microsoft.com/frontpage/
"Drag and drop" editing and many features; Bonus Pack includes graphics.

HomeSite for Windows 95 (shareware)
http://www.dexnet.com/homesite.html
Many features; US$40. Separate free version also available to download.

MACINTOSH

BBEdit (Bare Bones Software)
http://www.barebones.com/
Many Web authors and developers love this word processing program with HTML add-ons. HTML tools are included with the software on a CD-ROM for US$119. Download a "lite" version free.

HTML Editor (shareware)
http://dragon.acadiau.ca/~giles/HTML_Editor/Documentation.html
Simple, reliable; displays HTML tags in color-coded format. US$25. Download full version from:
ftp://cs.dal.ca/giles/

PageMill (Adobe)
http://www.adobe.com/prodindex/pagemill/main.html
Well liked by many Web developers for its ease of use and Macintosh "drag and drop" features.

PageSpinner (shareware)
http://www.algonet.se/~optima/pagespinner.html
Spiffy features and "drag and drop"; US$25.

BOTH WINDOWS AND MACINTOSH

Claris Home Page (Claris)
http://www.claris.com/products/products.html
Complete automated Web page production without HTML.

HoTMetal Pro (SoftQuad)
http://www.sq.com/products/hotmetal/
The Windows version is well-liked, but Mac users have been less enthusiastic. Download a free evaluation copy.

Internet Assistant for MS Word (Microsoft)
http://www.microsoft.com/word/fs_wd.htm
For MS Word 6.0 and higher; works within MS Word but may be confusing if you're not an MS Word expert. Free via download.

Netscape Navigator Gold (Netscape)
http://merchant.netscape.com/netstore/NAVIGATORS/
Combines the Netscape Navigator Web browser with a "drag and drop" HTML editor; requires a lot of RAM. Download from:
http://www.netscape.com/comprod/mirror/client_download.html

Designing Web content

> "If everything is highlighted, then nothing has prominence. I estimate that it costs the world economy about half a million dollars in lost user productivity every time we add one more design element to Sun's home page. It is the responsibility of the Web editor to prioritize the information space for the user and to point out a very small number of recommended information objects."
>
> — Jakob Nielsen, Sun Microsystems Distinguished Engineer,
> "Interface Design for Sun's WWW Site"
> http://www.sun.com/sun-on-net/uidesign/

Design means more than pictures. Every document, even a business letter, is designed, and Web pages are no exception.

A simple Web page may include no more than one heading and a short paragraph. The design of such a page is largely dictated by HTML. However, there are two things you should consider adding to each one of your pages:

- **Your e-mail address.** This is equivalent to signing your work on the Web, and it allows your online readers to contact you. People often send a Web author e-mail that corrects an error or suggests related sources, so listing your e-mail address on every page can bring benefits.
- **A link to your home page.** This is another way of signing your work. Anyone anywhere can link to any of your pages, so you

should never assume that a reader will come to a page of yours via a link from another page of yours. If readers can find your home page, they should be able to find more of your work (more about that below).

These two links usually appear at the bottom of the Web page. You might also include the date, especially on any page that you change regularly. It's standard practice to frame this information with the <ADDRESS> tags.

Example:

```
<ADDRESS>
<A HREF="mailto:mmcadams@well.com">
mmcadams@well.com</A><BR>
Visit <A HREF="index.html">Mindy's
HomePage</A><BR>
Last updated May 1, 1997
</ADDRESS>
```

Page design

People on the Web like to click more than they like to scroll. That means if you really want people to hang out at your Web site instead of someone else's, you should try to keep your documents short.

How long is too long? Web-savvy writers and designers agree that the limit is about 1,000 words per page.

Admittedly, not all content lends itself to a short, click-happy format. Research reports often can be broken up into sections or chapters, but sometimes the sections themselves are lengthy and cannot be divided further.

As a rule, try to reformat, rewrite, and repurpose your work into 1,000-word chunks (or smaller). When you find it impossible, follow these rules to try to hold readers' attention:

1. Keep your paragraphs short.
2. Use boldface and italics more than you would in print, to highlight key words and phrases that may catch a reader's attention.
3. Insert more headings than you would use in print (they scroll off the screen, so you don't need to worry about having too many).
4. Break out lists whenever you name more than two parallel or corollary items or ideas.

All these practices add variation to the text and increase the chances that readers who begin scrolling through your page at a fast clip (and they will, don't doubt it) will see something to make them stop and read closely.

Navigation

So now you have a dozen little 500-word chunks and you don't know what to do with them?

Therein lies the beauty of hypertext. By creating links in HTML, you can easily connect all your Web pages to your home page. What's more, you can connect them to one another.

If you have only a home page and a few additional pages, you may be satisfied with a simple list of links on your home page and a single link back from each of the other pages. But once you have five or more pages, you should consider a more sophisticated scheme. When a list of links is long, it becomes a liability, just like a long Web page: readers lose interest before they get to the end.

Begin to group your pages into sets of related material. For example, if you're a freelance writer who specializes in travel and food subjects, split your material into two sections. Describe each section briefly on your home page, perhaps highlighting your most recent work. Then send readers off — with a link — to the section that interests them most. Don't worry about which section is better for the series you wrote on the flavors of the Mediterranean; you can link to that from both sections.

For an even larger Web site, such as a newsletter with multiple issues online, be sure to consider the opportunities the Web provides that differ from those in libraries and other cataloguing systems. You are not limited to listing issues by number and by date (which isn't very helpful to browsing readers). Articles with related topics can be linked together; links to something new can even be added to an older article.

Navigation is simply getting around. Make sure that anyone who finds any of your pages can figure out how to get around to see your other pages.

If you're in charge of a Web site with changing content, the home page should reflect that. Readers are likely to bookmark the home page and check back to see what's new. Don't hide that information! Show it off, preferably near the top of the page.

A word about graphics

Pretty pictures deserve a lot of credit for making the Web popular and fun. But too many images on one page will make that page load very slowly, and people may not hang around to see what comes up.

When you have something to say, don't interfere with your message by scattering images all over your Web pages. Similarly, large background images and gaudy colors can get in the way.

You may be tempted to add a number of buttons, fancy borders, and three-dimensional titles just because you can. These things have their place, but think carefully about whether they really enhance what you're trying to get across.

A small, simple, original image repeated in a consistent manner can look very slick and professional, while a grab bag of mismatched clip art screams "Amateur!"

Putting your Web pages online

After you have created your Web pages, you must get them onto a Web server. The procedure for doing this differs depending on what kind of Internet account you have.

If your Web access is part of an account with a commercial online service, such as CompuServe or America Online, contact the service provider to find out what procedure to use.

With other kinds of full-service Internet accounts (SLIP/PPP), you may have to transfer your files by using file transfer protocol (FTP). Some Internet service providers offer other methods (some of which are simpler). Check with your ISP.

Transferring your files via FTP will be much easier if you use Fetch (Macintosh) or WS-FTP (Windows). You can download either of these free programs from: **http://www.shareware.com/**

If you have Web access through your job, you may not be permitted to put your own pages online. If that's so, consider getting your own personal Internet account.

If you're at a university, putting your Web pages online may be as simple as saving the HTML files and images to a certain directory. In other cases, you may have to contact someone who can set up a private directory on the university's computer for you. Contact the university computer services staff to find out what to do.

How to publicize your Web site

If you build it, will they come? Not unless they know about it. To let strangers know about your Web page, you will have to do some self-promotion.

The first step is to register your home page with the most popular search engines and directories on the Web (page 156; see also Chapter 4). This will ensure that people looking for something like your page will be able to find it. You may want to register some individual pages in addition to your home page, but that isn't necessary on all search engines.

From the search engine's or directory's home page, find the link for registering or listing a URL. Go to the appropriate page and follow the instructions there.

The more careful and specific you are when registering, the more people will be able to find your pages. For that reason, we don't recommend using a one-stop registration form such as SubmitIt! (http://www.submit-it.com/). Above all, don't make any typographical errors in your URLs! (It's safest to copy and paste the text of a URL to avoid mistakes.) Also be sure to describe your site accurately and well when you have the opportunity. If there's a word limit, stay within it. For directories that allow you to register your page in a specific category, take some time to consider which category is best.

You can also post an article announcing your pages to the newsgroup *comp.infosystems.www.announce*, if you're familiar with Usenet (see Chapter 6). Make sure that the subject line accurately

Most important search engines for registering your Web site:

AltaVista	http://www.altavista.digital.com/
Lycos	http://www.lycos.com/
Yahoo	http://www.yahoo.com/

Also important:

Excite	http://www.excite.com/
HotBot	http://www.hotbot.com/
Infoseek	http://www.infoseek.com/
OpenText	http://www.opentext.com/
WebCrawler	http://www.webcrawler.com/

To find other sites where you may want to promote your pages, see the directory at:

http://www.a1co.com/ (that's a numeral one, not a lowercase L).

(and concisely) represents the contents of your page. You can also search for other suitable newsgroups on search engines such as AltaVista (set the Search option to *Usenet*).

A great way to promote your Web site is to list it in the *sig* (signature file) that you attach to e-mail messages. That way, anyone who receives mail from you will know you have a Web page — including everyone on any mailing lists you belong to. If the topic of a mailing list is related to information on your Web pages, you can send a message to the list to announce your new pages (or, later, to announce a significant update).

Consider using a mailing-list search engine (such as **Liszt** at **http://www.liszt.com/**) to find a list suitable for announcing your pages (see Chapter 6 on listservs). The copy editors' list (Copyediting-L), for example, would be a fine place to publicize a page on grammar tips but a poor place to promote a page about photojournalism.

Under no circumstances should you announce your pages in an inappropriate place; that would only breed ill will toward you. Remember that there are now millions of Web pages on hundreds of thousands of sites, and yours will appeal only to specific groups of people. It's in your interest to seek out those groups and speak directly to them.

Although you won't need to know anything else to get started, you may want to learn more about HTML after you have created several Web pages. Everything you could ever need is available free on the Web, so happy surfing!

Writing for the Web: Additional resources

Introduction to HTML and URLs
http://www.utoronto.ca/webdocs/HTMLdocs/NewHTML/intro.html
A clear, straightforward reference by Ian Graham, author of *The HTML Sourcebook*; very clear explanations.

The Bare Bones Guide to HTML
http://werbach.com/barebones/
An excellent, exhaustive reference (but not a tutorial) to HTML 3.2 and the Netscape extensions, by Kevin Werbach.

Webreference.com
HTML tutorials:
http://www.webreference.com/html/tutorials.html
HTML specifications:
http://www.webreference.com/html/specs.html
Web graphics information:
http://www.webreference.com/graphics/

HotWired's Webmonkey
http://www.webmonkey.com/
Tons of tips in a how-to article format; particularly good information on tables and frames in the "HTML" section.

The Bandwidth Conservation Society
http://www.infohiway.com/faster/
Information on how to make your Web pages load faster, especially by tweaking your graphics.

The HTML Writers Guild
http://www.hwg.org/
A well-organized collection of tips, tutorials, and FAQs (answers to Frequently Asked Questions).

Yale C/AIM WWW Style Manual
http://info.med.yale.edu/caim/StyleManual_Top.HTML
High-level style advice; see also a critique of this manual at:
http://www.mcs.net/~jorn/html/net/klown.html

World Wide Web Consortium: HTML http://www.w3.org/hypertext/WWW/MarkUp/
This is the original source for all up-to-date HTML information (technical), but the site is difficult to navigate.

Introducing HTML 3.2
http://www.w3.org/pub/WWW/MarkUp/Wilbur/
All the details about the latest HTML draft specification (technical).

Further reading

Krol, Ed. *The Whole Internet: User's Guide & Catalog* (2nd ed.). Sebastopol, CA: O'Reilly & Associates, 1994.
http://www.ora.com/www/item/twi2.html

Lemay, Laura. *Teach Yourself Web Publishing with HTML 3.2: The Professional Reference Edition*. Indianapolis: Sams.Net Publishing, 1996.
http://www.lne.com/Web/Professional/index.html

Lemay, Laura. *Teach Yourself Web Publishing with HTML 3.2 in a Week* (3rd ed.). Indianapolis: Sams.Net Publishing, 1996.
http://www.lne.com/Web/HTML3.2/

Weinman, Lynda. *Designing Web Graphics*. New Riders Publishing, 1996.
http://www.lynda.com/dwg/dwg.html

Epilogue

"Remember that the technology, in and of itself does nothing. Rather, it makes it possible for you to shape your own world-within-the-world."

— Richard Seltzer, "Internet Advice for Newcomers"
http://www.samizdat.com/news20.html#newcomers

Learning to use the Internet efficiently and confidently is an accomplishment. But in the world of technology, the learning never stops.

The Internet is constantly surging ahead in new and often unexpected directions. New products, services, and technologies appear at such a breakneck pace that even high-tech professionals are hard pressed to keep abreast of the latest developments. One technology analyst recently claimed that a not-yet-released update of a popular Web browser had already been surpassed by a not-yet-released product from a competitor. For those who work at the leading edge of technology, it is a constant battle to remain in front.

We are regularly informed about developments — always just around the corner — that will transform the way we work and live:

- modems that will transmit data through radio waves, rather than through wires
- pocket computers that will run sophisticated applications such as videoconferencing
- miniature devices that will allow us to control our cars, home appliances, and office equipment via the Internet
- more — and more varied — electronic commerce.

Coping with all this change requires a continuing willingness to learn. We are still experimenting with the practical aspects of the Internet, and it is sometimes difficult not to be overwhelmed by the technology itself.

For writers, researchers, and journalists, the future of technology is not so much about smaller computer chips, faster modems, and the latest electronic gizmos, but rather about virtual offices and schools, online collaborations, and global communities — processes that are enabled by technology, but defined by people. Although technology will continue to move forward, people will embrace it only to the extent that it serves some practical human purpose.

Like other users of the Internet, information professionals can expect to have to continue learning. But — unlike the technicians who are bound by the rules of the technology marketplace — we have the luxury of selecting areas of learning that have practical and immediate value to our work.

INFO*nugget*

The market for electronic goods and services is expected to reach ten billion dollars or more over the next three years, with individual households pegged to have conducted 120 online transactions by the year 2000.

If you are a writer, researcher, editor, or journalist, your most important Internet skill will be to gain confidence in finding and using the myriad resources of the Net. Once you've learned the basics of online navigation, there are no mandatory benchmarks for mastering more — though there will always be more to discover.

One of the greatest opportunities for information professionals today is the possibility of helping to shape this new cyber world, as content creators and experts. Your own interests and abilities will determine whether this challenge is for you.

The authors of this book like to think that using the Internet is a bit like owning a piece of real estate. If it suits you, you can build a mansion — say, dozens of skillfully developed Web pages featuring your work. Or, you can just settle for a meadow — in which you ramble contentedly among the unruly, exuberant growth.

The greatest delight of the Internet is that it offers so many possibilities.

Appendix A

Lynx: A text-based Web browser

Lynx is a text-only browser that is commonly available on university- or library-based computers and public freenets. You may need to use Lynx as your Web browser if you are accessing the Web through a shell account (rather than a PPP or SLIP connection).

Because Lynx does not capture the Web's multimedia features, it is not most people's browser of choice. On the plus side, this very shortcoming also means that Lynx can be a faster way of navigating the Web. It has other practical features as well, such as its ability to automatically mail a document that is displayed.

Lynx has an excellent help function. Typing **h** for **help** gives you access to several general information guides, an explanation of the various keystroke commands, and the Lynx User's Guide.

There are also a number of powerful features within Lynx, such as the ability to search for a particular term within a document.

Find out more about Lynx's features by accessing the Lynx User's Guide from within the online **help** menu. Basic Lynx commands are listed below.

Navigating in Lynx: Key commands

You can navigate within Lynx by using the cursor (arrow) keys on your keyboard. These keys let you move to links within a document, which will be highlighted on your screen. Press **enter** or the right arrow key to display a Web page on the chosen topic.

Down arrow (or tab)	Highlight the next topic (or link)
Up arrow	Highlight previous topic
Right arrow	Jump to highlighted topic
Return, enter	Jump to a topic
Left arrow	Move up a screen (or back to the previous page)

Scrolling (moving up or down the page):

+ (or space)	Scroll down to next page
– (or b)	Scroll up to previous page

Other:

? (or h or H)	Help (screen)
a	Add current link to bookmark file
v	View bookmark links
=	View URL for link
d	Download current link
e	Edit current file
g	Go to a specified URL (brings up a prompt requesting the URL)
i	Show index of documents
m	Return to main screen
o	Set options (e.g., default address for mail)
p	Print file
Control G	Cancel input or transfer
/	Search currently displayed text
q	Quit
Q	Quick quit
z	Cancel transfer in progress
\	View source file (showing HTML tags)

Appendix B

Resources on the Web

The following selection of useful Internet links will be of particular interest to writers, researchers, journalists, editors, and students. Although the list is not comprehensive, it illustrates the range of resources on the Internet and, in many cases, may suggest starting points for research.

The list contains two sections: *Professional and Internet Resources* and *General Interest Resources.*

In *Part I: Professional and Internet Resources*, we have included sources that reflect the primary themes of this book. These include information about the Internet itself, as well as material directly relevant to information professionals. We have identified key reference areas — such as news sources, journalism links, and writing resources — and have developed these in some depth. Included in this section as well are sources pertinent to government, distance education, student information, and employment. The long list of Internet references will enable you to learn more about the technology and keep up with new developments.

In *Part II: General Interest Resources*, we have provided shorter lists of links to information on a broader range of subjects. Included here are topics that are frequently in the news; starting points for research in such areas as arts, sciences, and social sciences; and miscellaneous useful information resources.

These links are far from exhaustive; rather, they are highly selective. Deciding which general-interest topics and links to include was a major challenge. Our rule of thumb, if we had one, was to include the kinds of topics that we ourselves, as information professionals, want to know about.

Many of our favorite sources are highlighted in the chapters; for the most part, these are not duplicated here. We have assumed that, if you have taken time to explore the sites listed in the chapters, you will already have added your favorites to your personal hotlist. If not, be sure to refer back to the sites mentioned in the chapters, along with using this Appendix.

Contents

5. Media
6. Online Books
7. Online Newspapers and Magazines
8. Resources for Journalists
9. Resources for Writers
10. Resources for Editors
11. Resources for Students
12. Distance Learning
13. Job Resources

Part II: General Interest Resources

1. Arts and Culture
2. Business and Economics
3. Disability Information
4. Education
5. Entertainment
6. Environment
7. Health
8. History
9. Human Rights
10. Language
11. Law
12. Literature and Book Reviews
13. Locations
14. Mathematics
15. Politics
16. Science and Technology
17. Social Sciences
18. Sports
19. Travel
20. Women
21. Odds and Ends

We invite you to use the links listed here as starting points for Internet exploration. If we've been successful in introducing you to the Internet, you will soon have a hotlist of your own favorite resources. We hope that our list of sites will encourage you to develop your personal, and undoubtedly unique, perspective on the Internet.

Part I: Professional and Internet Resources

1. General reference

ACRONYMS

Acronym Dictionary. Offered as part of Carnegie Mellon University's English Server, this site lists acronyms in full text, so no searching is required.
http://english-www.hss.cmu.edu/langs/acronym-dictionary.txt

The Acronym Expander. Appropriately, this is probably the smallest Web site in the world. Type in an acronym, and it will tell you what it knows about who might own the mysterious letters.
http://habrok.uio.no/cgi-bin/acronyms

ATLASES

BigBook. U.S. addresses, including street maps. Astonishing!
http://www.bigbook.com/

MapQuest. Look up your friend in Miami or a place name you're not sure how to spell. This interactive atlas shows you the United States and major cities around the world. You can zoom in and find a building on a certain street, or zoom out to find out how to get there using major highways.
http://mapquest.com/

National Atlas Information System (NAIS). Source for Canadian geographical information.
http://www-nais.ccm.emr.ca/schoolnet/

Perry-Castaneda Library Map Collection. This is a major collection with more than 230,000 maps covering every area of the world. Maps for Bosnia, Middle East, Asia, Africa, etc.
http://www.lib.utexas.edu/Libs/PCL/Map_collection/Map_collection.html

Tiger Mapping Service. Provides a public resource for generating detailed maps of anywhere in the United States, using public geographic data. Includes a U.S. Gazetteer.
http://tiger.census.gov/

U.S. Gazetteer. The U.S. Census Bureau's official map service. Look up a place in the United States by name or zip code, then obtain census data for that location.
http://www.census.gov/cgi-bin/gazetteer

CITATION STYLE SHEETS

APA Style of Notation. Covers points of citation per the *Publication Manual of the American Psychological Association*, the preferred style guide in many social sciences.
http://www.uvm.edu/~xli/reference/apa.html

Beyond the MLA. Handbook for citations by Harnack & Kleppinger; includes models for documenting Internet sources.
http://falcon.eku.edu/honors/beyond-mla/#citing_sites

MLA-Style Citations of Electronic Sources. Uses the MLA style preferred by most university English departments.
http://www.cas.usf.edu/english/walker/mla.html

Pitsco's Launch to Citing Online Addresses. Pointers to a number of citation sources.
http://www.pitsco.inter.net/p/cite.html

DATABASES

(See also references in Chapter 5)

Database of Canadian Databases. Links to more than 60 databases of governments, foundations, and corporations, compiled by the Ryerson Institute for Computer-Assisted Reporting in Canada.
http://www.ryerson.ca/~ricarc/database.html

Internet Sleuth. From arts to zoology, search several online databases with just one query.
http://www.isleuth.com/

Research-It. This is an all-purpose reference site. Search language, financial, geographic and other useful tools.
http://www.iTools.com/research-it/research-it.html.

Webtaxi. Quick access to major search engines as well as access to specialized databases in arts, business, health, and other categories.
http://www.webtaxi.com

DICTIONARIES

The Dictionary of Phrase and Fable. The full text of E. Cobham Brewer's classic reference, which explains the origins of English phrases and defines characters from myths and fables.
http://www.bibliomania.com/Reference/PhraseAndFable.html

Hypertext Webster Interface. Simply type in the word you're seeking and the interface searches through Webster's online services to find a definition. You can link to many words contained in the definition. You can also look up the word in the thesaurus to get synonyms.
http://c.gp.cs.cmu.edu:5103/prog/webster?

Index of Online Dictionaries. Search service for comprehensive set of English and multilingual dictionaries. Links to A Web of Online Grammars.
http://www.bucknell.edu/~rbeard/diction.html

Notable Citizens of Planet Earth Biographical Dictionary. Facts on 18,000 figures from the past and present.
http://www.search.com/Single/0,7,200482-50072,00.html

One Look Dictionaries. Access to 79 dictionaries (at last count!), including science, medical, business, and other specialized dictionaries.
http://www.onelook.com/

Online Language Dictionaries and Translators. From Afrikaans to Zulu, more than 60 languages are represented with links to dictionaries that translate to and from English and any number of other languages.
http://rivendel.com/~ric/resources/dictionary.html

Robert Beard's Index of Online Dictionaries. If it's a language spoken by humans (or Klingons — even that *Star Trek* tongue is here!) you'll find a link to a dictionary from this site. Includes dictionaries in specialized fields.
http://www.bucknell.edu/~rbeard/diction.html

ENCYCLOPEDIAS

Encyclopedia Britannica. You can try out this mammoth resource for seven days for free, then you'll be sent information by e-mail on how to buy a subscription. You can retrieve full-text articles containing links to related articles in the encyclopedia, and also links to related sites elsewhere on the Web.
http://www.eb.com

World Factbook. Vital statistics on virtually every country in the world, compiled annually by the Central Intelligence Agency. Each country gets its own page with a map showing major cities and the capital, and including statistics on geography, government, the people, economy, and the military.
http://www.odci.gov/cia/publications/95fact/index.html

LIBRARIES AND LIBRARY RESOURCES

Beyond Bookmarks. Schemes for organizing the Web using traditional library classification systems.
http://www.public.iastate.edu/~CYBERSTACKS/CTW.htm

Canadian Information by Subject. An extensive subject tree with links to Canadian sites, compiled by the National Library of Canada. Subjects are arranged by the Dewey Decimal classification system.
http://www.nlc-bnc.ca/caninfo/ecaninfo.htm

Electric Library. This is a full-text service, meaning that entire magazine and newspaper articles and encyclopedia entries are displayed onscreen. You simply type in a subject keyword and the screen displays up to 30 items containing that word. It's free to search the library, which gives you the periodical's name and date so that you can look it up in a real public library. But there is a cost if you want to download the actual text.
http://www.elibrary.com

Infomine. This is a virtual reference tool that will be of particular interest to university-level researchers. More than 8,500 academic sources. Separate virtual collections exist for the broad disciplines of Biological, Agricultural and Medical Resources, Government Information, Physical Sciences, Social Sciences, and Humanities.
http://lib-www.ucr.edu/govpub/

Library of Congress Classification System. A California librarian has written an unofficial guide on how to understand the Library of Congress Classification System. Helps take the guesswork out of library research.
http://www.geocities.com/Athens/8459/lc.html

Library Resource List. List of 120 carefully selected sources. Developed for professional librarians, but of interest for its lists of reference and government sources.
http://www.state.wi.us/agencies/dpi/www/ref_res.htm

MELVYL. Library system of the University of California provides access to University of California library materials and a number of databases produced by libraries or organizations. Telnet-only access is gradually being integrated onto the Web. Some of the resources are available for U.C. affiliates only.
http://www.melvyl.ucop.edu/

My Virtual Reference Desk. Includes Virtual Facts on File, Virtual Newspaper, and Virtual Encyclopedia.
http://www.refdesk.com/

National Library of Canada. Subject access to Canadian information on the Internet.
http://www.nlc-bnc.ca/

SJCPL's Public Library Servers. This page has a searchable database of dozens of public libraries around the world that are online. You can also link directly to their home pages from a list of Web sites. Operated by the St. Joseph County Public Library in South Bend, Indiana.
http://sjcpl.lib.in.us/Databases/PubLibServFind.html

UnCover. This is "an online article delivery service, a table of contents database, and a keyword index to nearly 17,000 periodicals." It's free to search the database, but there is a fee for every article ordered. Articles are added the same day the publication hits the newsstands.
http://www.carl.org/uncover

Virtual Library. This is essentially a megalist of smaller lists arranged by subject, ranging from aboriginal studies to zoos. Each list is maintained by an expert in that field. The list links companies and organizations with sites related to the topic.

http://www.w3.org/hypertext/DataSources/bySubject/Overview.html

webCATS: Library Catalogs on the World Wide Web. Links to hundreds of online library catalogs around the world, arranged by region and library type.

http://library.usask.ca/hywebcat/

Z39.50. The Library of Congress has established a way to make the online catalogs of several libraries available in an easy-to-use format. Simply click on the library (from a listing of many universities in North America and Europe) and its search engine pops up on the screen. Every site looks the same. You can type in three searches at once, based on title, author, subject, and other categories you would normally find in a library catalog. The search results display as bibliographic entries.

http://lcweb.loc.gov/z3950/gateway.html

PHONE BOOKS

Canada 411. This service gives you Yellow Pages and White Pages listings for all the provinces and territories except Alberta and Saskatchewan.

http://canada411.sympatico.ca/

The Directory Organization. Phone, fax, and e-mail contact information for companies and individuals.

http://www.dir.org/

Infospace. Quickly find phone numbers and e-mail addresses.

http://www.infospaceinc.com/

Kapitol International Telephone Directory. Links to online White and Yellow Pages and fax directories from countries around the world. Sites are rated based on ease of use.

http://www.infobel.be/infobel/infobelworld.html

Switchboard. Provides phone numbers for 106 million residential listings and 11 million business listings in the United States.

http://www.switchboard.com

POSTAL CODES

Canada Post Postal Code Guide. Type in a Canadian address and find out its postal code. Conversely, type in a code if you don't know the address, and the guide will provide the location.

http://www.mailposte.ca/english/pclookup/pclookup.html

United States Postal Service. ZIP code lookup and address information. Find a zip code for an address, or find out what city belongs to a zip code.

http://www.usps.gov/ncsc/

QUOTATIONS

Bartlett's Familiar Quotations. From Chaucer to Grover Cleveland, find out who said what and when.

http://www.cc.columbia.edu/acis/bartleby/bartlett

Quotations Page. An eclectic collection of modern quotations.

http://www.starlingtech.com/quotes/

STYLE GUIDES

Elements of Style. Strunk & White's bible of good style, essential for writers and editors. The entire text is online, everything from forming possessives to omitting needless words.

http://www.columbia.edu/acis/bartleby/strunk/

Style Book of the University of Queensland Department of Journalism. Some good pointers on Australian English, and hints for tightening journalistic style.

http://www.uq.oz.au/jrn/stybook.html

THESAURUSES

Roget's Thesaurus. Type in your tired word and out comes a fresh alternative — or six.

http://www2.thesaurus.com/thesaurus/

2. Internet and computers

ELECTRONIC MAIL AND RELATED RESOURCES

Andrew Starr's Eudora Site. Good source of info for Eudora users. Also check out the official Qualcomm site.

http://www.amherst.edu/~atstarr/eudora/eudora.html

Beginner's Guide to Effective E-mail. All about how to write better e-mail.

http://www.webfoot.com/advice/email.top.html

BigFoot. Another people-finding source.

http://www.bigfoot.com

FAQ Finder (Frequently Asked Questions). Source for finding basic information on a wide range of topics.

http://ps.superb.net/FAQ/

The Net: User Guidelines and Netiquette — Index. Introduction to etiquette on the Internet with lots of good tips on using electronic mail and discussion groups.

http://rs6000.adm.fau.edu/rinaldi/net/index.htm

WebConferencing. David Woolley's site is probably the best place to find out about text-based online conferencing.

http://freenet.msp.mn.us/people/drwool/webconf.html

Whowhere? Find e-mail addresses worldwide and phone numbers in the United States.

http://www.whowhere.com

INTERNET FACTS

CyberAtlas. This source will help you track current and useful information on Web demographics and usage.

http://www.imagescape.com/new/users.html

The Open Market Internet Index. A monthly compilation of useful, interesting and just plain quirky Internet facts and figures.

http://www.openmarket.com/intindex/

Parallax Webdesign Internet Facts. A serious look at how the Internet is affecting global trade and communications. Includes figures on Internet use and profiles users in terms of demographics, education level, and home vs. office use.

http://www.echonyc.com/~parallax/interfacts.html

INTERNET STARTING POINTS AND GUIDES

(See also references in Chapters 3 and 4)

All-in-One-Search Page. Comprehensive search page that includes software searching.

http://www.albany.net/allinone/

Beaucoup! More than 800 links to sites useful to anyone doing research on the Web. Arranged according to broad categories such as media, reference, languages, literature, science and technology, and politics and government. The best feature is its direct search engine forms for looking up information on other sites.

http://www.beaucoup.com/

Cyberhound. This is another resource for searching the Web. The advantage here is that the sites have been selected as among the best by the publishers of Gale Directories, a respected source of information in the pre-Internet era.

http://www.thomson.com/cyberhound/homepage.html

eDirectory. Most search engines are so global that sometimes you can cast your net too wide. If you're only looking for country-specific information, you can connect to regional search indexes through this all-in-one site. The indexes are neatly arranged according to country.

http://www.edirectory.com/

Essential Links. Neatly organized links to search engines, other starting point directories, news sources, references, and cool Web sites.

http://www.el.com

Lycos Top 5% Web Sites. In addition to serving as a general purpose starting page, this site includes a search for the best of the best in a variety of categories.

http://www.pointcom.com/categories

Mansfield Cybrarian (Cornell University). Orderly and well-developed set of links to Internet sources selected and arranged by librarians. Includes access to full-text government information.

http://www.mnsfld.edu/~library/

Planet Earth. Search this virtual library using a graphic floor plan (or text version) or use its internal search engine to explore its database. Querying a subject pulls up 12 links to get you started on your information quest.

http://www.nosc.mil/planet_earth/info.html

Purely Academic. From the Dublin University Internet Society, this is a very good starting point if academic sites are what you are after. Emphasis is on providing direct links to actual research sources.

http://www.netsoc.tcd.ie/Background/

Starting Point. A simple, well-organized collection of links to sites in business, computing, education, entertainment, investing, magazines, news, reference, shopping, sports, travel, and weather.

http://www.stpt.com

Top of the Web. A selection of the best Web sites chosen by professional Internet surfer John December. Links are arranged by category (from art to software) plus a subject guide. Do a keyword search if you're stumped.

http://www.december.com/web/top.html

WebCentral. A comprehensive list of links to general topics (including journalism and writing) plus direct access to search engines, Web page review sites, and e-mail sites.

http://www.cio.com/WebMaster/lm_frontpage.html

Where the Wild Things Are. Librarian's Guide to the Best Information on the Net.

http://www.sau.edu/CWIS/Internet/Wild/index.htm

World Wide Web Yellow Pages
Descriptions of links to more than 200,000 Web sites.

http://www.superlibrary.com/newriders/wwwyp/

INTERNET TUTORIALS

Atlas to the World Wide Web. This is a good place to learn about the Web.
 http://www.rhythm.com/~bpowell/Atlas/toc.htm

Beginners Central. A top site for newcomers to learn about the Internet.
 http://www.digital-cafe.com/~webmaster/begin00.html

Best Information on the Net — Internet Training. Another training source.
 http://www.sau.edu/CWIS/Internet/Wild/Internet/Training/trindex.htm

BKC2SKOL. Librarian-developed introduction to the Internet. Very good set of lessons worth visiting for the subject references alone. There are lessons on science, health, business, etc.
 http://web.csd.sc.edu/bck2skol/fall/fall.html

Charm Net Learning page. This provides links to books, tutorials, and hint sheets for Internet learning as part of the home page for the Charm Net service provider in Baltimore, Maryland.
 http://www.charm.net/learning.html

Getting Technologically Savvy. Learn about online technologies. Topics include Internet searching, newsgroups, listservs.
 http://204.98.1.1/di/savvy.html

Internet Guides, Tutorials, and Training Information. A collection of useful guides from the Library of Congress, many for beginners.
 http://lcweb.loc.gov/global/internet/training.html

Internet Tourbus. Archives for a popular electronic mail course about the Internet. When you subscribe, you receive information via electronic mail about useful sites.
 http://www.worldvillage.com/tourbus.htm

Internet Training. These links are aimed at instructors who provide Internet training, but anyone can use the lesson plans and resources.
 http://www.december.com/cmc/info/internet-training.html

Learn the Net. A comprehensive guide to the Internet, including help with digging for data, using search tools, mailing lists, and databases, exchanging files, and developing Web pages.
 http://www.learnthenet.com/english/thetools/map.htm

Microsoft Library: Internet Resources. Well-organized Internet guide includes helps for beginners.
 http://library.microsoft.com/nethelp.htm

INTERNET UPDATES

The Blue Pages. Monthly reviews of sites on the Web, providing content summaries and ratings. Easy browsing by subject category.
http://www.thenet-usa.com/blue/blue.html

C*net. News and reviews with the latest from the computer world. Includes product reviews, hot Web sites, tips and how-tos to get the most from the Internet.
http://www.cnet.com/

NBNSoft. Detailed weekly reviews of the best that's new.
http://www.tricky.com/liz/

Netsurfer Digest. A weekly online magazine with the latest information on Internet-related topics. You can subscribe to the e-mail version.
http://www.netsurf.com/nsd/

Scout Report. This site gives a weekly round-up of what's new on the Web. It's operated by the University of Wisconsin at Madison and carefully screens new sites for value to researchers and educators. You can subscribe to a mailing list and receive the report, or you can read current and back issues on the Web site and follow the links directly.
http://www.cs.wisc.edu/scout/report/

ZDNet. Independent reviews of the latest Internet sites, computer software, hardware, and games. Advice and how-tos from beginners to advanced.
http://www5.zdnet.com/

MAGAZINES

COOL Doctor. Online magazine with articles on computers, the Web, the Internet, and software. Includes dictionary of computer jargon.
http://www.kww.com/cool/

Internet World. Notable source for Internet information.
http://www.iworld.com/

MacUser. Selected articles, columns, and features from the hard-copy version. Includes product news and reviews.
http://www.zdnet.com/macuser/

PC Computing. Online version of the hard-copy standby. Features include What's Hot, 1001 Downloads, 1001 Best Sites, and Tech Tips.
http://www.zdnet.com/pccomp/

TidBITS. Weekly electronic publication relating to the Mac and the Net.
http://www.tidbits.com/

Top 100 Computer Magazines. Links to online magazines about the Web, Internet, computers, and software.
http://www.internetvalley.com/top100mag.html

What's Hot on the Internet This Week. What's new, with a focus on information-rich sites from the El Dorado County Library. Recent listings have included Pulitzer Prize Winners for 1997 and a site featuring an historical atlas for the twenty-first century. You can browse the hotlist archives to find these and other hotlist selections.
http://www.el-dorado.ca.us/~lib-pl/thisweek.htm

Wired News. The latest from trendy Internet mag, *Wired.*
http://www.wired.com

MAILING LIST INFORMATION

Catalist Listserv Lists. Here you may browse for any of over 12,000 listservs. Search for lists by country or subject, or browse alphabetically.
http://www.lsoft.com/lists/listref.html

DaSilva's Mailing Lists. A searchable list of publicly available mailing lists. An updated list is posted monthly.
http://www.neosoft.com/internet/paml/

Deja News. Usenet news information and search tool.
http://www.dejanews.com

Liszt Newsgroups and Mailing Lists. Comprehensive service that enables you to search for newsgroups and listservs by subject and then subscribe to them from its search results screen.
http://www.liszt.com/

Vivian's List of Lists. A site developed around an original Internet resource for listservers called the "list of lists." The site also provides links to listserver software and mailing list providers.
http://catalog.com/vivian/interest-group-search.html

SOFTWARE

DNet Software Library. Can't find a certain kind of program? Search the software library by keyword to get what you need.
http://www.hotfiles.com/index.html

Jumbo! Shareware. Links to more than 93,000 shareware and freeware programs for all operating systems, including Web authoring tools, spreadsheets, audio, games, animation, screensavers, utilities, and more.
http://www.jumbo.com

Microlib Software Archives. Links to freeware and shareware for Windows, DOS, OS/2 and Macintosh operating systems, from the University of Texas at Austin Computation Center.
http://www.utexas.edu/cc/micro/microlib/

Tucows. Use this resource for downloading Internet software, including HTML editors, browsers, etc. Check "Browser Add-Ons" for software to use when capturing sites for downloading. WebWhacker is an example of an offline capture program.

http://tucows.com/

TECHNICAL HELPS AND TROUBLESHOOTING

Browser Plug-ins for Netscape. There are now more than 100 different plug-ins available to link many different software applications for the Web.

http://www.netscapeworld.com/netscapeworld/common/nw.plugintable.html

BrowserWatch — Plug-In Plaza! Browser plug-in info for all platforms.

http://browserwatch.iworld.com/plug-in.html

Computer Viruses Information. Jeff Frentzen has developed this resource for information on computer viruses.

http://www.pcweek.com/ir/0106/06jia.html

Internet Starter Kit for Macintosh. Online edition of the complete book for Mac users. Good source for pointers to Mac resources.

http://www.mcp.com/hayden/iskm/mac.html

MacFixIt. Practical, easy-to-use solutions for technical problems. Updated three times a week with hints from Mac users who contribute quandaries and tips. Topics are searchable by keyword.

http://www.macfixit.com

Scout Toolkit Latest Technology Pages. Check here regularly to find out about new Internet tools and tricks to make Net life easier.

http://www.cs.wisc.edu/scout/toolkit/latest/index.html

YIL's Surf School. Helpful lessons on a number of technical topics. You can also search for articles appearing in *Yahoo Internet Life*.

http://www.zdnet.com/yil/filters/surfjump.html l

WEB PAGE DEVELOPMENT

Bare Bones Guide to HTML. A handy reference to developing Web pages — in many formats and many languages.

http://werbach.com/barebones/

Homesite. Here's an example of a good, inexpensive editor for Windows 95. FrontPage, PageMill, Netscape Navigator Gold and HotDog Pro are other good editors. (See additional listings for HTML Editors in Chapter 8.)

http://www.dexnet.com/

HTML Goodies. A candy store for Web authors! Tutorials on everything from basic HTML to advanced tables and animated

GIFs. Includes "A Complete List of all HTML Tags and Commands" and "A Glossary of Computer/Internet Terms."
http://www.htmlgoodies.com

HTML Writers Guild. The site of "the first international organization of World Wide Web page authors and Internet Publishing professionals." Geared toward getting new members, but includes links to HTML resources, including writing HTML and design guidelines.
http://www.hwg.org/

The Icon Depot. Over 1,100 graphics for home pages: backgrounds, buttons, etc.
http://www.geocities.com/SiliconValley/6603

LynnsWeb Mastery. A terrifically useful page with pointers to the very best sites for Web page development.
http://fly.hiwaay.net/~nlf/graphics.htm

Terry Gould's Graphics. Download hundreds of free funky graphics for your home page: backgrounds, lines, bars, bullets, buttons, icons, and pictures.
http://webstrands.nas.net/list.html

Webmaster's Reference Library. Use the table of contents to find your way around this extensive information source for Web page development.
http://www.webreference.com

WebMastery. A collection of links to "the BEST Web resources" with free software and advice to help develop your home page. Includes graphics, clip art, sounds, HTML and other guides, resources for kids, and assorted tools to help you design your own graphics and animation.
http://fly.hiwaay.net/~nlf/graphics.htm

OTHER

B&R Samizdat Express. Internet-on-a-Disk, newsletter, electronic books. The newsletter provides interesting commentary and insights on Internet trends. The site also offers links to a number of useful business, education, and disability information sources on the Web. Eclectic, and well worth a visit.
http://www.samizdat.com

December Communications. Excellent set of resources on computer communications, including the monthly Computer-Mediated Communications online magazine.
http://www.december.com/

Electronic Frontier Foundation. This is an important source for

electronic information civil liberties groups. Net culture, censorship, privacy, and related issues are covered.
http://www.eff.org

Impact Online: Internet 101. Guide to the Internet for non-profit organizations.
http://www.impactonline.org/words/internet/index.html

The Informant. An example of a "personal agent." In this case, the agent (a computer program running at Dartmouth University) will track areas of particular interest to you. When you register for the service, you have the opportunity to enter up to three sets of keywords describing your area of interest. After identifying the top Web pages relevant to your topic, the program will then track the pages and inform you (via e-mail) of any changes occurring on your pages, and of any new "top" pages.
http://informant.dartmouth.edu

Internet Resources Newsletter. For academics, students, engineers, scientists, and social scientists, published by Heriot-Watt University in Edinburgh. Back issues provide an amazing list of resources of interest to professional researchers. Unfortunately, the list is not easily searchable.
http://www.hw.ac.uk/libWWW/irn/irn.html

Larry's InfoPower Pages. Larry Schankman provides an excellent overview of Web resources. Tour the net with a guide you can trust. Check out the best of social science sources and government information links, which are outstanding!
http://www.clark.net/pub/lschank

Odd de Presno Online World Resources Handbook. A practical guide to the online world. You can subscribe to regular updates via the Online World Monitor Newsletter. The newsletter provides well researched coverage of special topics, such as The Traveling Modem.
http://login.eunet.no/~presno/index.html

Red RockEater. Always thought provoking, Red RockEater is the brainchild of Philip Agre. He combines his own insightful comments (in "The Network Observer") with the republication of items that capture the social and political aspects of the Internet in a timely fashion. You can receive Red RockEater News by electronic mail.
http://communication.ucsd.edu/pagre/rre.html

3. Government Information

(See also references in Chapter 5)

CANADA

Canada Site (Government of Canada). Information on Canada and

its government. Links to dozens of federal departments, ministries, agencies, and Crown corporations. Includes telephone directory of federal government employees.
http://canada.gc.ca/

Canadian Government Information on the Internet. Compiled by a reference librarian at Mount Allison University, this comprehensive and well-organized site offers links to federal information alphabetically by subject (from Aboriginal People to Veterans), and provincial and municipal information by province. Also has links to discussion groups, library catalogs, and electronic journals.
http://www.lib.uwaterloo.ca/discipline/Government/CanGuide/

Canadian Parliament. Includes frequently asked questions about the House of Commons and Senate, visitor information, and a reference section.
http://parl30.parl.gc.ca/english/

Champlain. Search engine for Canadian government and legal information.
http://Champlain.GNS.CA/champlain.html

Federal Government Departments. Starting point to official Web sites for dozens of federal ministries, agencies, and Crown corporations.
http://canada.gc.ca/depts/major/depind_e.html

Prime Minister's Office. Information direct from the top. Fact sheets, news releases, and speeches from the prime minister of Canada. (You can even e-mail the prime minister.)
http://canada.gc.ca/english/pmo/index.htm

Statistics Canada. Not only the definitive source for official numbers, but also an excellent place to look for trends to yield story ideas. Arranges data according to population, economy, and the land. Includes full-text versions of *The Daily*, a daily newsletter of just-released statistics.
http://www.statcan.ca/start.html

Supreme Court of Canada. Searchable database of Canadian Supreme Court rulings (1993–97), also bulletins and decisions relative to the Charter of Rights and Freedoms.
http://lazio.crdp.umontreal.ca/Droit/CSC/index_eng.html

INTERNATIONAL

International Information on the Internet. Links to international agencies such as the European Union, Asian Development Bank, and United Nations. More than 30 countries' parliamentary sites are linked.
http://www.colorado.edu/libraries/govpubs/internat.htm

Organization of American States. Every country in the Americas (except Cuba) is a member of the OAS. The site includes news releases on OAS activities in the areas of democracy, business, human rights, the environment, and others. Information is available in English and Spanish.

http://www.oas.org/

POLITICIAN GOVERNMENT ADDRESS DIRECTORY

This directory contains the snail-mail address, fax/phone number, e-mail address, and Web page (where applicable) for leaders around the world.

http://www.trytel.com/~aberdeen/

United Nations Index. Official home pages of UN agencies are organized according to subject.

http://www.unsystem.org/

United Nations Statistics Division. Access selected data from member countries, compiled by the UN. Includes the *Monthly Bulletin of Statistics*, with numbers on economic activity, unemployment, consumer prices, and population from countries around the world.

http://www.un.org/Depts/unsd/mbsreg.htm

USA

Capitol Newswire. Claims to be the largest repository in the world of political, economic, and governmental news releases.

http://www.global-villages.com/capitolnewswire

Federal Government Information on the Internet. Compiled by a librarian for librarians, this collection of links to U.S. government information is useful for anyone doing research in the field. Some sites contain information available only for a fee.

http://www.unlv.edu/library/GOVT/

Full-Text State Statutes and Legislation on the Internet. Links to full texts of state constitutions, statutes, and legislation are available via the Web, FTP, telnet, and Gopher. Arranged by state; some states have more advanced resources than others.

http://www.prairienet.org/~scruffy/f.htm

Government Information Locator Service (GILS). Search U.S. federal government resources with a standardized search engine. GILS uses existing international standards for locating information.

http://www.usgs.gov/gils/

GPO Pathway Services. The Federal Depository Library Program has developed this site to guide librarians and researchers to U.S. government information. Browse topics, electronic documents, or search federal Web sites by keyword. Includes MoCat, a searchable monthly catalog of U.S. government publications.

http://www.access.gpo.gov/su_docs/aces/aces760.html

Historical, Social, Economic, and Demographic Data from the U.S. Decennial Census. Hosted by Harvard University, this site contains data from the census held every 10 years between 1790 and 1860.
http://icg.fas.harvard.edu /census/

The House of Representatives. News and background information on House activities, the legislative process, how to contact members, a schedule of events, and links to other government information.
http://www.house.gov/

Official Federal Government Web Sites. Links to dozens of federal departments, agencies, and services, compiled by the Library of Congress.
http://lcweb.loc.gov/global/executive/fed.html

OSU Government Information Sharing Project. Information on U.S. counties, census data, import/export, and school district data. Option for searching databases using selected categories.
http://govinfo.kerr.orst.edu/

The Senate. Information on members, committee activities, and legislative procedures.
http://www.senate.gov/

STAT-USA. Official economic news and statistics from the U.S. Department of Commerce. Includes the National Trade Data Bank, the U.S. Government's most comprehensive source of international trade data and export promotion information. Most data are available only by paid subscription. For individuals, it costs US$150 for one year, or $50 for 90 days.
http://www.stat-usa.gov/stat-usa.html

Telecommunications Act of 1996 Homepage (Benton Foundation). Benton specializes in communications policy issues and news. This Act is a comprehensive re-write of U.S. communications laws. The site provides a hypertext version of the Act and various related documents.
http://www.benton.org/Policy/96act/

U.S. Census Bureau. Official data on everything from aging to women-owned businesses, arranged alphabetically by subject. Includes news releases, population information, and every number you could possibly ever want.
http://www.census.gov

U.S. Legislative Information on the Net (Thomas). U.S. congressional information: the Congressional Record, bills, committee reports, etc.
http://thomas.loc.gov/

UMich Documents Center. Massive set of links for government information. Documents in the News provides helpful background links for current news topics

http://www.lib.umich.edu/libhome/Documents.center/

Webgator — Investigative Resources on the Web. A highly useful research tool that provides access to such investigative resources as courts, parole boards, databases, locators, records access (vital stats, motor vehicles, estates), adoptee resources, state licensing agencies, and more.

http://www.inil.com/users/dguss/wgator.htm

The White House. News releases, plus info on presidents past and present.

http://www.whitehouse.gov

4. Writing helps

GRAMMAR, ETC.

FOG Index. An established method to analyze written material to see how easy it is to read and understand.

http://www.fpd.finop.umn.edu/Related/Writing_Tips/Writing_Tips.html

An Online English Grammar. A comprehensive textbook-style document from a British educator.

http://www.edunet.com/english/grammar/fram-gr.html

A Web of On-line Grammars. Links to reference, learning and historical grammars for "as many languages as can be found on the Web," from Bengali to Welsh.

http://www.bucknell.edu/~rbeard/grammars.html

TUTORIALS AND GUIDES

Paradigm Online Writing Assistant. Geared towards university students preparing essays, this tutorial by a professor at Boise State University can help anyone plan a writing project, from an informal essay to a thesis. Get help deciding what to write, organizing material, editing your own writing, and documenting sources.

http://www.idbsu.edu/english/cguilfor/paradigm/

Purdue Online Writing Laboratory. Purdue University's online tutorial helps you write anything — research papers, business reports, personal correspondence. Covers how to develop an outline, how to paraphrase, and how to organize citations, among other things. Includes links to other university writing tutorials available on the Web and through e-mail.

http://owl.english.purdue.edu/writing.html

Undergraduate Writing Center. The University of Texas has compiled

links to handouts from online writing labs on everything from apostrophes to wordiness.
http://www.utexas.edu/depts/uwc/.html/handout.html

Writing Coach. The Write Place Software helps develop good writing skills. Includes writing tips and writing resources. Special pricing for students and academics.
http://surf.rio.com/~wplace/

5. Media

(News services, broadcast sources, and related links; see also resources listed in Chapter 5)

AJR NewsLink. Operated by the *American Journalism Review*, this has links to thousands of newspapers, magazines, and broadcasters. Claims to be the Net's most comprehensive news resource. Big selection of non-U.S. and campus newspapers.
http://www.newslink.org/

Associated Press (AP). Up-to-the-minute newscasts from the AP wire. Stories only go back a few hours, and include headlines as well as full-text features and transcripts of speeches and debates.
http://www.trib.com/NEWS/APwire.html

Canada NewsWire. Real-time Canadian news release database with around-the-world coverage.
http://www.newswire.ca/

Canadian Broadcasting Corporation (CBC). Program information and news items from English- and French-Canadian radio and television. Includes Newsworld and Radio Canada International.
http://www.cbc.ca/

The Canadian Press/Broadcast News. Canada's national newswire service publishes its headlines on the Web site. Not long on detail, but a good summary of what will be in tomorrow's newspapers.
http://www.canpress.ca/canpress/Overview.html

CANOE (Canadian Online Explorer). Home of several publications owned by Rogers and the Sun Media Corp., including *Maclean's, Chatelaine,* the *Toronto Sun,* and the *Financial Post.*
http://www.canoe.com/

CNN (Cable News Network). Read the top stories from news, entertainment, sports, business, travel, and weather. See video clips from the newscasts.
http://www.cnn.com/

Editor & Publisher Interactive. This site lists newspaper publishers with online services, as well as resources of interest to the news

media community. Includes headline highlights and the most frequently visited news sites.
http://www.mediainfo.com/edpub/e-papers.home.page.html

First Things First. Extensive list of news sources. Includes links to news services, wire services, and features. When you tire of the news, you can use this site to link to Dilbert.
http://www.refdesk.com/first.html

Media Literacy Project. Provides information and pointers to Internet resources on issues related to electronic media.
http://interact.uoregon.edu/MediaLit/HomePage

MSNBC. A digest of what's on the NBC networks.
http://www.msnbc.com/news/default.asp

National Public Radio. Transcripts from the day's top stories. Listen to live newscasts on the hour (requires a RealAudio player).
http://www.npr.org/

NeWo News Indices. An eclectic list of links to news sources from individuals, companies, and organizations ranging from Arabic News and Media to the Yankee News Desk.
http://newo.com/news/news_index.html

Pathfinder. Home to Time-Warner media such as *Time, Life, People, Money, Fortune, Sports Illustrated,* and CNN.
http://pathfinder.com

PointCast Network. A network of newspapers publishing online to provide a personalized news service. You must download software from the site, which is available only for Windows 3.1 or higher.
http://www.pointcast.com

Reuters. This respected news source puts out news summaries and headlines. There is no search capability, but they do archive material dating back one week.
http://www.yahoo.com/headlines/current/news/

Southam News. Links to home pages of members of the Canadian news chain: newspapers, magazines, and trade publications.
http://www.southam.com/

Vanderbilt Television News Archive. At this site, you can search for television news broadcasts dating back to 1968. Note that most of this archive has been developed as a Gopher site.
http://tvnews.vanderbilt.edu/abstracts.html

World Newswire. Top stories from many sources. Allows a quick scan of headline news. From this site you can also gain access to news in science, business, etc.
http://www.artigen.com/newswire/world.html

6. Online books

Association des Bibliophiles Universels (ABU). Its home page offers "as many French public domain texts as possible." Includes links to other services offering French texts.
http://web.cnam.fr/ABU/

B&R Samizdat Express. Internet-on-a-Disk, Newsletter, electronic books and Internet trends. This is a good source for electronic texts. The newsletter provides interesting commentary and unique insights on Internet trends.
http://www.samizdat.com

Bartleby Library. A digital library from Columbia University. Search *Bartlett's Familiar Quotations* and other well-known literary works.
http://www.columbia.edu/acis/bartleby/

Berkeley Digital Library Sun SITE. A Collection of digital material, including online books, photographs, archival documents, training materials, and other useful sources. Collections include medieval texts, *Nineteenth Century Literature* (a quarterly journal), letters and manuscripts of Jack London, a California Heritage photography collection, and an international collection of computer science technical reports. This is also a good source for information on how to develop digital collections.
http://sunsite.berkeley.edu/index.html

Bibliomania. Full texts of more than 40 classic novels, plus works of non-fiction and poetry.
http://www.bibliomania.com/url.html#publishing

Books on the Internet. Links to many online book sources, including McGraw-Hill, the Great Books Home Page, American Literature hypertext books, political, historical, and legal texts, classic fiction, and more.
http://www.lib.utexas.edu/Libs/PCL/Etext.html

Books Online: Titles. This site offers several different ways to search for books online.
http://www.cs.cmu.edu/booktitles.html

Computer and Internet Related Online Books Index. A truly amazing source for full-text computer- and Internet-related books.
http://home.earthlink.net/~jlutgen/cirob.html

Dial-a-Book Chapter One. This free service makes available (for online browsing) first chapters, tables of contents, and other excerpts of books on selected topics. With more than 360 books from over 92 publishers, this is a great way to sample before you buy.
http://www.psi.net/chapterone/

The English Server. Carnegie Mellon University publishes more than 10,000 humanities texts in many disciplines, from art and architecture to rhetoric. Also has links to academic journals, libraries, and sites about the Internet.
http://english-server.hss.cmu.edu/

History of Economic Thought. McMaster University in Hamilton, Canada has full-text versions of classic economic books by such authors as Karl Marx, John Stuart Mill, and Adam Smith, as part of its syllabus.
http://socserv2.socsci.mcmaster.ca:80/~econ/ugcm/3ll3/index.html

Internet Book Information Center. The latest book news, as well as an extensive guide to book-related sources on the Internet.
http://sunsite.unc.edu/ibic/

Literature Online (Lion). A fee-based collection of databases containing full texts of English and American literature: poems, plays, and novels. The site also has reference works, dictionaries, and bibliographies.
http://www.chadwyck.co.uk/lion/index.html

Malaspina Great Books. Links to full-text versions of great books, plus citations occurring on the Web, compiled by Malaspina University-College. Books are arranged by title, author, period, and topic.
http://www.mala.bc.ca/~mcneil/template.htx

Online Books (Web Communications). A list of links to sites with online books; compiled by Web Communications, the commercial Internet service provider.
http://www.webcom.com/power/online_books.html

Project Gutenberg. One of the original electronic text projects, this is a good source for literary works in the public domain.
http://kcmo.com/gdl

Scholarly Electronic Publishing Bibliography. References to online publishing of scholarly works, from the University of Houston.
http://info.lib.uh.edu/sepb/sepb.html

Universal Library Project. The goal of this project is to start a worldwide movement to make all the written works of humankind accessible over the Internet. Currently, 300 works in English are free for personal use.
http://www.ul.cs.cmu.edu/

7. Online newspapers and magazines

(See also references in Chapter 5)

E & P Directory of World Wide Electronic Newspapers. More than 1,600 links to online newspapers around the globe, compiled by Editor & Publisher magazine. Its database is searchable. Links are arranged by continent.
  http://www.mediainfo.com/ephome/npaper/nphtm/online.htm

Ecola Newsstand. A mega-site that offers separate indexes for newspapers, magazines, and computer publications, as well as links to thousands of electronic newspapers and magazines. At Ecola you can search for a publication by name.
  http://www.ecola.com/

Electronic Newstand. Substantial selection of articles from magazines, newsletters, newspapers, and more. Check out the Monster Magazine List!
  http://www.enews.com

Enter Magazine. This is a neat online magazine for those just starting out on their own and entering the work world. Useful topics include buying a car, cooking for yourself, and money management. Good resource for students.
  http://www.entermag.com

The Globe and Mail. Canada's national newspaper.
  http://www.globeandmail.ca/

HighWire Press. A number of academic journals from Stanford University Libraries, including *Science Magazine*.
  http://highwire.stanford.edu/

The Los Angeles Times. Full-text news, entertainment, business, and sports articles, plus a restaurant guide to eating out in L.A.
  http://www.latimes.com/

The New York Times. Registration is required for access to this valuable resource.
  http://www.nytimes.com/

Online Journals List. Compiled by the University of Texas Health Science Center, this list links you to sites of journals publishing online in fields of science, news, business, art, and entertainment.
  http://bioc02.uthscsa.edu/journal/journal.html

Ottawa Citizen. Another excellent online newspaper. In addition to daily news features, includes a wine guide, a directory of resorts and lodges for tourists, and free samples of Canada clip art.
  http://www.ottawacitizen.com/

Salon. Impressive e-zine about "books, arts, and ideas." Regular columns and news features about modern culture, media, entertainment, and literature.
  http://www.salon1999.com/

Serials in Cyberspace. Annotated links to many electronic journals sources. Largely academic focus.
http://www.uvm.edu/~bmaclenn

Suck. Well-written zine on pop culture.
http://www.suck.com

The Toronto Star. Canada's largest daily probably has the country's largest online newspaper, as well. Practically every article appears in full text, arranged by section headings. Copious graphics and photos take awhile to load, so be patient.
http://www.thestar.com

The Ultimate Collection of News Links. Links to hundreds of newspapers around the world, grouped according to continent and country.
http://pppp.net/links/news/

University of Chicago Press. Offers the *Astrophysical Journal* and *Child Development Abstracts and Bibliography.*
http://www.journals.uchicago.edu

Virtual Products. Canadian electronic publishing resources. Includes a number of full-text publications and publishing sources, including the Canadian Electronic Scholarly Network.
http://www.schoolnet.ca/vp/cesn

The Wall Street Journal. The full-text articles are available by subscription, but there are also links to free business-related sites.
http://www.wsj.com/

The Washington Post. This giant daily has searchable archives of articles.
http://www.washingtonpost.com

8. Resources for journalists

GENERAL

The Beat Page. From agriculture to weather, common newsroom beats are listed with links to sources for reporters covering the issues.
http://www.reporter.org/beat/

Canada NewsWire. Get fresh news releases from companies, governments, and organizations across Canada. Search the release archives for background.
http://www.newswire.ca/

CAR/CARR Links Page. Links to dozens of sites supporting journalists engaged in computer-assisted reporting. Includes story ideas, computer technology news, and discussion groups.
http://www.ryerson.ca/~dtudor/carcarr.htm

Columbia School of Journalism Library. Resources are geared to students, but are also useful for professional journalists.
http://www.columbia.edu/acis/documentation/journ/journnew.html

ETD Green Pages for Journalists. Links to resources for journalists covering the environment.
http://www.etd.ameslab.gov/etd/library/greenpages/Journalist.html

FACSNet. Resources for journalists covering public policy issues, organized by the Foundation for American Communications (FACS).
http://www.facsnet.org/

Finding Data on the Internet: A Journalist's Guide. Includes "Links to Potential Story Data" for sources of data, and "Statistics Every Writer Should Know," a quick math lesson on using figures.
http://www.nilesonline.com/data/index.shtml

Investigative Journalism on the Net. Well-organized set of links useful especially to Canadian journalists. Includes government resources and databases.
http://www.vir.com/~sher/julian.htm

A Journalist's Guide to the Internet. Online tutorials to help journalists learn the Internet at the beginner, advanced, and "extra" levels, produced by the Society of Professional Journalists.
http://www.ccrc.wustl.edu/spj/surf/surf.html

The KSG One-Stop Journalist Shop. Useful starting point, featuring journalists' tools of the trade and media criticism from the Kennedy School of Government.
http://ksgwww.harvard.edu/~ksgpress/journpg.htm

National Institute for Computer-Assisted Reporting (NICAR). NICAR offers training seminars to teach journalists to use electronic databases. The site includes "Computer-Assisted Reporting: A Practical Guide," adopted by several universities, which provides advice for both PC and Macintosh users.
http://nicar.org/

Student Press Law Center. This is "a nonprofit organization dedicated to providing legal help and information to the student media and journalism educators." Includes an online legal clinic with answers to FAQs about censorship, libel, copyright, and freedom of information (including getting access to public documents and meetings). The information is based on U.S. law.
http://www.splc.org/

University Wire. College journalists have their own online wire service, with stories added daily. There are also writing pointers, job openings, and links to college newspapers and student journalism organizations.
http://www.mainquad.com/uwire/

WebCentral Guide to Electronic and Print Resources for Journalists. A comprehensive guide to reference materials for journalists and other writers, including search tools, finding experts online, listservs, newsgroups, journalism associations and conferences, and print and online publications about the craft of writing.
http://www.cio.com/WebMaster/journalism.html

FINDING EXPERTS

Counsel Quote. Find a lawyer in the U.S. by posting a query for member lawyers to respond, or by searching their Experts on Call database. Site includes a list of legal story ideas posted by lawyers working in interesting fields.
http://www.counsel.com/counselquote/

Experts.com. Search the database of thousands of experts and consultants, who pay to be listed. Listings include only mailing addresses and phone numbers; no e-mail addresses.
http://www.experts.com

ProfNet. Experts at your fingertips on every topic imaginable. Send an online request for information and it will be answered by professors or other experts at universities, non-profit organizations, corporations, and government agencies around the world.
http://www.vyne.com/profnet/index.html

Sources. The long-trusted directory of Canadian organizations and experts is available online and easily searched. People pay to be listed so that they can get media coverage.
http://www.sources.com

Yearbook of Experts, Authorities & Spokespersons. Geared specifically for journalists, this is a searchable database of U.S. sources, indexed by subject keyword. People pay to be listed, and are available for interviews.
http://www.yearbooknews.com/

MEDIA ANALYSIS

American Journalism Review/NewsLink. This is a joint venture between *American Journalism Review* magazine, published by the University of Maryland Foundation, and NewsLink Associates, an online research and consulting firm. It includes weekly features from *AJR*, the worldwide online publication lists of NewsLink, and weekly original content created especially for online readers. It also includes an archive of back issues.
http://www.newslink.org/ajrguide.html

The Columbia Journalism Review. Back issues of the publication that critiques media coverage of current events.
http://www.cjr.org/

The Freedom Forum. Home to the nonpartisan, international foundation dedicated to free press and free speech.
http://www.freedomforum.org/

IGC: Media: Internet-Resources Collection. Maintained by the Institute for Global Communications, this site has good links to censorship and legal information related to communications. The media resources page has an activist focus and includes links to some alternative press sources.
http://www.igc.org/igc/issues/media/

Media and Communications Studies. Links to (mostly U.K.) Web resources for the academic study of media and communications. Developed by a professor at the University of Wales.
http://www.aber.ac.uk/~dgc/media.html

Media Watchdog. Emphasis on critiquing coverage and exposing biases in the mainstream media.
http://theory.lcs.mit.edu/~mernst/media/

The Poynter Institute for Media Studies. The site's Library Research Center allows searching full-text documents.
http://www.nando.net/prof/poynter/home.html

Project Censored. "News that did not make the news." Explores and publicizes significant news stories that have been effectively censored by the mainstream media. Online files date back to 1989.
http://censored.sonoma.edu/ProjectCensored/

ASSOCIATIONS

American Society of Journalists and Authors. ASJA members are independent nonfiction writers who must meet certain criteria. The site pertains only to the society and has no other links.
http://www.asja.org/

Canadian Association of Journalists. This site offers information on becoming a member of Canada's only national organization for professional journalists. Includes its own listservs, plus links to journalism-related sites.
http://marlo.eagle.ca/caj/

Investigative Reporters and Editors. Formed to help journalists tackle tough stories and issues. Search its Resource Centers collection of more than 11,000 investigative reporting stories, tip sheets, and other materials.
http://www.ire.org/

National Association of Black Journalists. Aimed at promoting and communicating the importance of diversity in newsrooms across the United States.

http://www.nabj.org/

National Association of Hispanic Journalists. Includes a chat forum for members to discuss issues pertaining to Hispanic journalists.

http://www.nahj.org/

National Association of Science Writers. Information on membership, its mentoring program, listservs, and a full-text version of its publication *Communicating Science News,* a guide on how to work with science journalists for scientists, physicians, and public information officers.

http://www.nasw.org/

National Press Club. The place where Washington journalists hang out (physically and cyberially). Lists club information, award winners, upcoming events such as guest speakers, and links to journalists' resources. It is a forum for discussing news, and is non-partisan.

http://npc.press.org/

National Writers' Union. This is the site of the trade union for freelance writers. Includes full text of NWU documents on everything from electronic rights to a sample standard journalism contract.

http://www.igc.apc.org/nwu/

Periodical Writers' Association of Canada. An organization for professional freelance writers, journalists, editors, and communications experts. Includes information on electronic copyright and the Hall of Shame, listing Canadian publishers who allegedly mistreat freelancers.

http://www.cycor.ca/PWAC/

The Reporters' Network. This organization exists only in cyberspace, with the goal to promote the Internet as a research and communications medium for working journalists. It compiles The Reporters' Network Media Directory, an e-mail directory of journalists, editors, producers, and freelance writers. Members must pay an annual fee.

http://www.reporters.net

Society of Environmental Journalists. Includes society publications and links to other sites useful to environmental journalists.

http://www.sej.org/

The Society for Professional Journalists. The largest professional organization for journalists in the United States, with over 14,000 members.

http://town.hall.org/places/spj/

9. Resources for writers

GENERAL

Gary Conroy's Technical Writing Page. An overview of technical writing resources on the Internet.
http://user.itl.net/~gazza/techwr.htm

Inkspot. An all-round resource page for writers. Includes *Inklings*, a free e-mail newsletter; a FAQ, tips, and advice for beginning writers; and resources for children's writers.
http://www.inkspot.com/~ohi/inkspot/

Instructor Resources (Writing). A resource for writing instructors with links to online composition journals, links to sources for technical and business communications, and a section on writing for the Net.
http://www.devry-phx.edu/lrnresrc/dowsc/instres.htm

io.Writing. Guides writers to other sites for help with finding an agent or publisher; offers reference material and answers to questions on grammar. Includes links to mailing lists, newsgroups, newsletters, publishers, and Canadian resources.
http://www.deepsky.com/~writing/Overview.html

Journal Writing Resources. Book references and other sources of information about keeping a personal journal.
http://www.spectra.net/~tbyrne/

Online Writery. Varied resources for writers, including writing programs, the screenwriters' network, and help for children's writers.
http://www.si.edu/start.htm

On-Writing's Internet Resource Guide. This is an especially valuable source for information on Web stuff for writers. The publication includes notes on writing courses, classes, and projects, as well as info on publishing e-zines.
http://www.on-writing.com/ezines.html

Poets & Writers. Comprehensive links for literary writers. Includes professional development (workshops and conferences, university writing programs), publishers, writing organizations, software and supplies, and literary magazines.
http://www.pw.org/

Script Tutor. Getting started with script writing, including demo versions of scriptwriting programs.
http://scripttutor.com

Society of Children's Book Writers & Illustrators. Information source and support for children's literature professionals.
http://www.scbwi.org

Teachers' & Writers' Collaborative. An organization to bring writers and teachers together to generate ideas and learning materials.
http://www.twc.org/tmmain.htm

Victory Page. Articles on how to write better, how to deal with critiquing, and where to go for online writing workshops.
http://www.crayne.com/victory/writetop.html

Writers' Resources. Very long list of resources for writers, including science fiction, scriptwriting, haiku, and more.
http://www.seanet.com/Users/warlock/writers.html

MARKETING AND PUBLISHING

Book Marketing Online. Geared more for publishers, this site also helps authors learn how to use the Internet to peddle their wares.
http://www.idealog.com/bmol01.html

Freelancers Online. Freelancers working in publishing and advertising can list free in this directory for employers to search. List yourself under such categories as magazine writer, travel writer, editor, proofreader, indexer, scriptwriter, copywriter, and so on.
http://haven.ios.com/~freelans/index2.html

Inkspot: Guidelines for Paying Markets: Hardcopy/Crossover Magazines. Part of the Inkspot writing home page (see entry under "General," above), this links to dozens of sites operated by hardcopy magazines showing writers how to submit queries and manuscripts.
http://www.inkspot.com/~ohi/inkspot/mktpaypaper.html

Internet Directory of Literary Agents. Lists agents representing fiction writers (in genres from adventure to young adult) and nonfiction writers (in fields ranging from agriculture to women's issues). Part of the WritersNet site (see entry below).
http://www.writers.net/categories-la.html

Internet Screenwriters' Network. Sources for screenwriters, including a directory of agents and marketing information.
http://screenwriters.com/screennet.html

Tips on Getting Published. Australian fiction author Sara Douglass helps would-be novelists get their words into print.
http://www.bendigo.net.au/~douglass/pubtips.html

The Writer's Marketboard. Browse the free listings from periodicals (both hard-copy and online) looking for freelance writers. Post your own writing proposals to be seen by editors paying for submissions. Includes fiction and non-fiction.
http://rain-crow-publishing.com/market/index.html

WritersNet. A non-commercial, free directory of published writers.

Non-fiction and fiction writers submit their own entries to this database. Potential clients searching for writers use the built-in search engine to find someone with appropriate experience. Includes a writing assignments bulletin board and a directory of literary agents.

http://www.writers.net/

INSPIRATION

Margaret Atwood's Home Page. The popular fiction writer dishes out tips and musings to budding scribes. Includes some of her lectures and book reviews, and an essay explaining the writer-editor relationship during the publishing process.

http://www.io.org/~toadaly/writing.htm

Pure Fiction. For writers of contemporary fiction or those who simply love to read. Aspiring authors are encouraged to use links here to help them write a bestselling novel. Includes lists of U.K. and U.S. literary agents.

http://www.purefiction.com/

ASSOCIATIONS

Canadian Authors' Association. Information on CAA publications, conferences, writing awards, and links to similar resources. Offers advice on contracts for freelance writers.

http://www.islandnet.com/~caa/national.html

SF Canada. The site of the former Speculative Writers' Association of Canada. Links to other science fiction writing sites.

http://helios.physics.utoronto.ca:8080/sfchrome.html

Society for Technical Communication. Members include writers, editors, publishers, and scientists. Includes information on conferences, competitions, seminars, and employment.

http://www.stc.org/

The Writers' Guild of America. Resources and tips for screenwriters. The WGA is a labor organization representing writers in the motion picture, broadcast, cable, interactive and new media industries.

http://www.wga.org

The Writers' Union of Canada. Members are published authors of fiction and non-fiction books. Includes information on membership, writing contests, book contracts, and literary agents.

http://www.swifty.com/twuc/

10. Resources for editors

EDITING TUTORIALS

Copy Editor Workshops. This site is maintained by *Copy Editor,* a

newsletter available by subscription in hard copy only. Courses are held by various groups in book, newspaper, and magazine copy editing, and some are summer institutes or correspondence courses.
http://www.copyeditor.com/workshops.html

CP Copy Talk. This newsletter on the Canadian Press home page calls itself "A Look at Writing," but it is mainly of interest to professional editors concerned with matters of style, consistency, word usage, spelling, and grammar.
http://www.canpress.ca/canpress/cpytlk.htm

The Editorial Eye. Home page for the commercial newsletter for editors (at press time, the newsletter was available in hard copy only, by subscription). Many how-to articles from back issues are free.
http://www.eei-alex.com/eye/

Magazine Copy Editing. Extensive syllabus from a course offered by magazine copy editor Mindy McAdams. The page includes links to a selection of Web sites related to editing and a reference to a mailing list for editors.
http://www.well.com/user/mmcadams/copy.editing.html

The Slot: A Spot for Copy Editors. Operated by an American copy editor, The Slot includes The Curmudgeon's Stylebook, with advice on spelling, style, usage, and grammar. It expands upon the Associated Press style book, which is mainly used by newspaper copy editors.
http://www.theslot.com

ASSOCIATIONS

American Society of Indexers. Includes FAQs about indexing, information on courses and conferences, and links to indexing-related sites.
http://well.com/user/asi/

Editors' Association of Canada. Information on membership, professional development seminars, and an annual award. Members include freelancers and in-house editors. Links to many editing-related sites.
http://www.web.net/eac-acr

Freelance Editorial Association. This America-wide association of freelance editors lists members in an online Yellow Pages for potential employers to search.
http://www.tiac.net/users/freelanc/index.htm

Indexing and Abstracting Society of Canada. Information on membership, publications, and links to resources for indexers.
http://tornade.ere.umontreal.ca/~turner/iasc/home.html

11. Resources for Students

GENERAL

Christina Demello's College and University Home Pages. Alphabetical and geographical listings of links to more than 3,000 college and university sites around the world.
http://www.mit.edu:8001/people/cdemello/univ.html

College Board Online. Access to SAT information and other useful tools, including a college cost calculator.
http://www.collegeboard.org

College Guides and Aid Home Page. Save you time and money during your search for colleges or student financial aid. This site offers recommendations on resources you can use each step of the way.
http://www.collegeguides.com/

CollegeNet. Information on colleges across the U.S.
http://www.collegenet.com/cnmain.html

CollegeView. Take virtual tours of more than 3,500 colleges in the U.S. Includes financial aid and career planning information.
http://www.collegeview.com

Ecola College Locator. Easy search for colleges and universities by location. Includes library and alumni pages.
http://www.ecola.com/college

.edu U.S. News Colleges and Careers. Apply to American colleges online, choose a grad school, find out about financing, and search top jobs for graduates.
http://www.usnews.com/usnews/edu/home.htm

Fastweb. Financial aid search throughout the Web. Free scholarship search.
http://web.studentservices.com/fastweb/

Kaplan's College Admissions. Ideas on how to save money, tips on filling out a college application form, and even a set of "flash cards" to help with college entrance exams.
http://www.kaplan.com/precoll/

MBA Page. A site intended to help you "survive and thrive as an MBA student." From Ohio State University, with contributions from hundreds of people at schools around the world.
http://www.cob.ohio-state.edu/dept/fin/mba.htm

Peterson's Education Center. This site offers information on colleges and universities, choosing a career, studying abroad, summer programs, distance learning, and many other areas.
http://www.petersons.com/

The Princeton Review. Information on top colleges and updates on tests such as the SAT and the LSAT. Sample test software.
http://www.review.com

studyabroad.com. Study Abroad Programs Directory: address and info on work and study opportunities abroad.
http://www.strudyabroad.com.

ESSAYS

Researchpaper.com. Claims to be "the Web's largest collection of topics, ideas, and assistance for school-related research projects." Lists more than 2,000 research topics. Its Writing Center features a how-to on writing papers. The discussion area links students working on similar research projects.
http://www.researchpaper.com/

Where the Wild Things Are — Hot Paper Topics. A librarian at St. Ambrose University in Davenport, Iowa has compiled links to current topics suitable for essays and articles.
http://www.sau.edu/CWIS/Internet/Wild/Hot/hotindex.htm

STUDY HELP

The Virtual Prof. Physics and chemistry professors at the University of Texas at Arlington provide personalized e-mail help to high school and university students. Basic help (such as sample tests) is free, while one-on-one sessions have a fee.
http://www.virtualprof.com/

The World Lecture Hall. This site links to pages from faculty around the globe who have class materials on the Web, such as lecture notes, exams, and course syllabi. Operated by the University of Texas at Austin.
http://www.utexas.edu/world/lecture/index.html

TEXTBOOKS

The Student Market. The art of used-book buying goes hi tech! Any U.S. university student can post notices to buy or sell textbooks. Buy from someone across campus or across the country.
http://www.studentmkt.com

CAREERS

Mapping Your Future. Students get help choosing a career and post-secondary courses, and applying for a student loan. Maintained by the American guaranty agencies who participate in the Federal Family Education Loan Program.
http://mapping-your-future.org/

Résumé Writing-ISU. Résumé writing tutorial for college students.
http://www.isu.edu/departments/enroll/resume.html

12. Distance learning

Canadian Distance Education Directory. Access to Canadian agencies in all provinces offering distance education courses and products.
http://is.dal.ca/~jmerry/dist.htm

CASO—The Internet University. Contains information on more than 700 courses offered online by colleges, universities, and other institutions.
http://www.caso.com

Distance Education Atlas. Links to a number of major distance education resources.
http://www.cet.hut.fi/atlas/disted.html

Distance Education Clearinghouse. Sponsored by the University of Wisconsin Extension, this is an award-winning site with wide-ranging information about distance education. The site includes news, course information, and pointers to professional resources.
http://www.uwex.edu/disted/home.html

Distance Education Consortium Web Page. From a consortium of U.S. universities. Search for programs, courseware, articles.
http://www.ces.ncsu.edu/adec/

Distance Learning on the Net. Well-designed Web site that includes an overview of distance education for those just getting started. Included as well are numerous links to institutions offering distance education courses.
http://homepage.interaccess.com/~ghoyle/

Distance Learning Resource Network. Developed by the Far West Laboratory for Educational Research and Development, this resource provides access to information, articles, and programs.
http://www.fwl.org/edtech/dlrn.html

Distance Teaching Resource Guide. From Globewide Network Academy, this site offers a teachers' resource guide and a searchable catalog of distance learning courses and programs.
http://www.gnacademy.org/

Getting Started With Distance Learning Bookstore. From the Academic Planning Services of Maine Online Bookstore, a list of books about distance learning (for those who are still fond of books!).
http://38.217.84.10/~lepine/book.html

ICDL Database. Distance education database from the Commonwealth of Learning. Information on over 31,000 distance learning courses, nearly 1,000 institutions teaching at a distance worldwide, and over 8,500 references to books, journals, articles, research reports, conference papers, dissertations and other types of literature relating to all aspects of distance education.

http://www-icdl.open.ac.uk/

The Internet University. A listing of over 500 courses available by computer, plus articles, information on course providers.

http://www.caso.com/

Peterson's Education and Career Center. Career info, studies abroad, and applications for colleges and universities online. Distance learning study tips are included here as well.

http://www.petersons.com/

Resources for Distance Education. A very long list maintained by Prof. Charles Darling: technology, journals, course providers.

http://webster.commnet.edu/HP/pages/darling/distance.htm

Spectrum Virtual University. An interesting selection of distance education courses, including courses on the Web and on writing. Best of all, the courses are free!

http://www.vu.org/campus.html

Teaching and Learning on the Web. Links to 426 distance education sites.

http://www.mcli.dist.maricopa.edu/tl/

Training & Development Online Resources. Long list of discussion groups related to learning and distance education.

http://www.tcm.com/trdev/faq/tdfaqolr.htm

United States Distance Learning Association. Fact sheet, research, chapter information.

http://www.usdla.org/

Wired University. Some courses and links to online learning institutions.

http://204.98.1.1/di/highered.html

13. Job resources

JOB-HUNTING HELP

Career Hotspots. Extensive list of career information sources.

http://www.bev.net/education/schools/admin/career-hot-spots.html

Career Resource Center. Contains more than 11,000 links to jobs and employers, plus job-related bibliographies, software, publications, and event calendars. Links are cross-referenced geographically.

http://www.careers.org/

The Riley Job Guide. Excellent starting point to begin your job search on the Internet. Includes tips on preparing résumés for the

Internet, and where to find job listings and career counseling online.
http://www.jobtrak.com/jobguide/

JOB LISTINGS

Academic Employment Network. Online job classifieds for U.S. teachers from kindergarten to university, indexed by subject, geographic area, and level of position.
http://www.academploy.com/

Creative Freelancers' Registry. A commercial site that has a database of freelancers with creative talents geared towards the book publishing industry. There is a monthly fee to list in the database. Registry includes ad copy writers, conceptual editors, copy editors, ghost writers, grant/proposal writers, indexers, interviewers, journalists, researchers, script writers, technical writers, and translators.
http://www.ghgcorp.com/cfr/

Editor & Publisher Classifieds. Dozens of job postings across the U.S. are available free to anyone looking for work in newspapers, from reporters and editors to advertising executives.
http://www.mediainfo.com:80/ephome/class/classhtm/class.htm

HRDC National Job Bank. Search jobs posted across Canada (by province and occupation) through regional employment centers. This site is operated by the federal government (Human Resources Development Canada).
http://ein.ccia.stthomas.on.ca/agencies/cec/jobbank/national/search.html

JobLink for Journalists. Part of the AJR NewsLink site (see entry under section 5, Media), this is a free, searchable listing of job openings in journalism. Includes entry-level and more advanced positions.
http://www.newslink.org/joblink.html

JobSAT. A Canadian-based service with a searchable database of jobs across North America. Also has links to job-hunting resources.
http://www.jobsat.com

The Monster Board. All-purpose job seekers' site. Boasts more than 50,000 free searchable job listings around the world. Search by location and discipline. Get career advice, read profiles about potential employers, and build your online résumé.
http://www1.monster.com

National Graduate Register. Canadian job-matching resource.
http://www.schoolnet.ca/ngr

RÉSUMÉ WRITING

ARCHEUS Guide to WWW Résumé Writing. Links to the best online full-text articles giving advice on writing résumés.
http://www.golden.net/~archeus/reswri.htm

Part II: General Interest Resources

1. Arts and culture

Artsedge. The U.S. arts and education information network from the Kennedy Center and the National Endowment for the Arts. Includes arts education news, links, database, and curricula for the performing and visual arts.
http://artsedge.kennedy-center.org

Canadian Arts, Culture, and Heritage Network. Gateway to selected Canadian heritage and arts resources.
http://cnet.unb.ca/achn/

ClassicalNet. An introduction to the world of classical music.
http://www.webcom.com/~music/

Guide to Museums and Cultural Resources. This guide, compiled by the Natural History Museum of Los Angeles County, lists museums and other cultural institutions around the world, according to continent. Tour a virtual exhibit, or find out how to visit a museum while on vacation. Links include "cybermuseums" that exist only on the Web.
http://www.lam.mus.ca.us/webmuseums/

World Wide Arts Resources. Billing itself as "the biggest gateway to the arts on the Internet," this site lets you choose from more than 460 arts categories: galleries and museums, film, theater and dance, antiques and crafts, and more.
http://wwar.com/

2. Business and Economics

ABC. Searchable directory of business information sources. Browsable by subject area, country, subject, industry, and geography.
http://www.abcompass.com/

Bloomberg News. Catch the latest stock quotes, market news, financial analysis, and business deals from the Bloomberg news service.
http://www.bloomberg.com

Canada Net Financial Pages. Canadian stock quotes from TSE, VSE, MSE and ASE.
http://www.visions.com/netpages/finance/finance.html

DBC Online. Real-time U.S. stock market information. The site also offers same-day government transcripts from Washington, Moscow, and the UN.
http://www.DBC.com/

The Economist. Selected articles from the current issue of the weekly newsmagazine. Receive free copies by e-mail of *Business This*

Week, a summary of the major business events worldwide, and *Politics This Week,* summarizing international political events.
http://www.economist.com

Hoover's Online. Access to Hoover's Masterlist database of over 9,000 companies. More detailed information available by subscription.
http:// www.hoovers.com/

International Monetary Fund (IMF). Search the publications database of this United Nations agency, and download full texts of some titles.
http://www.imf.org/external/

NewsPage. This commercial site is a daily business online news service. It covers 2,500 topics from more than 600 sources. News is arranged by industry (many in the high-tech field). Some full-text news items are available for free, but most are downloadable only by paying a monthly fee.
http://www.newspage.com/

Small and HomeBased Business Links. Launchpad for information on running a business from home.
http://www.ro.com/small_business/homebased.html

Strategis. Detailed information about Canadian industry: company information, business information by sector, technology, laws and regulations and consumer information.
http://strategis.ic.gc.ca/

VIBES—Virtual International Business and Economic Sources. Links to free international business information: full-text files, graphs, and statistical tables from government and private sources on Web and Gopher sites. Organized by topic, region, and country.
http://www.uncc.edu/lis/library/reference/intbus/vibehome.htm

WebEc. A compendium of academic economic resources on the Web, compiled by the University of Helsinki, Finland. The site is searchable and has a list of economic journals.
http://netec.wustl.edu/%7eadnetec/WebEc/WebEc.html#scm

World Bank (IBRD). Retrieve news releases, publications, and the annual report from the United Nations agency.
http://www.worldbank.org/

3. Disability information

Council for Disability Rights. Information on current legislation.
http://www.disabilityrights.org

Disability Mailing Lists. Includes Disabled Student Services in Higher Education.
http://www.vicnet.net.au/vicnet/Adrian/dislist.htm

Jim Lubin's Disability Information. Great list of Internet resources on disabilities developed by Jim Lubin, a quadriplegic who works nine hours a day at his computer.
http://www.eskimo.com/~jlubin/disabled.html

4. Education

AskERIC Service for Educators. An information service of the ERIC System (Educational Resources Information Center) based at Syracuse University. Among the services, educators can send e-mail requesting education information. The Virtual Library contains more than 700 lesson plans and educators' guides.
http://ericir.syr.edu

Canadian Association of Learned Journals. More than 40 Canadian academic journals are accessible from this site: either their tables of contents, or full-text articles. Subjects include law, history, engineering, public policy, and more.
http://www.ccsp.sfu.ca/calj/

The Chronicle of Higher Education: Academe This Week. Some articles are free, but the full-text version has a fee. The site has links to a forum on academic issues, job openings, events, and bestselling books. Includes page of new Web resources for academics, updated weekly.
http://chronicle.ment.edu/.index.html

Education Week Web Edition. The online edition of "America's Education Newspaper of Record." Full-text articles of education news, special reports, plus the monthly *Teacher Magazine*. Archived articles are searchable.
http://www.edweek.org/

Educom. Important resource for finding out about education and information technology.
http://www.educom.edu

FEDIX Opportunity Alert. Free e-mail service notifying subscribers of research and education grants from the U.S. government in their area of interest. Operated by Federal Information Exchange, Inc.
http://www.fie.com/

From Now On: The Educational Technology Journal. Valuable publication about technology and learning. Articles range from the "Disneyfication" of history to grant writing.
http://fromnowon.org

Global Campus. Educational institutions share resources on this database, with links grouped according to discipline. Maintained by California State University.
http://www.csulb.edu/gc/index.html

HighWire Press. Links to scientific journals compiled by Stanford University Libraries. One of this site's missions is to "foster research and instruction by providing a more direct linkage between the writers and readers of scholarly materials."

http://highwire.stanford.edu/

Kathy Shrocks Guide for Educators. This is a well-established Internet guide for classroom teachers.

http://www.capecod.net/Wixon/wixon.htm

OISE—Ontario Institute for Studies in Education/University of Toronto. Information on this graduate school of education, plus a page of links to Canadian Education on the Web, and CanGuide (OISE's Canadian database of provincial and territorial curriculum guides and resource documents).

http://www.oise.on.ca/index.html

SchoolNet. Comprehensive link to Canadian information related to education.

http://www.schoolnet.ca

United Nations Educational, Scientific and Cultural Organization (UNESCO). News releases; information on UNESCO programs and publications; worldwide statistics on education, science, and culture.

http://www.unesco.org/

U.S. Department of Education. Guides to the department; reports and links to educational organizations.

http://www.ed.gov

5. Entertainment

The Hollywood Reporter. Full-text articles on the online version of the entertainment trade magazine cost a fee, but there are links to entertainment industry sites with free information.

http://www.hollywoodreporter.com

HollywoodNet. Extensive reference to help you find your way around Hollywood. Includes links for writers.

http://www.screenwriters.com/indexmain.html

The Rock Guide. *Rolling Stone* magazine has a one-stop shop for information on music genres, artists, books and magazines, even concerts. You can even order tickets to shows.

http://www.rockguide.com/

6. Environment

CoVis Online Resources: Environmental Science. Links to information and education resources.

http://www.covis.nwu.edu/Geosciences/resources/environment.html

Envirolink. An environmental news service plus a clearinghouse of environmental information available on the Internet.
http://envirolink.org/

Environment Canada's Green Lane. Environment Canada's Web site provides information about current issues and access to Canadian regional environmental sites.
http://www.doe.ca

Environment Today. The Web's daily environment news and jobs source. News database and meetings database with information on hundreds of meetings on scientific and environmental topics.
http://enviro.mond.org/

Network Nuggets: The Environment. North American resources for learning about the environment.
http://www.etc.bc.ca/lists/nuggets/enviro.html

United Nations Environment Programme (UNEP). Search UNEP documents online, and follow links to other international environmental resources.
http://www.unep.org/

7. Health

Achoo. Contains the Internet Healthcare Directory, with more than 7,600 links to help organize the mountain of health care information on the Internet.
http://www.achoo.com/

AEGIS (AIDS Education). AIDS Education Global Information System. The "absolute latest information on AIDS and HIV."
http://www.aegis.com

American Medical Association. The AMA home page includes links to medical journals, plus a searchable database of more than 650,000 licensed U.S. physicians, according to name, specialty, and location.
http://www.ama-assn.org/

Canadian National Clearinghouse on Tobacco and Health. Provides access to an extensive database of Web documents on smoking and health.
http://www.ccsh.ca/ncth/index.html

CancerNet. Cancer information from the U.S. government's National Cancer Institute. This is a comprehensive resource documenting the latest research. Includes pointers to related global sites.
http://wwwicic.nci.nih.gov/

HealthWeb. Information on various health topics compiled by some

American universities. Includes descriptions of the condition, and links on where to find treatment, research, and more information.
http://www.ghsl.nwu.edu/healthweb/index.html

Home of WorldWide Wellness. Holistic health resources on the Internet.
http://www.doubleclickd.com/wwwellness.html

Medscape. Medical information, including mental health and Medline database.
http://www5.medscape.com/

Merck Manual. Look up medical ailments, their symptoms and treatments in this tried-and-true guide. Written for medical practitioners, but also understandable by lay people.
http://www.merck.com/!!sGkC23ajhsGkC63Aq2/pubs/mmanual/

NetVet. A place to start for healthy pets.
http://netvet.wustl.edu/

Internet Mental Health. Free encyclopedia of mental health information.
http://www.mentalhealth.com

Psychnet. From the American Psychological Association, this site offers the "PsychCrawler" search engine and useful brochures on psychology and mental health topics.
http://www.apa.org

The QuitNet. Need to stop smoking? From the Massachusetts Department of Public Health, this site provides lots of helps.
http://www.quitnet.org

World Health Organization (WHO). Statistics, reports, health advisories, and other useful information from the United Nations agency. Includes links to other health care sites.
http://www.who.ch/

8. History

English Server: History and Historiography. Site for full-text historical documents. Historical works are diverse, including material ranging from Bodleian Library manuscripts to the 1947 testimony of Walt Disney before the House Committee on Un-American Activities.
http://eng.hss.cmu.edu/history/

The History Net. This site is developed by the National Historical Society and Cowles Enthusiast Media. It contains a collection of feature articles from Cowles history magazines, such as *Historic Traveler, Civil War Times Illustrated,* and *World War II* magazine.
http://www.thehistorynet.com

Index of Resources for History. The University of Kansas Department of History has links to more than 1,700 sites of interest to historians.
http://ukanaix.cc.ukans.edu/history/

Internet Medieval Sourcebook. Extensive resource for medieval documents and information.
http://www.fordham.edu/halsall/sbook.html

The Smithsonian Museum. This site bills itself as "America's Attic"!
http://www.si.edu/start.htm

9. Human rights

Country Reports on Human Rights Practices. The U.S. Department of State writes annual reports on almost every country, assessing how well each one adhered to United Nations human rights laws based on incidents that occurred in that year. The reports are provided by U.S. embassies in the particular countries, and from other sources.
http://www.state.gov/www/issues/human_rights/1996_hrp_report/96hrp_report_toc.html

International Labor Organization (ILO). The site for this United Nations agency includes information on international labor standards and human rights.
http://www.ilo.org/

United Nations High Commission for Refugees (UNHCR). Information about UNHCR and refugees, back issues of *Refugees* magazine, news releases on refugees' situation worldwide, and a teacher's guide to use the site in class.
http://www.unhcr.ch/

10. Language

Center for the Advancement of Language Learning. Foreign language learning resources from the U.S. government. Some resources are intended for government personnel, but there are many good links here to Web resources.
http://www.call.gov/

Dave's ESL Cafe. English as a second language: links for teachers and students.
http://www.pacificnet.net/~sperling/eslcafe.html

The Human-Languages Page. "A comprehensive catalog of language-related Internet resources." Each one of dozens of languages has a collection of links to online translating dictionaries, tutorials to learn the language, newspapers and texts in that language, and schools that teach the language.
http://www.june29.com/HLP/

Temas. Spanish language learning resource.
http://www.umr.edu/~wdechent/Temas/

Web of Online Grammars. Links to online grammar resources for more than 20 languages. Here you will find Russian, English, Greek, Hebrew and many more language learning helps.
http://www.bucknell.edu/~rbeard/grammars.html

WWW Resources for French as a Second Language Learning. Learn to conjugate verbs, test your French grammar, and find other resources for learning French.
http://www.uottawa.ca/~weinberg/french.html

11. Law

GENERAL

Decisions of the International Court of Justice. Information on the United Nations' World Court is presented by the Cornell University Law School. There are full texts of some decisions, plus information on the court, its judges, and the United Nations Charter.
http://www.law.cornell.edu/icj/

FedLaw. Comprehensive source for legal research links. This site includes hypertext references to a number of legal information documents and sources, such as *Roberts' Rules of Order*, an Internet directory, and a "Finding Missing Persons" page.
http://www.legal.gsa.gov/

FindLaw. U.S. legal resources arranged under broad categories such as legal subject index, law firms and lawyers, cases and codes, legal news and reference material, and foreign and international law.
http://www.findlaw.com

International Centre for Criminal Law Reform and Criminal Justice Policy. Joint initiative from University of British Columbia, Simon Fraser University, and the Society for the Reform of Criminal Law, this resource provides links to sites dealing with criminal law.
http://www.law.ubc.ca/centres/crimjust.html

LawCrawler. This comprehensive search engine finds law resources on the Web, including statutes and laws, judicial opinions and case law, government resources, law schools, law reviews, legal publishers, consultants and experts, law firms and lawyers, law libraries, student resources, legal employment, and other law indexes.
http://www.lawcrawler.com/index.html

LegalDocs. This is a source for U.S. legal documents such as contracts and wills. Includes assistance in completing the forms.
http://legaldocs.com

Oyez Oyez Oyez. From the U. S. Supreme Court, information about major constitutional cases in the U.S. In some cases, actual proceedings are available in RealAudio format.
http://oyez.at.nwu.edu/oyez.html

U.S. House of Representatives Internet Law Library. Links to U.S. federal laws, state and territorial laws, laws of other nations, treaties and international law, law school library catalogs, attorney directories, and law book reviews and publishers.
http://law.house.gov/

Virtual Canadian Law Library. Includes links to national and international legislation, Canadian law libraries, firms, faculties, publishers, directories, and conferences.
http://www.droit.umontreal.ca/doc/biblio

COPYRIGHT

Canadian Copyright Law. Copyright lawyer Lesley Ellen Harris answers questions about copyright law, both from what users of copyright material should know, and how creators such as writers can protect themselves.
http://www.mcgrawhill.ca/copyrightlaw

Copyright and E-mail. Copyright information with a special focus on e-mail.
http://www.mindspring.com/~isenberg/paper1.html

Copyright and Fair Use Site. Stanford University's resources on U.S. copyright, including statutes, guidelines, Web sites, and mailing lists.
http://fairuse.stanford.edu

The Copyright Website. Award-winning source of information on U.S. copyright.
http://www.benedict.com/index.html

U.S. Copyright Office Home Page. Offering general information and publications on U.S. copyright, including online forms to register copyright for your writing.
http://lcweb.loc.gov/copyright/

12. Literature and book reviews

Author! Author! Lists of authors on the Web, pages dedicated to literature, and libraries online.
http://www.li.net/~scharf/author.html

Bibliofind. Search out-of-print book titles by keyword.
http://www.bibliofind.com

Bookport and Internet Book Fair. Links to reading lists and bibliographies, publishers' and booksellers' Web pages, and online books.
http://www.bookport.com

The Bookshelf. Book collecting and preservation, and a calendar of book-related events. Access to booksellers' catalogs and lots of related links.

http://www.auldbooks.com/biblio

BookWire. This site lives up to its billing as The First Place to Look for Book Information on the World Wide Web. Includes list of authors on tour, reading discussion groups, book reviews, and links to online resources for book people to help market books.

http://www.bookwire.com/

Fiction Addiction. Book reviews for popular fiction.

http://www.iol.ie/~westrock/fiction/

Children's Literature Web Guide. Outstanding children's literature source with many useful links for writers.

http://www.ucalgary.ca/~dkbrown

CM: Canadian Review of Materials. Reviews Canadian books, videos, and other materials for children and young adults.

http://www.mbnet.mb.ca/cm

Internet Book Information Center. Myriad book resources, including a Guide to Book-Related Resources on the Internet and The IBIC Journal. "Selective, opinionated Guides to current and classic books, organized by author or genre." Includes links to world literature sources.

http://sunsite.unc.edu/ibic/

SharpWeb. Society for the History of Authorship, Reading, and Publishing. Research source for those with an interest in the history of books.

http://www.indiana.edu/~sharp

ONLINE BOOKSTORES

The Amazon Bookstore. Search one million titles and order them by e-mail. The site is updated daily with reviews of the latest releases. A personalized service notifies you by e-mail when your favorite author releases a new title.

http://www.amazon.com

BookWeb: Bookstore Directories. Search for bookstores inside and outside the U. S. Lots of specialty bookstores.

http://www.bookweb.org/directory/

13. Locations

Black World Today. Chronicles the daily social, political, cultural, and economic realities of Black communities and countries.

http://www.tbwt.com/index2.htm

Canadiana. Canadian resources page: Canadian publications online, exchange rates, travel, technology, and more.
http://www.cs.cmu.edu/Unofficial/Canadiana/

CIA World Factbook. Published annually in July by the U.S. Central Intelligence Agency, this is a great resource for factual information about many countries. Look under "CIA Publications."
http://www.odci.gov/cia/

CIA Publications Handbooks. This resource, based on a search engine called Harvest, allows you to search multiple references: the World Fact Book, Handbook of International Economic Statistics, Chiefs of State, and Cabinet Members of Foreign Governments.
http://www.odci.gov/Harvest/brokers/odciweb/query.html

City.Net. Comprehensive guide to cities around the world.
http://www.city.net

Country Maps from W3 Servers in Europe. Access to information on countries in Europe using clickable maps. Includes access to information on European cities and information servers.
http://www.tue.nl/europe/

The European Institute for the Media. An indispensable source of information for global journalists. Full-text research reports for many Eastern European countries.
http://www.eim.org

Hotzones. Information for journalists (and others) who might be traveling to hazardous zones, such as Bosnia and Cambodia. Information includes health and safety tips, plus contact telephone numbers gleaned from journalists familiar with the region.
http://moon.jrn.columbia.edu/NMW/hotzones/

National Geographic's Cartographic Division. Useful source for maps of the world. Includes political maps, facts, flags and country profiles.
http://www.nationalgeographic.com/ngs/maps/cartographic.html

OzSource. Australian resources for arts, literature, politics, geography, geography, history, media, indigenous people and statistics.
http://www.gu.edu.au/gwis/hum/acs/hum_acs_ozsource.html

UK Guide. Includes travel, London guide, newspapers, and education links.
http://www.cs.ucl.ac.uk./misc/uk/intro.html

U.S. State Home Pages. Links to official U.S. state home pages.
http://www.globalcomputing.com/states.html

Yahoo Canada. Comprehensive links to Canadian information.
http://www.yahoo.ca

14. Mathematics

Math and Science Gateway. This Cornell Theory Center hotlist is for maths and sciences.
http://www.tc.cornell.edu:80/Edu/MathSciGateway/

WWW Virtual Library Mathematics List. Links to general resources, specialized fields, math department Web servers, math software, and electronic journals.
http://euclid.math.fsu.edu/Science/math.html

15. Politics

CNN/Time AllPolitics. Political news and views, including poll results, special reports, and Web Watch links to political parties and other political sites.
http://allpolitics.com

Doug Ingram's News & Politics Page. Links to sources on the left, the right, and various other ideologies.
http://www.shrubbery.com/ingram/politics.html

Internet Resources for Political Science. Extensive links to useful political science sources, including news sources, U.S. and foreign governments, and think tanks.
http://www.aum.edu/home/academics/schools/sciences/pspa/hotlinks.htm

Mother Jones. Worth reading even if you don't agree with the left-leaning political views.
http://www.mojones.com/

Political Science Resources. Source for international political information, political theory links, newsgroup archives, etc.
http://www.keele.ac.uk/depts/po/psr.htm

RealCom National Politics & Personalities. Links to political parties around the world, plus some off-the-wall political sites and collections of resources based on ideologies at all points on the political spectrum.
http://www.rtis.com/nat/pol/

16. Science and Technology

Biological Sciences World Wide Web Server. This site from California State University attempts to "consolidate existing WWW biological science teaching and research resources."
http://arnica.csustan.edu/

Eisenhower National Clearinghouse Science. Intended as a teaching resource, this site is a good starting point for a wide range of science topics. Links include hotlists for chemistry, earth science, life sciences, physics, and space science. There are also links to museums and zoos.

http://www.enc.org/

Frank Potter's Science Gems. A well-organized collection of links to 2,000 of the Web's best science resources.

http://www-sci.lib.uci.edu/SEP/SEP.html

Inquirer's Guide to the Universe. An interactive online exhibit, with a helpful list of space science resources.

http://www.fi.edu/planets/planets.html

inScight. A daily information service with the latest science news. Includes an archive. Compiled in conjunction with *Science*, the weekly magazine published by the American Association for the Advancement of Science.

http://www.apnet.com/inscight

The MAD Scientist Network. Scientists from around the world will field questions in different areas of science. There is a FAQ archive where you can answer such questions as, "Has the massive black hole in the center of our galaxy been confirmed?" Includes links to sites for learning about science.

http://medinfo.wustl.edu/~ysp/MSN/

Math and Science Gateway. This Cornell Theory Center hotlist is for maths and sciences.

http://www.tc.cornell.edu:80/Edu/MathSciGateway/

New Scientist. News, jobs, and more from *New Scientist* magazine. A leading science and technology site on the Internet.

http://www.newscientist.com/

Philadelphia Inquirer Health and Science Magazine. Full texts of articles published every week on science and medicine.

http://sln.fi.edu/inquirer/inquirer.html

Science in the Headlines. Science news headlines and background information from the National Academy of Sciences.

http://www2.nas.edu/new/newshead.htm

Selected Sites in the Sciences. A guide to science sources from the Health Sciences Librarian at University of North Carolina.

http://www.iat.unc.edu/guides/irg-26.html

Smithsonian Institution. Information on the institution's exhibits, galleries, and research centres.

http://www.si.edu/start.htm

Today at NASA. Daily updates of the space agency's activities, including press releases and links to current NASA missions.

http://www.hq.nasa.gov/office/pao/NewsRoom/today.html

The Tree of Life Home Page. Extensive resource for the life sciences. An example of a distributed knowledge system where many people from around the world contribute information about life on the planet.

http://phylogeny.arizona.edu/tree/phylogeny.html

17. Social sciences

Coombsweb Social Sciences Server. Maintained by the Australian National University, this is an electronic repository for social sciences, humanities, and Asian studies research and related bibliographies. This is also the home of the Buddhist Electronic archives. This is an important resource, but plan to spend some time finding your way around.

http://coombs.anu.edu.au/

H-Net Humanities and Social Sciences Online. Central storehouse for humanities and social sciences information that has been developed as an international cooperative initiative. An annotated database of links to extensive history and social studies sources.

http://h-net2.msu.edu

Millennium Institute. State of the world with respect to population and available resources.

http://www.igc.apc.org/millennium/

Research Engines for the Social Sciences. Very thorough set of links to social science sources. Includes many links to Canadian sources and to news, journalism, and statistical sites.

http://www.carleton.ca/~cmckie/research2.html

Social Science Information Gateway. Includes a searchable database of social science sources.

http://www.clark.net/pub/lschank/web/mu-scref.html

Social Sciences Directories. From Western Connecticut University, Internet directories for anthropology, geography, economics, political science, sociology, etc.

http://www.wcsu.ctstateu.edu/socialsci/homepage.html

Statistical Sources. Developed by Larry Shankman, this is an extensive set of links to many important statistical resources on the Web for economics, business, health, census data, etc.

http://www.clark.net/pub/lschank/web/govstats.html

WebEc. WWW resources in economics: a comprehensive resource for economics information, including the history of economics.

http://netec.wustl.edu/%7eadnetec/WebEc/WebEc.html#scm

18. Sports

College Sports Online. Resources for fans to follow major U.S. college football and basketball teams, including links to local newspapers that cover the teams.
http://www.collegesports-online.com/

My Virtual Reference Desk—Sports Sites. Links to sports information and news.
http://www.refdesk.com/sports.html

19. Travel

Fare Tracker. A source for finding the lowest fare for flight tickets. Registration required.
http://expedia.msn.com/pub/faretrkr.hts

Fine Travel Magazine. Online e-zine with free full-text articles on selected destinations around the world. Aimed at appealing to travelers, not tourists.
http://www.finetravel.com/finetrav/

Fodor's. The perennial travel experts provide a personalized trip planner, giving tips and information on cities and countries worldwide. Read full-text seasonal articles on destinations around the globe.
http://www.fodors.com

Lonely Planet. Online source for off-the-beaten-track travel information.
http://www.lonelyplanet.com.au/lp.htm
http://www.lonelyplanet.com.au/contents.htm (low graphics)

Passport Services. For U.S. travelers, this is a source for obtaining downloadable forms for passports and birth certificates.
http://travel.state.gov/passport_services.html

Reed Traveler.Net. Geared to travel agents but useful to anyone planning a trip, with airline timetables, hotel reservations, and corporate discounts. Includes Travel Weekly Online, links to about 1,000 travel-related sites on the Web.
http://www.traveler.net/

World Travel Guide. Search alphabetically for world travel information.
http://www.wtgonline.com/

20. Women

Canadian Women's Internet Association. Motherhood, sisterhood, spirituality, and more.
http://www.women.ca/more.html

FeMiNa. Web directory for women and girls. Lots of topics, from sports to spirituality.
http://www.femina.com/

WebGrrls. Directory to women's sites on the Web.
http://www.webgrrls.com/

21. Odds & ends

About Work. Topics include First Jobs, Work From Home, Entrepreneurs, Company Life, Career Shift, and Out of Work. Don't miss the Bitch & Moan feature!
http://www.aboutwork.com

Consumer's Resource Handbook. This publication from the U.S. Office of Consumer Affairs includes advice to consumers and contact information for consumer protection. This is a hefty, and very popular, guide. There are literally thousands of names, addresses, and phone numbers for corporations, trade groups, and consumer protection agencies.
http://www.pueblo.gsa.gov/

Consumer World. Over 1,400 consumer resources on the Internet.
http://www.consumerworld.org

DisInformation. Stories on media manipulation, political and environmental issues, new science, the far right, conspiracy theories, UFOs, and other interesting stuff. Also check out the e-zine with pros and cons on featured topics. An interesting site for an alternative look at the news.
http://www.disinfo.com

Food and Drink Hotspots. When you're tired of surfing and want some food!
http://www.bev.net/education/schools/admin/food-drink-hot-spots.html

http://www.kn.pacbell.com/wired/grants/grant_res.html

Kelley Blue Book Used Car Guide. Popular source for used car price information. The site offers new car prices as well.
http://www.kbb.com/

National Fraud Information Center. One organization that monitors fraud on the Internet recently reported discovering approximately 500 variations on get-rich-quick cyberscams.
http://www.fraud.org

Robin Garr's Wine Lovers' Page. A lovingly done site from a wine-loving journalist. You can even submit a wine-related question and have it answered by e-mail within 24 hours.
http://www.iglou.com/why/wine.html

Weathernet. Sponsored by the Weather Underground, this site offers forecasts, advisories, and links to weather information.
http://cirrus.sprl.umich.edu/wxnet/

Appendix C
Citing online sources

"It seems like a no-brainer: When doing a story about a World Wide Web site, tell the reader or listener where to find it. But the question of when to give out a Uniform Resource Locator, or URL — a home page or e-mail address — is still muddy territory for the media as style and usage rules are being formed in an effort to keep up with evolving technology."

— JULIE GAMMILL GIBSON, *AMERICAN JOURNALISM REVIEW*, NOVEMBER 19, 1996

How and when to clutter up a tight, well-written news story with a long and awkward URL is only one of many new issues facing writers, researchers, and journalists who want to use Internet resources in their work.

For journalists and writers

Journalists and writers need guidelines about how to quote people's comments from e-mail and newsgroup postings, as well as how to cite facts and figures obtained from Web sites and home pages. Such guidelines are emerging slowly and sporadically at news organizations and publishing companies, and — at least among journalists — a consensus has yet to develop.

When asked how they cite online resources, journalists describe a variety of approaches. Some report that they quote from e-mail messages freely without identifying that the quotes were obtained electronically. After all, they point out, journalists rarely specify whether quotes were obtained over the telephone or in a personal interview, and they don't want to treat e-mail any differently. Others are forbidden by their editors from treating e-mail messages as anything other than leads. All direct quotes must be obtained the old-fashioned way, by telephone or in face-to-face interviews. Still other journalists say they quote from e-mail messages and newsgroup postings, but only by adding qualifiers such as "said someone who identified herself as Jane Doe in a message posted to the Internet newsgroup *misc.kids.*" They admit such qualifiers make their prose less than graceful.

Another issue that journalists have debated concerns electronic discussion groups. Does a news professional have the right to publish quotes pulled from e-mail messages or newsgroup postings without first asking permission from the author of the message? Some argue that newsgroup postings cannot be considered private because millions of people around the world can read them, so journalists are free to quote from them in their stories. Others argue that people should not find themselves quoted in a news story unless they have been asked for, and have given, permission.

The Associated Press in the United States is among those organizations that have developed formal policies for online resources. In a document circulated in 1996 by Bill Dedman, the director of computer-assisted reporting for the Associated Press, reporters were told the following:

> Respect the privacy of individuals, who may not be aware that their comments in electronic forums could be distributed by journalists. Do not quote private individuals or public figures from online communications unless you verify the identity of the author and assure yourself that the author meant to speak publicly. Often it's best to contact people online, then to conduct an interview by telephone or in person. If you have online discussions to gather information, make sure the other party knows you are a working journalist.

(For more details about AP's policy, see Appendix F.)

There is not yet much consistency among news organizations either about how to cite facts and figures pulled from the World Wide Web or whether to include URLs in news reports. Broadcasters do everything from reading out complete URLs while displaying them on the screen to telling their viewers to use search engines to find the sites. Some publications publish an index where URLs mentioned elsewhere in the text can be cited in full.

For researchers

Researchers have made more progress in agreeing on how to cite online references in formal footnotes and bibliographies. There are now several resources online where such guidelines are outlined.

One of the most popular sites is **Bibliographic Formats for Citing Electronic Information**, located at:

http://www.uvm.edu/~ncrane/estyles/

The site provides a guide called *The Handbook for Citing Electronic Resources* by Xia Li and Nancy Crane. Its guidelines are based on the American Psychological Association (APA) Embellished Style and the Modern Language Association (MLA) Embellished Style. The guide includes suggestions for citing everything from journal articles and individual works to newsgroup postings and e-mail messages.

Another site, the **Web Extension to the American Psychological Association Style** (WEAPAS), suggests modifying APA style to accommodate Web resources. Look for this site at:

http://www.beadsland.com/weapas/

WEAPAS (which considers itself a "work in progress") includes lots of good advice and links to other papers about the reasons behind each of its suggested modifications.

Another site also applies APA style to online resources. Called the **APA Publication Manual Crib Sheet**, it's located at:

http://www.gasou.edu/psychweb/tipsheet/apacrib.htm

Finally, there is a site that extends MLA style to electronic communications. It's called the **MLA-Style Citations of Electronic Resources** and is located at:

http://www.cas.usf.edu/english/walker/mla.html

Copyright issues

"Nearly all of the information you find via electronic sources has copyright protection. Electronic journals, news wires and electronic versions of print material have the same copyright protection as material that has been traditionally published. You should work under the assumption that information posted to news groups and discussion lists is copyrighted ... The best alternative is to secure the permission of the creator of the work you wish to quote."

— RANDY REDDICK AND ELLIOT KING, *THE ONLINE JOURNALIST*. ORLANDO, FL: HARCOURT BRACE, 1995, P. 209.

Copyright, once considered a boring topic for seminars and conferences, is now attracting widespread attention, thanks to the Internet. The dissemination of information and programs over the Net has raised many questions about how copyright applies to online material. The debate has been as confusing as it as been helpful. While many of the copyright violations on the Net have to do with pirating software, there are other problems too of more concern to writers, researchers, and journalists.

Essentially, copyright is the exclusive right, protected by law, of any author of a creative work to control the copying of that work, whether it includes a copyright notice or not. While the details of copyright laws vary from jurisdiction to jurisdiction, most allow for some limited use of short excerpts of copyright material for what is called "fair use" in the United States and "fair dealing" in Canada. They also allow use of material considered "in the public domain." It's how those two exceptions are interpreted regarding online material that is causing the most debate.

The first question is how much of an online publication can be excerpted and quoted verbatim without permission under the rules about fair use. Downloading or printing material for personal use is allowed under the fair use provisions of copyright laws. But if you want to distribute something to someone else online or off, only short excerpts of someone else's work can be reproduced for such purposes as criticism, commentary, news reporting, scholarship, or research.

The second question is whether any information online can be considered in the public domain. Experts disagree about this. Brad Templeton, the publisher and editor of the electronic newspaper *ClariNet e.News*, has published a FAQ on the myths of copyright in which he says:

> Nothing modern is in the public domain anymore unless the owner explicitly puts it in the public domain. Explicitly, as in you have a note from the

FYI The full FAQ outlining the myths of copyright and links to other resources about copyright can be found at: **http://www.clari.net/brad/copymyths.html**

author/owner saying, "I grant this to the public domain." Those exact words or words very much like them.

Some argue that posting to Usenet implicitly grants permission to everybody to copy the posting within fairly wide bounds, and others feel that Usenet is an automatic store and forward network where all the thousands of copies made are done at the command (rather than the consent) of the poster. This is a matter of some debate, but even if the former is true (and in this writer's opinion we should all pray it isn't true) it simply would suggest posters are implicitly granting permissions "for the sort of copying one might expect when one posts to Usenet" and in no case is this a placement of material into the public domain.

A detailed FAQ about copyright as it applies in the United States has been put together by a lawyer in California named Terry Carroll. It includes lots of links to other valuable resources about copyright and to Carroll's most recent update on the laws. It can be found at:

http://www.aimnet.com/~carroll/copyright/faq-home.html

One of the more extensive sites for information about copyright and fair use is one at Stanford University. It includes information and links related to the use of copyrighted material by individuals, libraries, and educational institutions. It can be found at:

http://fairuse.stanford.edu/

FYI The **United States Copyright Office** has a Web page at the Library of Congress Web site where you can information, forms, and even a list of answers to commonly asked questions. It's at: **http://lcweb.loc.gov/copyright/**

Information about copyright laws as they apply in Canada can be found at the Web site for the **Canadian Intellectual Property Office** at:

http://info.ic.gc.ca/ic-data/marketplace/cipo/welcome/welcom_e.html

Appendix E

Censorship issues

"One need look no further than any ... newspaper to believe that the 'Net consists of a bunch of teen-aged boys who, when they're not breaking into NORAD defense computers around the world, are staring at pictures of naked women on their Internet screens all day while they trade E-mail with tips on how to blow up the Pentagon ... The reality is far different. Tens of millions of people sign on to the Internet every day to do research. Companies are discovering new ways to compete globally through the Internet. Global knowledge access throughout the Internet has become fundamental to the regular working lives of many millions of people. Science, business — our entire world — is transformed as the whole of human knowledge becomes available in electronic form. And yes, some fringe elements use the Internet too."

— JIM CARROLL, *GLOBE AND MAIL*, MARCH 21, 1995

How to control the fringe elements who use the Internet to distribute child pornography and instructions for building pipe bombs is a question that has received considerable attention in recent years.

Trying to control all the digital bits of information that people exchange over the Internet every day is not only technically impossible — it would be the equivalent of tapping everyone's phone all the time just to catch a few obscene phone callers.

Yet, many people who don't understand the technical impossibility of such a measure are demanding it be done. Some commercial services have responded by trying to ban some Internet newsgroups from their service. But these are feeble attempts that do little to stop such activities as the distribution of pornography online.

Some of those most determined to stop the flow of offensive material online are parents who do not want their children looking at hard-core porn on their home computers. In an effort to meet their concerns (and make some money, of course), several companies have developed programs that promise to make the Net safer for children. Each operates a little differently, but essentially, all block access to sites believed to contain obscene and pornographic material and prevent users from sending out personal information or embargoed words to public discussion groups. For a review of several such programs (including CyberPatrol, CyberSitter, KinderGuard, and NetNanny), and links to information about how to get them, check out the following site, maintained by the watchdog organization **SafeSurf**, located at:

http://www.cnet.com/Content/Reviews/Compare/Safesurf/index.html

Appendix F

Associated Press policy for using electronic services

These rules apply to the Internet, commercial online services, and other electronic resources used by staff of The Associated Press.

The guidelines are intended as guardrails against careless use of the new electronic vehicles.

Some of the points should seem obvious, because our old values of accuracy and responsibility remain the same. Other rules will seem new, as the technologies are new.

But no rules can protect us entirely. Use common sense, be cautious, and think before you act. If you're not sure, ask for guidance. What you do on a computer can be awfully hard to take back.

1. Accounts on AP's electronic services are intended to aid the business and professional activities of AP staff. The accounts are for business use only, the same as AP portable computers and cellular phones. If you have private business to conduct, use a private account. Although you can access the AP accounts from home, this is not a license to connect for personal use.

   Remember that connecting to electronic services uses a limited resource that costs the AP money. The same Internet connections and dial-up ports are needed to file and distribute AP text, photos, graphics, audio, video, and data.
2. Each account is assigned for use only by the AP staffer. Sharing accounts is not permitted. No generic or departmental accounts will be assigned. Choose a password that would be difficult to guess (not any form of a family name or birthdate, not a word in any dictionary). The system will require you to include two characters not in the English alphabet, and to change your password frequently.
3. Conduct business on electronic services as if you are appearing at a public meeting representing the AP, or writing a letter on company letterhead. After all, every message sent with an AP account is stamped "ap.org." What you write, even in private e-mail but especially in posts to lists and Usenet newsgroups, could be forwarded to millions of people, and no doubt will be saved somewhere by somebody. Many mailing lists that are erroneously thought of as private are routinely archived on Usenet newsgroups or the World Wide Web, which are public. Even World Wide Web servers collect at least part of the addresses of all users visiting them. And any user of AP's Internet server can see generally what activity any other user is

doing. In short, if you wouldn't want your online activity to be shown on CNN or in Times Square, don't do it on the Internet or America Online.

4. AP has longstanding rules against News employees participating in political activities or taking sides on matters of public debate. These rules apply to electronic communication as well. Do not express opinions about products, companies or individuals. Non-news employees, who may be unaccustomed to these rules, should remember that Internet readers won't know whether a user from ap.org is a newsperson. Even what a non-News employee does can reflect on AP's newsgathering.
5. To do their work, AP staff need to participate in electronic discussion groups on professional or technical topics. Posting to other groups of general interest should be limited to seeking information. For example, a reporter doing a story on prostate cancer may post to a medical group, or a group for older men. Or a technician may seek help on a software discussion group.
6. When participating in discussion groups, be sure the reader knows that you are not stating AP policy. Someone reading a message from you@ap.org won't know AP's organizational structure. If complaints or questions come to you because you are identified as an AP employee, refer them to the appropriate supervisor.
7. Act as if the laws on libel and privacy apply to electronic communications. Remember that the laws of other jurisdictions may be more restrictive than your own. Respect the privacy of individuals, who may not be aware that their comments in electronic forums could be distributed by journalists. Do not quote private individuals or public figures from online communications unless you verify the identity of the author and assure yourself that the author meant to speak publicly. Often, if you contact someone online, it's best to conduct an interview by telephone or in person. If you have online discussions to gather information, make sure the other party knows you are a working journalist. Although some Web pages and browsers allow sending of what's called anonymous e-mail, send only mail with your name and AP affiliation attached.
8. Apply the strictest standards of accuracy to anything you find on electronic services. The Internet is not an authority; authorities may use it, but so do quacks. Make certain a communication is genuine before relying on it as a source for a news story. More than one person may share an e-mail address, and e-mail addresses and Web page sponsorship can easily be faked. Ask yourself, "Could this be a hoax?" Do not publish on the wire any electronic address without testing to see that it's a working address, and satisfying yourself that it is genuine. Apply, in other words, your usual news judgment.

9. Respect the copyrights of individuals and organizations, including the AP. Do not forward or post anyone's material without permission. Do not post or send to individuals any proprietary AP material, including news stories, photos, graphics, audio, video, data, or any internal communication.
10. Abide by the courtesies of the electronic community. Courtesy requires basic technical competence. For example, be careful not to send a message to a mailing list that was intended for only one user. If you subscribe to a mailing list, keep a copy of the message telling you how to unsubscribe. Don't type in all caps; people will think you're shouting. Avoid the "flame wars" that easily erupt when conversations are conducted online. And, because AP's Internet server has limited capacity, clean out your mailbox and home directory routinely, and log off when you're not using the system.

Glossary

Anonymous FTP One of the Internet's main attractions is its openness and freedom. FTP (*F*ile *T*ransfer *P*rotocol) Internet sites let you access their data without registering or paying a fee.

Applet A small program written in a computer language called Java. Applets can be embedded in HTML pages to produce animations, calculations, and other dynamic elements.

Archie A search tool that helps you locate information stored at hundreds of anonymous FTP sites around the Internet.

ASCII (Ask-ee) *A*merican *S*tandard *C*ode for *I*nformation *I*nterchange, plain text without formatting that's easily transferred over networks. (Got a question? Just ASCII.)

Backbone The main communication line that ties computers at one location with those at another. Analogous to the human nervous system, many smaller connections, called *nodes* or *remote sites*, branch off from the backbone network. (Don't slip a disk!)

Bandwidth An indication of how fast information flows through a computer network in a set time. Bandwidth is usually stated in thousands or millions of bits per second. See Ethernet.

Baud Unit of speed in data transmission; maximum channel speed for data transmission.

BinHex A method for converting non-text files into ASCII. BinHex is one of the ways of coding a file (such a word processed file) for transfer through electronic mail. MIME and Uuencode are two other ways of coding messages for e-mail transfer.

Bit A single-digit number in base-2, specifically, either a 1 or a zero. The smallest unit of data that can be handled by a computer. It takes eight bits (a byte) to represent one character (e.g., a letter or number) of text.

BITNet One of the precursers of the Internet, BITNet stands for Because It's Time Network. BITNet involved a network of educational sites, and many listserver discussion groups originated on BITNet.

Bounce Return of e-mail that contained a delivery error.

Bozo filter A program that screens out unwanted and irritating incoming messages. (Both messages and filter can be breaches of netiquette.)

bps Bits per second: a measure of how fast data are moved from one place to another. For example, a 28.8 modem can move 28,800 bits per second.

Browser A software program that is used to access various kinds of Internet resources. Netscape and Internet Explorer are examples of Web browsers.

Bulletin Board A computerized "meeting space" where individuals log onto a (usually) quite small computer and exchange messages and computer programs.

Byte A set of bits that represent a single character. There are eight bits in a byte.

kilobyte (KB) = 1,024 bytes of data
megabyte (MB) = 1,048,576 bytes
gigabyte (GB) = 1,000 megabytes
terabyte (TB)= 1,024 gigabytes

CCITT The Consultative Committee for *I*nternational *T*elegraph and *T*elephone makes technical recommendations concerning data and telephone communications systems.

CD-ROM Compact *D*isk *R*ead-Only *M*emory. CD-ROM can hold the equivalent of 1,500 floppy disks. It is the most popular carrier of interactive multimedia programs that feature audio, video, graphics, and text.

Chat and Talk A chat program lets you electronically "converse" online with many people simultaneously. A talk program is like a personal telephone call to a specific cybernaut — only in text. See IRC (Internet Relay Chat).

CIX Commercial *I*nternet e*X*change, a group of companies providing a range of specialized services, such as financial data, for a fee.

Client A desktop personal computer that communicates with other PCs and larger computers, called *servers* or *hosts*.

Client/server computing Combining large and small computers in a network so data are readily available when and where they are needed. For example, in a retail store, information is collected from customers at point-of-sale terminals. Then it is directed to a server in the store and forwarded to a larger enterprise server for inventory management and other functions.

CNRI Corporation for *N*ational *R*esearch *I*nitiatives, an organization that is exploring different ways to use a national information highway.

Computerphobe Someone who is afraid of using computers. (Now, who could that be?)

Cookie A piece of information sent by a Web server to a Web browser as a kind of memory device. A cookie enables the server to tell where you left off in a previous interaction, or what set of preferences you might have chosen. Cookies allow the computer to "remember" login or registration information, and they allow customized information to be sent to the user.

Copyright The legal right granted to a copyright owner to exclude others from copying, preparing derivative works, distributing, performing, or displaying original works of authorship of the owner. Copyrighted works on the Internet are protected under national and international laws. Examples of copyrighted works include literature, music, drama, pictures, graphics, sculpture, and audio-visual presentations.

Cybernaut Someone who explores the vast world of cyberspace where only the brave dare venture.

Cybernetics In 1948, Norbert Wiener coined this term to describe the "entire field of control and communication theory, whether in the machine or in the animal." *Cyber-* has become a popular prefix for many Internet terms: cyberlingo, cyberwonk, cybercast. (What hath Norbert wrought!)

Cyberspace Word coined by William Gibson in his 1984 sci-fi novel, *Neuromancer*. Refers to all the sites that you can access electronically. If your computer is connected to the Internet or a similar network, then it exists in cyberspace. Gibson's style of fiction is now called *cyberpunk*.

Daemon Web software on a UNIX server; a program running all the time in background, providing special services when required.

Dedicated line A telephone line that is leased from the telephone company and used for one purpose. In cyberspace, dedicated lines connect desktop systems to servers.

DES The *D*ata *E*ncryption *S*tandard represents a set of criteria for providing security for transmitted messages. Standards like this lay the groundwork for electronic commerce over the Internet.

Dial-in connection A way to access a computer on the Internet using a PC, telephone line, and modem. Slower than connecting directly to the Internet backbone, but provides accessibility from many sites and does not require specialized equipment.

Domain The system of organizing the Internet according to country or type of organization, such as educational or commercial. For instance, an educational institution such as The Franklin Institute Science Museum in Philadelphia, USA would have ".edu" as a suffix to its domain name (sln.fi.edu). Other typical suffixes include ".com" for commercial organizations and ".org" for non-profit groups.

Domain Name System (DNS) The scheme used to define individual Internet hosts.

Download When you transfer software or other information from the Internet to your PC. *Upload* refers to transferring content to a server from a smaller computer or a PC.

E-mail Electronic mail. The term has several meanings: the network for sending messages; the act of sending a message electronically; and the message itself. It all comes down to using a computer network to send electronic messages from one computer user to another. Fortunately, all the electronic junk mail you receive is environmentally friendly since it generates no paper — unless you print it.

Electronic commerce Buying and selling products and services over the Internet.

Ethernet (Not an illegal fishing device.) A common type of network used in corporations. Originally limited to 10 million bits of information per second, technical improvements have raised Ethernet bandwidth (how fast information flows through a computer network in a set time) to 100 million bits of information per second — in concept, enough speed to transfer the entire contents of the *Encyclopaedia Britannica* in one second.

E-Zine A Web-based electronic publication.

FAQ List of *F*requently *A*sked *Q*uestions (and answers) about a particular topic. FAQs can usually be found within Internet discussion groups that focus on specific topics. Read FAQs before asking a question of your own — the answer may already be waiting.

Finger A program that provides information about someone connected to a host computer, such as that person's e-mail address.

Firewall A mechanism to keep unauthorized users from accessing parts of a network or host computer. For example, anonymous users would be able to read documents a company makes public but could not read proprietary information without special clearance.

Flame rude or ludicrous e-mail. Advice: Don't reply to flames, just extinguish them by deleting.

Freenet A community computer network, often based on a local library, that provides Internet access to citizens from the library or sometimes from their home computers.

FTP *F*ile *T*ransfer *P*rotocol is a program that lets you transfer data from an Internet server to your computer.

Gateway A system that connects two incompatible networks. Gateways permit different e-mail systems to pass messages between them.

Gigabyte A unit of data storage that equals about 1,000 megabytes. A CD-ROM holds about two-thirds of a gigabyte (650 million bytes). That's enough space to hold a full-length motion picture. (Don't forget the popcorn.)

Gopher A system that uses menus and special software on host computers so that you can more easily navigate around the Internet. The area of navigation is referred to as GopherSpace.

GUI *G*raphical *U*ser *I*nterface, software that simplifies the use of computers by letting you interact with the system through graphical symbols or icons on the screen rather than coded commands typed on the keyboard. Microsoft Windows and the Apple Macintosh operating systems are the two most popular GUIs.

Hacker The best reason of all to put up a firewall. Originally, some of these pranksters breached computer security systems for fun. Computer criminals have created chaos on computer networks, stealing valuable data and bringing networks down for hours or days. See DES (Data Encryption Standard).

Home page The main page for a site on the Internet. Businesses, organizations, and individuals may post home pages to the World

Wide Web. Also can be the first page that appears when you call up your browser.

Host A server computer linked directly to the Internet that individual users can access.

Hotlists Frequently accessed URLs (Uniform Resource Locators) that point to Web sites. Usually organized around a topic or for a purpose, e.g., a hotlist of search engines on the Web.

HTML *H*yper*T*ext *M*arkup *L*anguage; the codes and formatting instructions for interactive online Internet documents. These documents can contain hypertext, graphics, and multimedia elements, including sound and video.

Hypermedia Multimedia and hypertext combined in a document.

Hypertext An electronic document that contains links to other documents offering additional information about a topic. You can activate the link by clicking on the highlighted area with a mouse or other pointing device.

Information Highway Also referred to as I-Way, Internet, Infobahn, Autostrada, National Information Infrastructure (NII), Global Information Infrastructure (GII). The network is currently "under construction" to make existing computer systems more efficient at communicating and to add new services, such as electronic commerce, health information, education, polling — just use your imagination.

Infrastructure The base on which an organization is built. It includes the required facilities, equipment, communications networks, and software for the operation of the organization or system. But most important, it includes the people and the relationships that result.

Internet An interconnection of thousands of separate networks worldwide, originally developed by the U.S. federal government to link government agencies with colleges and universities. Internet's real expansion started recently with the addition of thousands of companies and millions of individuals who use graphical browsers to access information and exchange messages. See Mosaic.

InterNIC The *Inter*net *N*etwork *I*nformation Center. The NIC is run by the U.S. National Science Foundation and provides various administrative services for the Internet.

Intranet A private, internal network for a company or organization that uses the same kind of software that is used on the Internet. A company intranet, for example, could be used as the basis for an internal electronic mail network and for posting company procedures and announcements in the form of Web pages.

IP *I*nternet *P*rotocol is the communications language used by computers connected to the Internet.

IP number A unique address assigned to a computer on the Internet. Individual domain names (such as *nasa.gov*) are all associated with an IP number that designates the location of the computer. IP numbers are made up of four parts separated by dots, e.g., 145.122.241.2.

IRC *I*nternet *R*elay *C*hat, a software tool that lets you hold keyboard conversations. See Chat and Talk.

ISDN The *I*ntegrated *S*ervices *D*igital *N*etwork defines a new technology that delivers both voice and digital network services over one "wire." More important, ISDN's high speed enables multimedia and high-end interactive functions over the Internet, such as video-conferencing.

ISP *I*nternet *S*ervice *P*rovider: a company or institution that provides access to the Internet. Most often, an ISP will sell dial-in access to a computer that is connected to the Internet.

Java A programming language invented by Sun Microsystems that is specifically designed for writing programs that can be quickly downloaded to your computer and run. It is possible to write a Java program to do many of the things we currently use a personal computer for, such as word processing.

Knowbots An intelligent program or "agent" that you can instruct to search the Internet for information about a particular subject. While still in their infancy, these agents are the focus of intense software research and development.

LAN *L*ocal *A*rea *N*etwork, a collection of computers in proximity, such as an office building, that are connected via cable. These computers can share data and peripherals such as printers. LANs are necessary to implement client/server computing since the LAN allows communication to the server.

Listserv; Listserver An electronic mailing list used to deliver messages directly to the e-mail addresses of people interested in a particular topic, such as journalism.

Luddite Person who believes that the use of technology will diminish employment.

Lurking The practice of reading about a newsgroup in order to understand its topics and tone before offering your own input.

Mbone *M*ulticast back*bone* is an experimental system that sends video over the Internet.

MIME (Not Marcel Marceau.) *M*ultipurpose *I*nternet *M*ail *E*xtensions, an enhancement to Internet e-mail that lets you include non-text data, such as video and audio, with your messages.

Modem (*Mo*dulator-*dem*odulator) A device that allows your computer to connect to another computer over telephone lines.

Mosaic This sophisticated, graphical browser application lets you access the Internet World Wide Web. After the introduction of Mosaic in 1993, the use of Internet began to expand rapidly.

Multimedia Multiple forms of communication including sound, video, video-conferencing, graphics, and text delivered via a multimedia-ready PC.

Net surfing The practice of accessing various Internet sites to see what's happening. (A whole new world for the Beach Boys!)

Netiquette Standards of behavior and manners to be used while working on the Internet. For example, a message in ALL CAPS can mean the sender is shouting.

Network People connected via computers to share information.

Newbies Newcomers to the Internet.

Newsgroup The Internet version of an electronic discussion group, where people can leave messages or post questions.

Newsreader A program that helps you find your way through a newsgroup's messages.

Newsserver A computer that collects newsgroup data and makes it available to newsreaders.

NFS The *N*etwork *F*ile *S*ystem lets you work with files on a remote host as if you were working on your own host.

NNTP *N*etwork *N*ews *T*ransport *P*rotocol, an extension of TCP/IP protocol; describes how newsgroup messages are transported between compatible servers.

NSFNet Large network run by the U.S. National Science Foundation. It is the backbone of the Internet.

Packet A collection of data. Packet switching is a system that breaks data into small packets and transmits each packet independently. The packets are combined by the receiving computer. (Danger! We may have crossed over into geekspace.)

Point Of Presence (POP) A method of connecting to an Internet service locally. If a service company has a POP in your area, then you can connect to the service provider by making a local call. POP is also used for *P*ost *O*ffice *P*rotocol.

Postmaster The person at a host who is responsible for managing the mail system.

PPP *P*oint-to-*P*oint *P*rotocol connects computers to the Internet using telephone lines; similar to SLIP.

Protocol Rules or standards that describe ways to operate to achieve compatibility.

Public domain software Computer programs you may use and distribute without paying a fee. *Shareware* is distributed at no cost, but you are expected to pay the author a fee if you decide to keep and use it.

Resource hog A program that eats up a large amount of network bandwidth.

Router A device that acts as a traffic signal to direct data among different networks. Routers often have enhanced processing capabilities that enable them to send data on an alternative path if one part of the network is busy.

Server Equivalent to a host, a machine that works with client systems. Servers can be anything from PCs to mainframes that share information with many users.

Service provider A company that provides a connection to the Internet.

SIG *S*pecial *I*nterest *G*roup. (Also nickname of Wagnerian opera hero.)

sig Signature file. A combination of characters that can be automatically appended to any outgoing electronic message — e.g., the sender's name, address, phone/fax numbers, or a humorous or thought-provoking quotation.

SLIP *S*ingle *L*ine *I*nternet *P*rotocol is a technique for connecting a computer to the Internet using a telephone line and modem. Also called Serial Line Internet Protocol. See PPP.

Smiley Manipulating the limited potential of keyboard characters to show goodwill, irony, or other emotions with a "smiley face." There are a number of text-based effects, for example, (–: and ;–).

SMTP *S*imple *M*ail *T*ransport *P*rotocol, the Internet standard for transmitting electronic mail messages.

Sneakernet The 1980s way of moving data among computers that are not networked, by storing data on floppy diskette and running the disks from one computer to another. (Very good for the cardiovascular but not the information system.)

SNMP *S*imple *N*etwork *M*anagement *P*rotocol is a standard of communication of information between reporting devices and data collection programs. It can be used to gather information about hosts on the Internet.

Spamming Indiscriminately sending a message to hundreds or thousands of people on the Internet, e.g., unsolicited junk mail. Not good netiquette.

Streaming Audio, video, and text available for viewing on your computer even as it is in the process of downloading to your system from a Web site.

T1 Telecommunications lingo for digital carrier facility used to transmit information at high speed. (T1 is to the Web what passing gear was to the '64 Cadillac.) If you want to turbocharge your network backbone, many companies are expanding to the even faster T3 service.

TCP/IP *T*ransmission *C*ontrol *P*rotocol/*I*nternet *P*rotocol; communication rules that specify how data are transferred among computers on the Internet.

Technogeek A person who is so involved with computers and the so-called "virtual world" as to have only a tenuous hold on the real world. (But then again, what is reality?). Similar terms: nerd, propeller head, and techie.

Telnet Software that lets users log on to computers connected to the Internet.

Token ring Featured on LANs (Local Area Networks) to keep control messages (tokens) moving quickly among the users.

UNIX Software operating system that provides the underlying intelligence to Internet servers. Mosaic and other browser programs have helped increase Internet usage by hiding the complexities of UNIX from the average cybernaut.

URL Abbreviation for *U*niform *R*esource *L*ocator, the Internet addressing system. (What's your URL?)

Usenet *Use*r *Net*work, an array of computer discussion groups, or forums, that can be visited by anyone with Internet access.

Virus Destructive computer program that invades by means of a normal program and damages the system.

WAIS *W*ide *A*rea *I*nformation *S*ervers search through the Internet's public databases for specific information. For instance, you could locate information about a particular medical breakthrough by searching through the research libraries of teaching hospitals connected to the Internet. (WAIS and means!)

Web site A sequence of related Web pages normally created by a single company or organization.

Webster Habitué of Web sites and other cyberplaces.

White Pages Because they remind people of the old telephone book, services that list user e-mail addresses, telephone numbers, and postal addresses.

Winsock *Win*dows *Sock*et, an extension program designed to let Windows applications run on a TCP/IP network.

Worm This computer program replicates itself on other systems on the Internet. Unlike a destructive virus, a worm passes on useful information. (Maybe we're fishing too deeply!)

WWW The World Wide Web is a hypertext-based collection of computers on the Internet that lets you travel from one linked document to another, even if those documents reside on many different servers.

Index